Living with Insecurity
in a Brazilian Favela

Living with Insecurity in a Brazilian Favela

Urban Violence and Daily Life

R. BEN PENGLASE

Rutgers University Press

New Brunswick, New Jersey, and London

Library of Congress Cataloging-in-Publication Data
Penglase, Ben.
    Living with insecurity in a Brazilian favela : urban violence and daily life / R. Ben Penglase.
        page   cm
    Includes bibliographical references and index.
    ISBN 978-0-8135-6544-6 (hardcover : alk. paper)—ISBN 978-0-8135-6543-9 (pbk.)—
ISBN 978-0-8135-6545-3 (e-book)
    Marginality, Social—Brazil—Rio de Janeiro. 2. Violence—Social aspects—Brazil—Rio de
Janeiro. 3. Urban poor—Brazil—Rio de Janeiro. 4. Caxambu (Rio de Janeiro, Brazil)—Social
conditions. 5. Rio de Janeiro (Brazil)—Social conditions. 6. Slums—Brazil—Rio de Janeiro.
7. Squatter settlements—Brazil—Rio de Janeiro. 8. Drug traffic—Social aspects—Brazil—Rio
de Janeiro. 9. Police brutality—Brazil—Rio de Janeiro. I. Title.

HN290.R5P46 2014
307.3'364098153—dc23

                                                                        2013042859

A British Cataloging-in-Publication record for this book is available from the British Library.

Visit our website: http://rutgerspress.rutgers.edu
Manufactured in the United States of America

For Erika, the residents of Caxambu,
and all the victims of violence in Rio de Janeiro

Contents

Acknowledgments

Many people have helped me with this project, over the course of many years. I am sure that I have forgotten many, but there are some that I cannot fail to single out. Erika Grinius convinced me that we really had to live in Caxambu, and read many, many drafts. Without her support and encouragement, this book never would have happened.

Aquele abraço also goes to the people whom I call Clara, Zeca, Seu Lázaro, Pedro, Dona Elsa, Dona Carmen, Anacleto, Tia Naná, my landlord Seu Nogueira, and all the residents of the place I call Caxambu. Without their help, patience, and encouragement this would not have been possible. They welcomed two gringos into their neighborhood and made sure that I rarely got lost and always felt like part of the family. In exchange they only asked me to "tell it like it is." It was only long after my fieldwork was completed that I became aware of how often they were helping me without my even knowing it. My debt to them is enormous, not just for helping me (and putting up with my endless questions) and inviting me into their homes and into their celebrations, but for teaching me how to live.

Many other people have also been vital in introducing me to Brazil. Thanks must go to my parents, who exposed me to Brazil as a young boy, and who made me an anthropologist (as well as a Carioca *de coração* and a Flamenguista) before I was aware of it. Gilza, Marquinhos, and Elisabete also made me curious, at an early age, about lives that were so close to mine yet also so distant. Years later, Paul Chevigny, Juan E. Méndez, and James Cavallaro at Human Rights Watch reintroduced me to Brazil and reinstilled my curiosity and admiration for the Cariocas and other Brazilians who strive to make Brazil better, more humane, just, and no less vibrant.

Thanks also go to Gilberto Velho, Elizabeth Leeds, Alba Zaluar, Marcos Alvito, Lícia Valladares, and all the anthropologists and sociologists in Brazil who provided me with invaluable advice, inspiration, and encouragement. Nilza Waldeck, Rita Moriconi, Marisa Leal, and Márcia and Fernando at the Fulbright office in Rio were also a great source of help. Viva-Rio was an immense help at various stages of my research.

A group of friends whom I met in Rio were, and continue to be, a source of inspiration and friendship. Luke Dowdney never let me forget what the whole point of such a project is, or should be. When I was living in Caxambu, Desmond Arias, Erica Windler, Peter Beattie, Luciana Lopez, Lígia Mefanoli, Amy Chazkel, James Woodard, and Jerry Dávila all provided shelter, great conversation, insight, and many *saideiras*.

As this book has come together, it has taken many different forms and has been read to and received responses from many people. At Harvard, Lucia Volk, Maria Clemencia "Mencha" Ramirez, Kathleen Gallagher, Haley Duschinski, and Bret Gustafson kept me on my feet, intellectually and emotionally. Kay Warren and David Guss also gave me critical feedback on this manuscript at an early stage. Thanks go to the many people who have organized and participated in panels and talks with me. They are too many to mention, but if you read this book and parts of it seem familiar, yet better, it is because of your help. Chapter 2, for instance, grew out of a talk given on a panel organized by Bernie Perley and Tracey Heatherington. Colleagues and friends at various institutions have also been immensely helpful, especially the Latin American writing group at Texas Christian University, which included Bonnie Frederick, Steve Sloan, Peter Szock, and Edna Rodríguez-Plate. At Loyola University Chicago, Kathleen Adams and Ruth Gomberg-Muñoz have provided constant helpful advice and support.

I would also like to thank my editor and the staff at Rutgers University Press. Marlie Wasserman has been tremendously helpful and supportive. The anonymous reviewers of the manuscript also provided essential assistance. Thanks must also go to Margaret Case for her careful copyediting and attention to detail.

Portions of this book have appeared in articles that I have published elsewhere. Some of Chapter 2 was previously published, in a different form, in R. Ben Penglase, "The Bastard Child of the Dictatorship: The Comando Vermelho and the Birth of 'Narco-Culture,'" originally published in *The Luso-Brazilian Review* 45 (1) 2008: 118–145, © by the Board of Regents of the University of Wisconsin System, reproduced courtesy of the University of Wisconsin Press. Parts of Chapter 4 were published in Ben Penglase, "States of Insecurity: Everyday Emergencies, Public Secrets and Drug Trafficker Power in a Brazilian Favela," *PoLAR: Political and Legal Anthropology Review*, 32 (1) 2009: 407–423. Portions of Chapter 5 appeared, in a substantially altered form, in Ben Penglase, "Invading the Favela," in William Garriott, ed., *Policing and Contemporary Governance: The Anthropology of Police in Practice*, 2013, Palgrave Macmillan, reproduced with permission of Palgrave Macmillan (www.palgrave.com).

Two influences on this book are, sadly, no longer around to read the final product. David Maybury-Lewis saw the scholarly promise in me, and along with Ken George, Bill Fisher, Sally Falk-Moore, and Michael Herzfeld, helped make me into an anthropologist. David's commitment to both anthropological inquiry and social justice continue to inspire many, including me. Begoña Aretxaga provided the initial theoretical inspiration for this project and continues to be a formative influence on my thinking. I like to think that she'd be amused at how she haunts these pages.

**Living with Insecurity
in a Brazilian Favela**

1

"To Live Here You Have to Know How to Live"

> There are lots of things here that
> you can't tackle straight on. But you
> also can't walk around with your
> head down all the time. That's what's
> important: knowing what you can
> directly challenge and what you can't,
> while keeping your head up.
> —Sônia

On one hot and drowsy day, I was sitting in Dona Carmen's backyard. Dona Carmen was one of my neighbors in Caxambu, a *favela* (squatter neighborhood), in the northern part of Rio de Janeiro, Brazil.[1] Dona Carmen supplemented her husband's retirement pension by selling meals to people in the neighborhood. The food could be taken home on paper plates wrapped up in tinfoil (known as *quentinhas*) or eaten under the shade of a mango tree in Dona Carmen's backyard, where her chickens, grandchildren, and a large pet German shepherd named Hulk chased each other in circles, creating an atmosphere of friendly chaos. I was sitting on a concrete stool next to Dona Carmen's open-air kitchen, and had just finished a plate of chicken with rice and beans, when Dona Miriam, a woman from the neighborhood, came into the yard and began to talk with Dona Carmen. Dona Carmen listed to the woman's complaints but also had one eye on the television, which was showing an evangelical Protestant talk show.

Though I had been living in Caxambu for several months, I had never met Dona Miriam.[2] It was clear that barely concealed underneath her flow of complaints to Dona Carmen—her husband had lost his job, the police had recently tried to extort money from her son—Dona Miriam was curious about what I was doing in a neighborhood that few wealthier people, and even fewer foreigners, visited. After a while Dona Miriam began to talk with me and with another couple sitting nearby. Dona Miriam already knew who I was, not an unusual occurrence in a neighborhood where almost everyone knows everyone else, and where despite my ability to speak Portuguese, my wife and I stood out for our obvious foreignness, making us objects of intense local gossip from the moment we moved in.

Dona Miriam began our conversation by asking me how I liked the neighborhood. This was not a naïve question, simply aimed at making pleasant conversation, and it was one that I had been asked more than once. Residents of Rio's favelas, as I show in more detail throughout this book, are highly attuned to the stereotypes that outsiders have of their neighborhoods as dangerous and violent areas. Without quite realizing how deeply I had internalized the opposite trope that favela residents use to counter these negative stereotypes—that favelas are actually safer and friendlier than Rio's crowded streets and anonymous middle-class apartment buildings—I answered, as I often did, that I liked how friendly everyone was.

Dona Miriam looked at me skeptically, perhaps wondering if I really knew what I was talking about or whether I was being honest with her. She persisted, asking: "But don't you think it's difficult to live here?" I agreed, and again dodged the issue that neither of us was openly acknowledging. Instead, I remarked upon what favela residents often hold out as the real challenges to their daily lives: that sometimes the house where I lived had no water, and that it was irritating that the only way to get home at night was by foot, as there was no public transportation and taxis would never drive up the hillside on which Caxambu was built.

My reference to the difficulty of entering the neighborhood at night had, as I had intended, caught her attention. Without openly saying so, I had touched upon a raw nerve: the difficulties created by exclusion of favelas from regular urban infrastructure (such as water and sewage systems), the poverty of many of the neighborhood's residents and their social and racial marginalization were compounded by the violence that resulted from favela-based drug trafficking and corrupt policing. The drug trade, which uses favelas as stockpiling points for a citywide trade in cocaine and marijuana, creates the all-too-frequent possibility of shoot-outs between the police and drug dealers, especially at night as sales heat up and as many residents take to their homes. Drug trafficking also deeply influences how favelas are represented in the media, as they become depicted as "fortresses for drug dealers."

Dona Miriam looked surprised at my answer, and turned to Dona Carmen, exclaiming: "This guy comes and goes in the neighborhood at night?" "Sure," Dona Carmen replied, winking at me, "everyone here knows him. He's friends with everyone." The young man sitting at the nearby table joined in the conversation, saying, "See, in order to live here, you have to know how to live."[3] Dona Miriam chuckled, seemingly satisfied with this exchange, and then went on to ask me more personal questions about where I was from, how long I'd lived in Caxambu, and where my wife was working.

Social Tactics and States of (In)security

This snapshot from my ethnographic research is unremarkable in and of itself. But it opens a window onto a major theme of this book: the experience of living in what I call a state of (in)security. When Dona Carmen commented that I could come and go in the neighborhood at night because I was "friends with everyone," she was referring to the security that comes from living in a neighborhood where almost everyone knows everyone else and where most forms of crime are severely repressed by the local drug traffickers. The friendliness of Caxambu's residents, and the broader network of reciprocal support and mutual aid, produced a context of stability. As we will see in later chapters, local drug traffickers participate in social networks of mutual assistance. At the same time, though, drug dealers also deliberately manipulate fear of crime in an attempt to legitimate their authority. As a result, in one sense, the neighborhood was secure. But Dona Carmen, Dona Miriam, and I all knew that this security was predicated upon a larger context of unpredictable and all-too-often lethal violence, as well as a larger context of exclusion.

The multiple types of violence that mark everyday life in Caxambu have produced a social universe that is deeply contradictory and ambivalent, both safe and dangerous, familiar and unpredictable. Residents of favelas such as Caxambu are distinctly aware that their neighborhood is the product of generations of social and economic marginalization. Living in such a neighborhood stigmatizes the residents of Caxambu as *favelados*. They also know that living in a favela exposes them to the risk of being caught in the cross fire of gun battles between police and rival drug gangs. Yet Caxambu, like all favelas, is a self-built neighborhood (Gilbert 1998; Holston 1991), and residents are often justifiably proud of the generations of sweat and hard work that they have put into building the neighborhood's homes, stores, corner bars, streets, alleys, and sidewalk stoops.

The neighborhood is thus a deeply intimate place, or what Caxambu's residents often call a *morro familiar*, meaning a morro (hillside, the term locally preferred to *favela*) that is both familiar and family-based.[4] Yet people in Caxambu are confronted with the paradox of living in a space that is both deeply familiar and yet also often unpredictably dangerous. The conversation that I described above—acknowledging the difficulties inherent in daily life without directly stating what those difficulties are—is one example of "knowing how to live" in such a neighborhood.

This book addresses these "ways of knowing"—what I refer to, following Michel de Certeau, as "social tactics"—that residents of one favela neighborhood in Rio de Janeiro use to address the multiple forms of violence and the resulting social contradictions that impinge upon their daily lives. Certeau's distinction between *tactics* and *strategies*, and his emphasis on identifying "ways of operating" or focusing on how people actually make use of what they have, provide crucial analytical tools to understand daily life in neighborhoods such as Caxambu (1984, 34–42). For Certeau, strategies are the schema used by the powerful: they seek to produce regularity and stability; they are predicated on the ability to establish relations of exteriority by which social actors can produce, manipulate, and control situations. Tactics, on the other hand, are the ways of operating of the powerless: they are ruses or tricks that do not necessarily challenge or resist systems of power but function within them. Tactics are aimed at carving out temporary spaces of autonomy and seizing momentary opportunities to create, however briefly, advantages for those who can "seize on the wing the possibilities that offer themselves at any given moment" (1984, 37)

Knowing how to live in Caxambu demanded a tactical approach to social life. It was predicated, perhaps above all, on using the neighborhood's spaces and social relations in ways that did not *bater de frente* (hit straight on, or directly challenge), the more powerful. Daily social life in this neighborhood did not necessarily mean resisting the will of the more powerful or fighting against structures of exclusion such as racism and class exclusion. Instead, knowing how to live meant maintaining a constant attentiveness to how to dodge, evade, or turn to one's advantage the obstacles that life placed in one's path.

The residents of Caxambu pay close attention to knowing how to live, not only because their daily margins of survival are often slim and the obstacles that confront them powerful but also because of where they live—in a neighborhood classified as a favela. As squatter neighborhoods, favelas can be seen as tactical spaces: as I explain in more detail below, though residents did not own the land that they lived on, shanties were often tolerated and unofficially accepted. In most cases, favela residents did not collectively demand title to their land; thus favelas were, themselves, "ruses" or "tricks" that allowed the urban poor to carve out improvised spaces where they and their families could live. At the same time, in such a tactical space daily life was characterized by a deep insecurity and vulnerability, and residents did seek unofficial and informal connections to local politicians, employers, and elites.

Many favela residents responded to these challenges by emphasizing creativity, improvisation, and the ability to carve out zones of temporary autonomy and pleasure while not engaging in a potentially costly battle with larger and more powerful structures of authority. Paying attention to how social tactics are used by favela residents to live with insecurity also complicates answers to a series of simple dichotomous questions about the effects of violence and insecurity in Latin America. Debates about whether favela residents accept or reject violence, whether they cooperate with drug traffickers or are coerced into assisting them, seem to miss the point. A tactical approach to insecurity—predicated upon, as Seu Lázaro once told me, "não se metendo em briga de cachorro grande" (not getting in the middle of a fight between big dogs)—means not taking sides, deliberately, so as to maximize one's longer-term survival.

The social tactics deployed by Caxambu's residents as they live with insecurity are, in this sense, an elaboration of a deep cultural repertoire, a way of living with insecurity that Rio's urban poor have elaborated for generations. Although neoliberal economic reforms and the drug trade have produced new forms of insecurity, Rio's poor and nonwhite citizens have long lived in a context where many larger aspects of their lives are often beyond their control. Many of the residents of Caxambu, for instance, are the descendants of slaves who had little control over their own labor. Living with insecurity by elaborating social tactics is thus in part a response to the built urban form of favela neighborhoods and to the deep historic forms of racial and class exclusion. But it is also a response by residents to the symbolic place that favelas have occupied in Rio's social imaginary. Since squatters first erected shacks on Rio's hillsides more than one hundred years ago, favelas have come to symbolize difference and disorder, pockets of racial and class difference located within the center of Rio.

Favelas and the Social Imaginary of Rio: From Terror to "Pacification"

Because many favelas in the city of Rio are located near, or even within, wealthier neighborhoods, they have had a visibility that many other poor neighborhoods have not had. They have come to symbolize both the best and worst of Rio—both its "authentic" Afro-Brazilian traditions such as samba and carnival, since many favela residents are the descendants of slaves, and Brazil's savage class and racial inequalities. Caxambu, then, was not just a neighborhood with its own particular history of occupation and specific sets of social relations, but a favela, a mythical or hyper-real place laden with symbolism and conveying larger sets of meanings about the nature of Brazilian society.[5] Two moments from the relatively recent history of Rio capture the place that favelas have occupied in the city's social imaginary.

On Monday, September 30, 2002, large parts of the city of Rio were brought to a standstill as panic spread throughout the city. Shop owners closed their doors, claiming that young men armed with AK-47s had appeared at their doors early in the morning, identifying themselves as members of a favela-based drug gang and ordering them to shut down. As rumors spread, schools closed and sent students home, bus drivers refused to drive their routes, restaurants, banks, and shopping malls closed. News reports claimed that the shut-down had been ordered by the imprisoned drug trafficker Fernandinho Beira Mar in retaliation for having been transferred to a more secure prison facility. Regardless of the specific motives, a more general fear that violence was spilling beyond the confines of Rio's favelas triggered a cascade of panic. The owner of a bakery in the upper-middle-class neighborhood of Botafogo explained why he closed down this way: "Some people stopped working because of rumors that armed criminals would come down from the favelas; others shut down because they saw that the neighboring stores had closed" (*Estado de S. Paulo*, September 30, 2002).

In what quickly came to be called the holiday of terror, the boundaries that had seemed to contain Rio's violence appeared to be collapsing. Images of heavily armed drug traffickers in the city's favelas were common on television or in newspapers. But young men armed with AK-47s were never seen downtown or in the city's chic beach-front areas. It was also common practice for drug traffickers to order businesses in favelas to close when a powerful drug dealer was killed. But drug traffickers had never exercised this influence in the "regular" city (Penglase 2005).

Favelas had become iconic symbols of a broad sense of insecurity and concern with personal safety shared by many residents of Rio, and this shutdown would not be the last time that violence appeared to spill beyond the borders of the city's favelas. Later in 2002, drug traffickers reportedly threw a hand grenade at the Rio Sul shopping center, one of the city's fanciest, and machine-gunned the Palácio de Guanabara, the state governor's office. These events were associated with favelas in press reports, and favelas seemed to symbolize a broader collapse of public security. Favelas were territories beyond the control of the state and yet in the center of the city, a safe zone for drug-trafficking gangs whose violence threatened the city as a whole.

In 2011, a very different image of favelas was splashed across newspapers and television screens. On Sunday morning, November 13, approximately three thousand police officers and soldiers moved into the favela of Rocinha and also occupied the neighboring favelas of Chácara do Céu and Vidigal. Not only is Rocinha one of the largest favelas in the city of Rio, and perhaps all of Latin America, but its location near wealthier neighborhoods meant that the drug business there was highly lucrative. The massive police occupation had been anticipated for weeks. In a prior operation, soldiers and police had occupied the favelas of the Complexo do Alemão, and reporters had claimed that drug traffickers from Alemão had fled to Rocinha. Rocinha had also been in the news in August 2010, when an early-morning shootout between drug traffickers from the favela and the police in the streets outside the favela ended with a group of drug dealers invading the Hotel Intercontinental and taking several hotel employees hostage before eventually surrendering.

On the day of the operation, the governor of Rio declared that it marked an historic occasion. Governor Sérgio Cabral stated: "I believe that this is an historic and emotional day for all of Brazil, and especially for the city of Rio. We have recovered this territory for the 100 thousand people who live in Rocinha . . . people who need peace." (*O Globo*, November 13, 2011). The massive operation occurred without a single shot being fired, and no drug traffickers were arrested.[6] In the days after the occupation, though, police apprehended and confiscated a large number of guns, including automatic rifles, and quantities of cocaine and marijuana. The international press saw a larger significance: the occupation of Rocinha, the *New York Times* declared, was "a pivotal effort by the government to assert control over lawless areas of the city ahead of the 2014 World Cup and 2016 Olympic games" (*New York Times*, November 13, 2011).

The joint police and army operation to occupy Rocinha was dramatic, but it was only one of a series of occupations of favelas that had begun in 2008. In a shift in policing strategies in favelas, Governor Cabral and his secretary of public security, José Maria Beltrame, began a policy called Unidades de Polícia Pacificadora (UPP or Police Pacifying Units). According to the police, the goals of the UPP policy were threefold: to retake territory controlled by drug traffickers; to provide public safety to favela residents; and to "contribute to the breaking of the 'logic of war'" that had characterized the city of Rio (www.upprj.com).

The strategy was straightforward. First, favelas would first be occupied by the police's elite battalion, the Batalhão de Operações Especiais (BOPE or Special Operations Battalion), often in conjunction with the army. They would search the neighborhoods for drug dealers, weapons, and illegal narcotics. After this initial period of military-style occupation, policing would then be handed over to a new favela-based police unit, the UPP, which would establish a base in the favela and carry out community-based policing. Unlike past practice, the police presence in favelas with UPPs would be permanent. The UPPs would also be staffed by newly minted police officers straight from the police academy, in order to break prior patterns of police corruption. Finally, the UPP was to include a "social UPP," or UPP-2, which would extend city services to favelas, seeking to transform them into "regular" neighborhoods.[7]

The UPP policy was no doubt motivated by the efforts of Rio's authorities to change the image of the city in advance of the 2014 World Cup and the 2016 Olympic Games, as the *New York Times* reported. The Brazilian Olympic delegation led by President Luiz Inácio "Lula" da Silva, which met with the International Olympic Organizing in Copenhagen in 2009 during the final stages of the selection process, included the police captain in charge of the first UPP (Carvalho 2013, 288). But for Rio's state government, the UPPs also symbolized a larger transformation, as part of an effort to reverse decades of the city's economic and political decline.[8]

A conjuncture of events seemed to mark a major transition in Rio's economic and political fortunes. In late 2007, President Lula announced the discovery of the Tupi deep-sea oilfield off the coast of the northern part of the state of Rio.[9] The economy of the state of Rio was also bolstered by a major commodity boom, which allowed Brazil to weather the 2008 global economic crisis. Public security seemed to be improving: Rio's homicide rate, while still high by international standards, had been dropping since the early 2000s (Waiselfisz 2007). The state's political forces were also in unprecedented alignment. In 2007, the governor of the state of Rio, Sérgio Cabral, and the mayor of the city of Rio, Eduardo Paes, were from the same party (the Partido do Movimento Democrático Brasileiro), which was a political ally of President Lula's Partido dos Trabalhadores.

Rio's political and economic leaders saw improving public security as essential to consolidating positive economic change and presenting Rio as a global city. A widespread perception of insecurity had come to be seen not just as a public safety issue but also as a drain on the city's economy, negatively impacting tourism and investment in local businesses. Favelas were to blame, it was said, and the UPP policy sought to dramatically change the perception of these neighborhoods as zones of criminality. José Luiz Alquéres, the president of the Commercial Association of Rio, made the connection between the UPP policy and the drive to change Rio's image explicit: of all the policies implemented to improve the business climate and quality of life in Rio, the one that drew the most attention to positive changes, he stated, was the establishment of the first UPP in the favela of Dona Marta in December 2008 (2011, 68). In favelas, the UPP policy was highly popular, and yet it met with deep skepticism. Residents of favelas occupied by the police have praised improvements in their public safety. At the same time, they have also expressed concern about whether the policy will be long lasting (Carvalho 2013).[10]

The UPPs and the "pacification" of favelas were the product of a particular coming together of political and economic events in the city of Rio—not the least of which was the hosting of the final games of the 2014 World Cup in the iconic, and recently privatized, Maracanã soccer stadium, located in a neighborhood ringed by favelas, including Caxambu. But they are also an example, if a dramatic one, of a larger regional trend. As Daniel Goldstein has argued: "Under the neoliberal regimes of the last few decades in Latin America . . . national states have increasingly been required . . . to adopt the role of security providers for global capital. . . . Nations that cannot provide guarantees of 'security' to transnational corporations risk an investment downturn, as foreign companies and financiers may refuse to do business there" (2010, 493).

In 2002, favelas were seen as symbols and causes of a broader collapse of public security. By 2011, they were the stages upon which Rio's state government demonstrated a dramatic improvement not only in public safety but also in the quality of life of the city of Rio. Because the UPP policy in Caxambu was put in place after I finished fieldwork, I cannot comment on how the UPPs have affected the lived experience of insecurity in Rio's favelas.[11] In the chapters to come, however, I show how they build upon a larger and deeper set of images and understandings of favelas. Several elements are striking. First, in keeping with a long tradition, the UPP policy depicts favelas as distinctive spaces, areas that require different forms of governance. The city of Rio is seen as split between the regular city and favelas, which are by definition irregular and pathological. Second, even as the pacification policy seeks to reverse a prior pattern of police confrontation with drug dealers, it perpetuates the rhetoric of warfare: favelas are enemy territory, to be retaken by military means. When they occupy a favela, the police always hoist the Brazilian flag, as if until that moment favelas had been part of a separate nation. Finally, residents of favelas are seen as passive objects controlled by more powerful forces—whether favela-based drug dealers or the police—rather than as subjects with their own experiences, voices, and demands. They are seen as either powerless pawns or guilty accomplices in what is often depicted as a war.

Favelas and the "War in the Hills"

In recent decades, the city of Rio de Janeiro has been depicted as experiencing a unique, and drastic, form of urban violence: a war that is not a war, or an undeclared civil war, centered in the city's favelas. For example, in a documentary film, a police captain assigned to the elite BOPE battalion stated:

> On April 20th I arrived at police headquarters before sunrise, and I was standing on the veranda looking at the *morros*, right? I noticed that there were tracer bullets flying from one hillside to the other. It was a war between drug dealers, and they were using tracer bullets, right? And then I thought to myself, in what other city of the world that is not at war would you see such a scene? Because there's no civil war in Rio de Janeiro. What we are living through is a war in the hills, a war between policemen and traffickers, or between traffickers themselves. (Salles and Lund 1999)

This way of speaking of urban violence in Brazil—characterizing it with a war metaphor—pervasively frames the multiple types of violence encountered by favela residents. As with any ideological construct, the war metaphor should be examined for what it hides as much as for what it reveals. If Rio is often described as experiencing a war, then this is a distinctly paradoxical and unique form of contemporary urban warfare.

There are three particular characteristics of this "peacetime war" that shape daily life in Caxambú and generate sets of questions that I address throughout this book. First, unprecedented levels of violence are occurring not under a totalitarian or dictatorial regime, but in a time of ostensible democracy. Second, urban violence is highly unevenly distributed over Rio's landscape. The third important feature of urban violence in Rio de Janeiro, connected to the first two, is how it generates radical uncertainties and senses of insecurity.

In 1985, Brazil emerged from over twenty years of military dictatorship. The return to electoral democracy produced both hope and anxiety. Brazilian social movements mobilized for the rights of the formerly excluded, such as indigenous people, the rural landless, and Afro-Brazilians. There was a heated political debate about public security and anxiety about the nature of social change in a deeply unequal society. The transition to electoral democracy also occurred without a thoroughgoing reform of the police and justice systems. A blanket amnesty for politically motivated crimes during the dictatorship allowed former political prisoners and left-ist guerrillas to regain their political rights. But the amnesty also meant that policemen who had committed acts of violence and human rights abuses as part of the dictatorship's repressive apparatus remained on the job. On a larger scale, Brazil was in the midst of a Latin America–wide convergence of three forces: increased global flows of capital and commodities, the rapid expansion of neoliberal economic policies, and an expansion of the regional drug trade.

One result was that throughout the 1980s and 1990s, Rio saw a rapid escalation of crime, especially homicide. Homicide is often taken as the prime measure of crime, since corpses are easily countable, whereas other indicators of crime depend on whether the victim reports the crime to the police, which Brazilians are often loath to do. Yet homicide is, of course, only one measure of urban violence, and is subject to manipulation.[12] Criminologists have also long pointed out that feelings of insecurity are often only loosely linked to actual rates of crime. Nonetheless, the rapid escalation of homicide during the 1980s and 1990s was shocking. Nationally, between 1977 and 1994, the homicide rate increased by 160 percent (Peres 2004, 19). The increase in homicide among young people during the 1990s was particularly dramatic: in the state of Rio, in the decade between 1989 and 1999 the homicide rate for those aged fifteen to twenty-four increased an amazing 217 percent (*Jornal do Brasil*, August 17, 2000).[13]

Not only did violence expand at a time of democratization but two other aspects of urban violence in Rio—features that distinguish the violence experienced in Caxambu and other poor neighborhoods in Rio—also stand out. First is the highly uneven distribution of homicide. Simply put, being male, a teenager or young adult, black or of mixed race, and living in a poor neighborhood make one far more likely to be the victim of homicide. Though statistics simplify the complexity of living in a militarized and criminalized neighborhood, producing the illusion that violence can be measured and controlled, they make this pattern clear. According to a study by Julio Waiselfisz, the nationwide homicide rate for those aged fifteen to twenty-four in 2004 was more than double the average homicide rate (2007, 8).[14] In the state of Rio, the homicide rate for fifteen-to-twenty-four-year-olds in 2000 was 107.6 per 100,000, a death rate almost equivalent to that of countries experiencing civil war (*Globo*, May 10, 2002).[15] The concentration of homicide in poor neighborhoods such as Caxambu is also clear. In 1996, for example, the homicide rate for young men in the wealthy neighborhood of Leblon was 12.7 per 100,000, while that of working-class Bangú was 120 per 100,000, ten times greater (Cano 1997). The city's black and mixed-race males are particular targets of this violence.[16]

It is also important to point out that the police play a major role in producing such extreme levels of homicide. In the 1990s, the police in Rio de Janeiro were responsible for approximately 10 percent of all homicides. Police violence is, of course, not an exclusively Brazilian phenomenon. Yet comparing police shootings in Rio to other cities indicates the lethality with which Brazilian police operate. In 1995 the police in Rio killed, on average, one person a day (*Globo*, April 12, 2001).[17] By comparison, in Los Angeles between 1985 and 1989 the police killed an average of twenty-five people annually, while in New York the average number for that period was twenty-three. According to Martha Huggins, "The Rio police annually kill almost as many civilians as all U.S. police forces do combined, although Rio's population is five and one-half million and the U.S. population is over 250 million" (2000, 116).

Police killings are concentrated in poor neighborhoods such as Caxambu. Statistics indicate that not only are police shootings of civilians more likely to occur in favelas but police shootings in favelas are also more likely to be lethal than in nonfavela areas. For example, between 1993 and 1996, the majority of killings by the police occurred in favelas, although the favela population is less than one-fifth of the city's total. Investigations have also repeatedly shown that despite police statements claiming that shootings in favelas occur in the context of gun battles with criminals, many shootings are executions. Ignacio Cano has shown that in at least half of the killings of civilians by police in Rio's favelas, the victim had four or more bullet wounds, mostly in the shoulder, chest, and head, indicating that the police often shoot to kill, not to disarm. Victims of deadly police force were hit from behind 65 percent of the time (Huggins 2000). Further belying the claim, often made by the police, that there are more killings of suspects in favelas because favelas are more dangerous to patrol are statistics that show the police are actually *less* likely to die in favelas than in nonslum areas. Knowing how to live in Caxambu, then, meant knowing how to live in a highly lethal neighborhood, particularly if you were young, male, and black or of mixed race.

Many factors account for the rapid increase in rates of crime and, in particular, for the high incidence of police killings. The legacy of impunity for violent state actors, and a lack of an effective judicial oversight of police violence—combined with a much larger collapse of Brazil's judicial system—are all important factors. The most important reason, though, is the territorialization of the city's drug trade in poor neighborhoods such as Caxambu. Beginning in the late 1970s, there was a regionwide boom in cocaine production in Latin America as Colombian cartels responded to shifts in demands for drugs by US consumers and changing policies of interdiction. Brazil quickly became both an important transshipment point for drugs destined for the United States and Europe, and an important local market as cocaine became a drug of choice among the city's elites. According to Alba Zaluar, so much cocaine became available so quickly that one of her informants recalled that in 1984 "it snowed in tropical Rio" (Zaluar and Ribeiro 1995, 95).

As the drug trade boomed, several large drug-dealing groups, such as the Comando Vermelho (CV, or the Red Command), came to power in Rio's favelas (Arias 2006; Gay 2005; Misse 2006; Penglase 2008). Because Rio's favelas house the city's working poor, they are often located near main transportation corridors or, in the city's wealthier southern zone, adjacent to the neighborhoods of the wealthy. Favelas were also historically excluded from regular police patrolling, and had a long history of antagonism between favela residents and the police. The criminal organizations that emerged in the city's favelas—which rapper and activist MV Bill has argued are best conceived of as *narco-varejo* (narco-retail) operations, rather than gangs or mafias (Athayde, Bill, and Soares 2005)—realized that favelas could be strategic stockpiling points for the distribution of cocaine to wealthier customers in other parts of the city of Rio. The relatively cheap price of cocaine—at least compared to the price paid by users in the United States and Europe—also meant that there was a small but significant customer base in favelas themselves. Favela-based traffickers also took advantage of the state's unwillingness to provide public safety in poor neighborhoods by repressing crime in favelas while harshly punishing anyone who cooperated with the police.

With the escalation of the drug trade, it became common for the police to describe their actions in the city's favelas in terms of urban warfare, often drawing comparisons with combat zones in foreign countries. For example, after a six-hour-long shoot-out between the police and drug traffickers in the Tijuca neighborhood during which four people were killed, the commander of the military police said: "We don't carry out policing. We carry out *combate de guerra* (warfare). The criminals have incredibly powerful weapons, worthy of Osama bin Laden" (*Globo*, April 2, 2002).

It is important to state, as most residents of Caxambu and of Rio's other favelas would insist, that the drug trade in Rio's favelas is only a small part of a larger whole that extends far beyond these poor communities. Only a few favelas make up the bulk of the trade, and the vast majority of favela residents do not participate directly in the drug trade at all. The residents of Caxambu also insist that the demand for drugs does not originate in their neighborhood, and that no one in Rio's favelas possesses the financial and political resources needed to ship drugs vast distances. In an interview, the rapper MV Bill, a resident of the favela of Cidade de Deus, expresses feelings similar to those of many residents of Caxambu: "The real *traficantes* (drug dealers) are in the Zona Sul [the wealthier part of Rio], the owners of boats and planes that bring the drugs. People who live in favelas and have some involvement in the drug trade are just soldiers. Soldiers in an army of blood" (*Extra*, October 24, 1999).

It is also essential to understand the distinctiveness of Rio de Janeiro's social and urban topography. In the United States and Europe, the neighborhoods of the poor are often distant from those of the wealthy, located either in the abandoned inner city or in distant working-class suburbs (Wacquant 1993; Wilson 1987). In contrast, Rio de Janeiro's traditional wealthy neighborhoods such as Copacabana and Ipanema are built on land squeezed between the ocean and the coastal mountain range, and poor favelas are often located on the outskirts of wealthy neighborhoods or even on hillsides within some of the city's most elite areas. This has led to what some observers have called the *carioca* pattern of urban development: a pattern that combines socioeconomic distance with spatial proximity—within what is, to my mind, one of the most breathtakingly beautiful cities in the world (Ribeiro 1996).[18]

The carioca pattern of urban development means that even though violence is highly concentrated in the city's favelas and poor neighborhoods, it can never entirely escape the attention of those who live in wealthier areas. The sociologist Luiz Eduardo Soares has summed up the paradoxical situation of Rio, a city marked by extreme inequalities and yet one where lives that are distant in socioeconomic terms are not always so easily separable:

Insecurity has spilled itself over the city. Fear, today, is a democratic sentiment. . . .
In Rio de Janeiro, the politics of privilege imposed itself for decades, as in all of

Brazil. But the human geography complicated the strategy of elitist isolation. The topography located favelas in the heart of wealthy neighborhoods. The daily interactions between classes made Rio a unique city. . . . In Rio there is no besieged citizenship: we are all part of one battlefield, immense, beautiful, and terrifying. (Soares 2000, 45)

Following Soares's lead, my approach is to interrogate simple assumptions about the invisibility or separation of the lives of the poor from those of the wealthy. Favelas are often depicted as separate territories. Yet they are the product of a larger process by which Rio's urban poor have been incorporated into the city's structure, even if in an informal and marginalized manner. This approach requires rethinking common arguments about the poor as being excluded from the city—assuming, for instance, that favelas are an example of the "prisonization" of poverty (Wacquant 2008).

Further, Soares encourages a focus on the sentiment of fear and insecurity. Soares might be right in stating that insecurity is a "democratic sentiment" and Rio can be thought of as an "immense battlefield." But insecurity and urban violence are experienced in very different ways in different social contexts. In a pioneering analysis, Teresa Caldeira and James Holston argued that a powerful sense of insecurity is widespread among Brazil's population (1999, 694). The fear of crime leads residents of Brazil's cities to restrict their movements, abandoning some public spaces and attempting to privatize others, and to support private responses to crime such as hiring security guards or supporting death squads. Urban violence has increasingly generated a set of discourses and practices that are reshaping how Brazilians think about and experience their social universe. In this sense, violence should be thought of not simply as destructive but also as productive, generating new meanings, emotions, practices, and forms of subjectivity (see, of course, Foucault 1977).

Yet there are many reasons to doubt that the experience of insecurity is equally shared by the middle-class residents of São Paulo's gated communities, whom Caldeira so aptly described, and Rio's favela dwellers, with whom I lived. Generalizing that a rise in violent crime has produced a blanket state of fear collapses social, racial, and regional difference. It also risks simplifying the complexity of daily life, particularly in poor neighborhoods such as Caxambu. In the neighborhoods of São Paulo studied by Caldeira, people had a pervasive sense of fear, yet the crime they experienced was mostly petty. By contrast, people who live in poor favelas in Rio such as

Caxambu often have very direct experience with violent crime. Many residents of Caxambu told me that seeing dead bodies was not uncommon. But they experienced, in their daily lives, a mixture of both security and uncertainty, a sense of safety and yet a worry about the possible appearance of lethal violence.

The third distinctive characteristic of urban violence in Caxambu is this ambiguous and ambivalent component of daily life—a state of (in)security. Urban violence in Rio shares much in common with what Carolyn Nordstrom has called dirty wars, where contending forces "use the construction of terror and the absurd as a mechanism for gaining or maintaining sociopolitical control over a population" (1992, 261). Unlike Sri Lanka or Mozambique, the cases Nordstrom focuses on, Brazil was not experiencing a declared civil war. But during the 1990s and early 2000s, it was commonplace to hear the city characterized as experiencing a war—but one whose causes and outlines are blurred and unclear.

The Brazilian filmmaker João Moreira Salles noted that when he visited Sarajevo he immediately thought of Rio, not because Sarajevo was similar to Rio but because it was so different. Salles felt that unlike Rio, the civil war in Sarajevo, as atrocious as it was, was openly acknowledged as a war; there were clearly defined ideological positions, and the war was ending through a peace process. The streets of Sarajevo felt safer than those of Rio, and the police presence less obvious. The main difference between Sarajevo and Rio, Salles stated, was the nature of the violence: "Theirs has an ethnic and religious basis, and is impregnated by the history of at least a thousand years. Ours . . . ours is an incognito." Yet, he pointed out, between April of 1992 and November of 1995, some 11,600 people were killed in Sarajevo. During the same period, 13,000 murders occurred in Rio (2001).

If imagery and experiences of warfare pervade much of daily life Rio's favelas, then we have to ask: what type of war is this and what are its effects? How is war experienced when conflict is not characterized by clear dichotomies or obvious battle lines? If there is a war in Caxambu and Rio's favelas, the identities of the combatants are clear: they are police, the local drug gangs, and other drug gangs vying for control of their rival's territory and drug distribution points. But clashing ideologies or political visions are not competing against each other there, and it is often unclear how the different sides are aligned. Police corruption and the actual involvement of some policemen in the drug trade produce scenarios that are shifting and opaque: the police and the drug dealers can be allies, can work together against other police or other drug dealers, or can quickly switch sides.

Anthropology of Violence in Latin America's "Age of Insecurity"

The increase in violent crime in Rio during the 1990s was part of a larger regional trend. According to Diane Davis, "violence could even arguably be considered the central—if not defining—problem in contemporary Latin America" (2006, 178). Across the region, as the Cold War ended in the 1980s, countries emerged from civil wars or authoritarian dictatorships. With the advent of democracy, Kees Koonings and Dirk Kruijt argue, "one might cynically state that violence is being democratized in Latin America" (1999, 11). For twin processes were taking place: there was a turn from protectionist economic policies to those favoring global free market competition, and rates of crime and interpersonal violence dramatically escalated. Violence has long been integral to state formation in Latin America. In the 1980s and 1990s, though, several new factors influenced the shape of violence. First, economic policies implemented throughout the region led to greater inequality. Second, one of the legacies of decades of civil war and dictatorship was a broad pattern of impunity for violent acts committed by the police and other security forces. Third, the expanded cross-border trade of goods enabled by neoliberal economic reforms also created new opportunities for drug trafficking and other forms of transnational organized crime.

As Desmond Arias and Daniel Goldstein note, "violence pervades much of Latin America, but the configuration and politics of that violence differ substantially from place to place" (2010, 21). An overview of several countries presents the larger pattern. In El Salvador, for instance, the number of homicides in 1995 matched, or perhaps even surpassed, the annual death rate during that country's civil war (Moodie 2010, 46). Likewise, when Guatemala's civil war officially ended in 1996, violent crime dramatically increased in many rural areas. Shockingly, Guatemala's homicide rate in 2005 exceeded the average number of people killed each year by political violence during the country's armed conflict (O'Neill and Thomas 2011, 11). As David Stoll has observed, for many Guatemalans, the end of the genocidal civil war coincided with a situation of greater anxiety about violence, though this time the perpetrators were criminals and not soldiers (2008, 188). Ellen Moodie likewise noted that in postwar El Salvador, life was characterized by a "new climate of risk" that some Salvadorans felt was "worse than the war" (2010, 21). Overall, Latin America is experiencing what Davis has called an "age of insecurity" (2006).

As crime rates have increased, so has the scholarly examination of violence. Scholars from a wide variety of fields have noted the negative impact that violence has upon citizenship, politics, and the nature of democracy. Guillermo O'Donnell, for example, has argued that some Latin American states have been unwilling or unable to extend full rights and citizenship to all their inhabitants. This has produced what he calls a "low-intensity citizenship," where poor and marginalized people live in a formally democratic state, yet cannot expect fair treatment in the courts or by the police (1993, 1361). In a similar formulation, Teresa Caldeira and James Holston have argued that Brazil can be characterized as a "disjunctive democracy," where citizens are free to vote in free and fair elections and yet cannot count on the state to guarantee civic rights such as the access to a fair trial, protection from arbitrary arrest or police abuse, or even the right to life (1999).

As I have attempted to understand how these processes impact the daily lives of the residents of Caxambu who I came to know, three arguments from the anthropological analysis of violence in Latin America have been guideposts for the analysis that follows. First, anthropologists have shown that the lived experience of violence is often one of deep ambiguity and uncertainty. Ellen Moodie, for instance, demonstrates how postwar violence in El Salvador was characterized by "radical uncertainty" (2010, 15). During the civil war, the structural causes of conflict were relatively clear. Postwar life in El Salvador, Moodie argues, is characterized by a pervasive sense of "not knowing," where daily life is characterized by individual risk taking in the face of an unpredictable social world. Likewise, Linda Green argues that one of the pervasive effects of the conflict in Guatemala was the creation of a state of fear, where the lines between combatants and civilians were increasingly blurred. For instance, young men who served in the army returned to their natal villages, populated by indigenous people similar to those whom they had been ordered to kill (1998). Aldo Civico, in his research with Colombian paramilitaries, notes an analogous way in which violence produces profound ambiguity. Paramilitaries are not formally part of the military, yet cooperate closely with the Colombian army in its war against leftist guerrillas. Paramilitaries, Civico states, "arise, grow, and develop in the shadows, that is, in a gray area where the borders between legality and illegality are blurred and confused" (2008, 135). Similarly, Daniel Goldstein argues that poor urban people in Bolivia, who are vulnerable to criminal violence and lack access to public services, feel that their social world is insecure. This daily world, Goldstein argues, "is highly unstable, characterized more by fragmentation and unpredictability than by order and routine" (2012, 5).

In such situations, understanding the effects of violence requires remaining attentive to what is not said, and to what is actively not known. Goldstein, in attempting to track the absence of the state in a poor barrio in Bolivia, calls such an endeavor a "hauntology" (2012). In my experience in Caxambu, I have found that similar absences, cloudy ambiguities, and ambivalences pervasively structure daily life. Residents of Caxambu, for instance, have to actively "not know" many things about the drug dealers with whom they share their neighborhood and who, in some cases, are their relatives, friends, and neighbors. In the chapters that follow I explore the larger social and historical context that has produced such ambivalences. For example, just as favela neighborhoods are both the product of racial and class exclusion and yet also affordable homes for the poor, where many have lived for generations, local drug dealers are also both "other," in that they are seen as having chosen a life of violence and crime, and yet are often well known, having grown up with residents of the neighborhood. They haunt the neighborhood while, at the same time, they are also deeply familiar. Rather than attempt to explain away such contradictions, or reveal the truth hidden under layers of ambiguity and uncertainty, I try to show how these contradictions and silences are socially created.

This brings me to my second guidepost. Anthropologists have argued that it is problematic to see violence as a pathological disruption of an otherwise peaceful social order. Instead, violence should be seen as part of a larger social context characterized by peace and conflict, domination and cooperation, contestation and agreement. Kay Warren has made the point forcefully, arguing that the danger of seeing the world as a stable system disrupted by instability is that this perspective "plays out to be (as often as not) a defensive support of the status quo of power arrangements" (2002, 381). Nancy Scheper-Hughes and Philippe Bourgois have likewise argued that rather than seeing peace and violence as opposites, they should be arranged analytically along a continuum. The social order enforced in spaces like public schools, hospitals, or nursing homes, they point out, can enable more dramatic forms of violence (2004, 19).[19]

Copious ethnographic observation has fleshed out these claims. Scheper-Hughes showed how residents of a poor shantytown in northeastern Brazil experienced routine forms of violence, what she calls everyday violence, such as not being counted in the census or being mistreated in public hospitals, which then enabled more of what she calls visible forms of violence such as infant mortality and death-squad killings of supposed criminals (1992). Daniel Goldstein, in his research in Bolivia, has shown how violence is not necessarily a breakdown of the social order, or a failure of the state. Goldstein argues that residents of Villa Pagador, a poor neighborhood outside of Cochabamba, lynched suspected criminals not only in an attempt to create public safety in their neighborhood but also to draw attention from the government (2004). Violence, in this sense, is not some sort of remnant of an uncivilized past. Instead, Goldstein argues, lynchings fit well within a neoliberal context, where austerity policies force cutbacks on public services and individuals are called upon to take responsibility for their own protection (2003). In her research in El Salvador, Moodie likewise argues that sensations of insecurity do not represent a breakdown of the social order, but are integral to a neoliberal context where an individual's ability to manage risk is seen as an important skill (2010).

In my research in Caxambu, I saw repeatedly how stability and instability, violence and peace, and safety and insecurity, all went hand in hand. The challenge for me in the chapters to come—the counterpart to hearing silences and to knowing what is not known—is to portray how daily life could be characterized by quotidian routine and dangerous interruptions of violence, a sense of safety and yet feelings of insecurity. For example, an afternoon sitting outside a street-corner bar in Caxambu could swing quite suddenly, as it did for me more than once, from a friendly chat with neighbors to a moment of panic, as the police drove up the hillside and fired their guns at drug dealers running down an alley, then back to "normal" life. Police violence was not unusual or uncommon. But it was also deeply disruptive to daily life. Inspired by the anthropologists I cite above, I attempt to show how in such a situation violence and peace, order and disorder are flipsides of a larger social context.

My third guidepost expands upon this understanding of violence and disorder as connected to peace and stability. Anthropologists have repeatedly shown how violence and insecurity can be productive by creating meanings, emotions, social relations, and forms of subjectivity. Rather than examining violence as a series of discrete events, the goal is "to locate it within a set of practices, discourses and ideologies, to examine it as a way to deploy power" (Nagengast 1994, 111). Arthur Kleinman has argued that violence can be a force that can order social worlds. He points out that this deeper form of violence is "perhaps all the more fundamental because it is hidden or secret violence out of which images of people are shaped, experiences of groups are coerced, and agency itself is engendered" (1997, 239). Anthropologists applying this concept in Latin America have examined, in particular, how concern with crime and violence produces discourses about security that, when deployed upon "dangerous" people or spaces, can create behaviors, experiences, and forms of being.

Elana Zilberg, in her research in El Salvador and Los Angeles, has shown how zero-tolerance policing, war-induced migration, and anti-immigrant policies were all part of a process that created a transnational gang threat (2011). Zilberg shows how the Los Angeles police force took an increasingly draconian approach to gang activity in the 1990s. As it adopted zero-tolerance practices, the LAPD transformed many common practices carried out by young men in immigrant barrios—standing in groups on a street corner, wearing clothes or making gestures indicating membership in a particular group—into illegal activities. Young men who did not comply with this attempt by the police to discipline barrio residents were singled out for particular punishment. Many of these men had left El Salvador as children, migrating to the United States to flee the political and economic chaos of civil war. When they were arrested and deported to El Salvador, they then were instrumental in creating the gangs—such as the MS-13 and 18th Street—that the police sought to control. As she states: "A politics of paranoia—be it of illegal aliens, gangs, or terrorists—relies on fictional realities to drive draconian agendas at the same time as it brings those fictions into being. It feeds into the proliferation of the very monsters it seeks to eliminate" (2011, 236).

Daniel Goldstein has drawn particular attention to how security and violence have reshaped daily life in Latin America (Arias and Goldstein 2010; Goldstein 2010). As countries throughout Latin America shifted from dictatorships to democracies during the 1980s, they also implemented neoliberal reforms that entailed drastic cuts to state spending on public services, the privatization of formerly state-owned companies, and the opening of local economies to global competition. At the same time, many countries in Latin America experienced rising rates of crime. Security, Goldstein argues, became a way to call upon fear to manage the crises of neoliberalism and its attendant forms of violence (Goldstein 2010, 487). On the one hand, the state could use concern with security to justify its coercive activities. At the same time, though, neoliberalism entailed devolution from the state of many of its responsibilities onto citizens, who increasingly became responsible for protecting themselves. Security, Goldstein argues, has become a "framework for organizing contemporary social life" that affects "the subjects of anthropological work and . . . the contexts within which that work is conducted" (Goldstein 2010, 488).

Inspired by this approach, I show how violence and insecurity produced social practices, meanings, and forms of being in Caxambu. As I explain in greater detail in Chapter 2, a broad discourse about insecurity stigmatized and criminalized the favelas of Rio as sites of violence and insecurity, as threats to the rest of the city. For this very reason, residents of Caxambu systematically rejected the term *favela* for their neighborhood, using instead the more neutral word *morro*, or hill. The images stigmatizing favelas enabled forms of policing and broader patterns of racism, exclusion, and marginalization that deeply shaped daily life.

At the same time, though, a focus on the lived experience of insecurity reveals a more complex picture. As Goldstein points out, security can be appropriated and redeployed by people who are the targets of state neglect, violence, and crime (2012, 121–165). In Caxambu, concerns about security and insecurity permeated daily life, as residents, drug traffickers, and the police all attempted to offer their own definitions of what security meant, how it could be provided, and by whom. I examine insecurity in Caxambu as such a contested site. I look, in particular, at the lived experience of insecurity, one that entailed both feelings of security and simultaneously of fear, one that produced people who were both familiar and strange, and one that made the neighborhood a site of both safety and danger.

The early twentieth-century Brazilian journalist, dandy, and bon-vivant João do Rio once quipped that Brazil's real national motto was not "order and progress"—the positivist slogan on the Brazilian flag—but "order in the disorder" (do Rio 1997, 236). I have often felt that this is the challenge in portraying daily life in Caxambu. Daily life in a neighborhood like Caxambu, where almost everyone knew each other and where many people were closely linked through ties of kinship and friendship, was a far cry from the images of favelas as violent, chaotic war zones. And unlike some poor neighborhoods in El Salvador, Guatemala, or Bolivia, daily life in Caxambu was not permeated by feelings of insecurity. Instead, most residents generally felt, most of the time, safe and secure. Life in a poor neighborhood where people had few resources and worked long hours was also often boring and tedious. But at the same time, the drudgery of daily life was sometimes punctuated by moments of joy and pleasure, and intense moments of danger. The inhabitants of Caxambu all knew that their daily routines could be suddenly interrupted by potentially lethal violence from the police or drug dealers.

João do Rio's challenge is to show how this unpredictability also contained a certain type of order, had its own logic. I would add that a further challenge is to show the disorder in the order: to show how a larger context of racial and class exclusion, a deeper structure of invisible structural violence, established the often unquestioned parameters of daily life in Caxambu. Safety and danger, unpredictability and order, violence and peace, were inextricably linked in daily life, producing a state of (in)security. In what follows I do not try to explain this state, but portray it, describe it, and perhaps give a sense of what it felt like. In particular, I turn to storytelling, narrating how I experienced (in)security but also letting the residents of Caxambu tell their stories.

In this book, I keep the analysis focused on daily life in Caxambu as I experienced it. My guiding concern is to explore how favela residents view their lives and worlds, how police and drug traffickers affect them, how other less visible forms of violence shape their lives, but also to show the joy and resilience of the people I came to know. In doing so, I have been guided by what Michael Jackson called "radical empiricism" (1989). That is, empiricism in the sense that I have focused on what I saw and heard, on the actual events that occurred, radical in the sense that what I saw and heard was the product of my own specific positioning. Another observer at a different time, and of a different gender, race, or social class, would probably have seen and heard otherwise. My focus has been a classic anthropological question: how do people in Caxambu understand their lives? What does violence mean to them, and how does it fit with all the other aspects of their daily struggles and joys?

The methodological challenges here are two: first, how to depict both order and disorder in ways that do not reify one as the normal counterpart to the other; and second, how to depict a situation of uncertainty and unpredictable violence when I myself was part of the story. Kay Warren has suggested one approach. She argues that ethnographers should present "narratives of absence and displacement that capture the contradictory currents of change" (2002, 391). This is the approach that I have pursued, centering each chapter in this book around particular narratives, or ethnographic vignettes, that do not present a stable, coherent social world disrupted by violence, nor do they show a chaotic world where no rules apply. Rather, I have tried to present stories that can show how both security and insecurity, order and disorder, coexist, as people struggle to make sense of and cope with the instabilities they experience. It has become fairly common, in the analysis of urban violence, to argue that violence produces "epistemic murk" (Taussig 1986) or "everyday states of emergency" (Scheper-Hughes 1992). A radically empiricist approach leads me not to simply evoke these tropes, as powerful as they are, but to examine the particular social interactions where these states were generated and describe, as best I can, the meanings and emotions that they generated—to examine as precisely as possible how the residents of Caxambu experienced and understood the order in the disorder.

Ethnographic Representation and the Paradoxes of Daily Life

Though this is a book about urban violence, most of the more violent incidents that I examine happen off stage. There are several reasons why this is so. I am not interested in describing violent acts to shock the reader, engaging in what Nancy Scheper-Hughes and Philippe Bourgois have called a pornography of violence that both attracts and repels the reader, yet that disables critical analysis (Scheper-Hughes and Bourgois 2004, 1). As Bourgois argues, harrowing descriptions of violence can "reinforce negative perceptions of subordinated groups," while failing to reveal "the chains of causality that link structural, political, and symbolic violence in the production of an everyday violence that buttresses unequal power relations" (Bourgois 2004, 433). Instead, I am interested in the lingering effects of more traumatic events, in what happens after the shooting is over, so to speak.

I was also not present when some of the more extreme incidents of violence occurred. Like most residents of Caxambu, I was careful about protecting my safety, generally avoiding the neighborhood late at night and going indoors when the police were raiding the neighborhood or when a contentious drug deal was happening. I felt that it was more important to participate in the strategies that residents used to avoid violence than to attempt to be an eyewitness to dangerous incidents. Directly witnessing violence might have made me seem more heroic, yet it would have been extremely dangerous and would have made my neighbors think I was a fool.

Throughout the book, then, the focus is mainly on residents of Caxambu who do not directly participate in the drug trade, and upon the small, mundane ways that violence shapes their lives. I have focused every chapter around particular "moments of crisis," or what Sally Falk Moore called diagnostic events, which help to convey what it is like to live in a state of (in)security. These moments do not reveal smooth functioning of a social order, but instead the "ongoing contests and conflicts and competitions and the efforts to prevent, suppress, or repress these" (1987, 730). At these moments the established social order and senses of security and predictability are called into question, and indeterminacy is most apparent. These are also moments when tensions in the relationship between large-scale structures and individual agency is most acute, when conditions seem impossible and yet the imperative to do something is unavoidable. These moments, though, present no easy resolution, no clear guideline into knowing how to live in Caxambu. Instead they are moments of absence and displacement that exemplify the challenge of living in a state of (in)security.

In Chapter 2, I compare two such moments from my fieldwork to describe how discourses of insecurity shaped both my research and daily life in Caxambu. The first moment of crisis was the first time that I was stopped and searched by the police. Being searched by the police was an almost archetypal ethnographic moment, one which seemed to give me a deeper rapport with residents of Caxambu, and which seemed to make tangible larger forces such as policing and the drug trade. The second incident, when I was embroiled in a long-simmering dispute, shows how daily social life is also often full of uncertainty, ambiguity, and danger. To make sense of these two incidents, I show how they were shaped by a discourse of insecurity that takes favelas to be prime symbols of disorder and danger.

Chapter 3 examines how the built space of the neighborhood mediates local social relations. This chapter is organized around another fieldwork moment, a discussion between Seu Lázaro, an older man and local community leader, and Tubarão, a drug dealer, over whether or not Tubarão should wear his gun while sitting with me in Seu Lázaro's backyard. Here the focus turns from the citywide discourse of insecurity to a more local context, examining how Caxambu's local history is reflected in the stories that residents tell about their neighborhood. I show how lived experiences are founded upon an older, larger contradiction between the neighborhood's officially illegal yet unofficially tolerated status, what Boaventura de Sousa Santos has called the basic insecurity of Rio's favelas (1977, 91). This local context produces profound ambiguities, as the space of the hillside is deeply familiar, literally the product of generations of work by Caxambu's residents, yet also a zone of exclusion.

I also explore how this contradiction enables the emergence of drug traffickers, who flourish in this "alegality" or "extralegality." Social relations between people who inhabit the morro of Caxambu, especially young men involved in drug trafficking, are paradoxical, as these young men are both well known to everyone, yet are seen as dangerously seduced by a world of crime. I call these young men dangerous intimates. The way that residents of Caxambu speak about their neighborhood as a big family, though, does not simply reflect its history or disguise actual inequalities. Instead, I show how the discourse of a familiar hillside is also a tool that residents can use as they attempt to manage relationships with local drug traffickers.

In Chapter 4, the focus turns more directly onto the relationships between residents of Caxambu and local drug dealers, examining the structures of authority that drug traffickers create. This chapter examines what happened when the drug dealer Tubarão shot a local man and also shot and killed Seu Lázaro's pet dog. Building upon the analysis of the relationship between order and disorder, I argue that drug traffickers in Caxambu do not impose their power through brute coercion, nor by establishing a clear statelike structure of rules. Instead, they rely upon what I call a strategy of abnormalization as they both insist upon a set of rules that determine how favela residents must interact with them, yet also consistently violate these rules. As drug traffickers attempt to appropriate security and insecurity, they have a profound impact on local understandings of gender and authority.

Chapter 5 examines how policing shapes daily life in Caxambu. Here, too, I do not look at the more extreme cases of violence in Caxambu. Instead, I examine mundane interactions between the police and favela residents, showing how militarized forms of policing reshape experiences of racism and social discrimination. Using the idea of criminalization—or the

attempt to redefine everyday practices as crimes—I argue that prior interpretations of police violence in poor neighborhoods have failed to truly
understand how police practices affect daily life. The police, I argue, produce a new form of prejudice, the prejudice of criminalized space, which
overlaps with and also reshapes older forms of racial and social discrimination. An ethnographic look at police practices on the ground also shows
that the police are neither absent from poor neighborhoods like Caxambu nor do they simply cordon off the wealthy from the poor. Instead,
I show how policing often works symbiotically with drug-trafficker violence as they both produce forms of disorder that both try to turn to
their advantage.

Chapter 6 concludes the analysis of Caxambu's state of (in)security, not
by offering a sense of closure but by juxtaposing the meanings and memories attached to three different parts of the top of the hill that Caxambu is
built on: a sidewalk where a girl named Estela was killed; a bust of Brazil's
former president Getúlio Vargas; and a large cross that sits in front of Caxambu's long-abandoned Catholic church. In each of these three cases, it is
possible to see the productive qualities of Caxambu's state of (in)security
by examining how violence, in Allen Feldman's term, "semiotizes" spaces
and objects (1991). The meanings and memories attached to these three
places are opaque, contradictory, and in many ways phantasmagorical.
They serve as final reminders of how the transnational drug trade, broader
flows of legal and illegal commodities, clashes between the police and drug
dealers, and competing notions of security or the lack of it reshape local
places and social relations. At the same time, as the residents of Caxambu
attach their own meanings to their neighborhood, they engage in social
tactics that help them navigate the wider state of (in)security, not challenging more powerful forces such as the police or local drug dealers, yet quietly insisting on their own agency, identity, and pride.

Participant-Observation, Narcocultures, and the Law of Silence

Rio's drug trade has undergone significant changes since the time I conducted my fieldwork in Caxambu. The late 1980s and early 1990s were,
perhaps, the high point of the consolidation of the drug trade in the hands
of the CV. By the late 1990s and early 2000s, when I did my fieldwork,

serious rivalries within the CV led to a splintering of the organization. As the CV splintered, rival organizations (the Terceiro Comando and the Amigos de Amigos) took advantage of the group's divisions and fought for control over favelas, becoming major forces in their own right.

By the early 2000s, new actors emerged: elements of the police and other agents of the state moved directly into organized crime, establishing groups called *milícias* (McLeod-Roberts 2007; Zaluar and Conceição 2007). Unlike the CV, milícias do not focus exclusively upon drug trafficking, but pursue a wider and more traditional strategy of organized crime, demanding payments by favela residents for the provision of safety and seeking to profit by regulating and organizing favela-based forms of extra-legal economic enterprises, from drug trafficking to unregulated transportation. The more recent UPP policy of permanent police occupation of favelas will, no doubt, provoke even more changes in the structure of drug dealing.

Though the drug trade in Rio is highly dynamic, the CV and Terceiro Comando have left a deep legacy on daily life in Rio's favelas, producing what might be thought of as a narcoculture. As one aspect of this legacy, Rio's drug-trafficking organizations have had a profound impact upon language, which filters through the rest of this book and deeply shaped my research. Marguerite Fietlowitz has shown how the violence unleashed by Argentina's military dictatorship produced a new lexicon, one that distorted and reshaped perceptions of reality and that remains one of the most profound and lasting legacies of the dictatorship (1999). Rio's drug-trafficking organizations have similarly reshaped the language used in the city's poor hillside neighborhoods, producing a linguistic culture where reality is often opaque and ambiguous.

The terms used to talk about drug trafficking and drug traffickers, for example, are highly ambivalent and characteristically amorphous, drawing variously upon imagery of warfare, the language of corporate management, romanticized folk legends, and much more diffuse imagery. The most common term used to describe drug dealers, and which the drug dealers use to describe themselves is *bandido*, meaning bandit and evoking the famous outlaws whose exploits defying the police and elite delight Brazil's poor, especially in the northeast. A particularly famous example was Lampião (Chandler 1978), whose legends have become the stuff of Brazilian folklore (Slater 1982). Rio de Janeiro also has its share of famous Robin Hood–like bandits, such as the mythical Charles 45, made famous by a song by pop singer Jorge Ben. Drug traffickers are also often called *malandros* (hustlers), evoking the romanticized image of the stylish rogue or man-about-town often celebrated in samba songs for his ability to live at the margins of the legal world, creatively avoiding the discipline of wage labor. An array of other terms used describe drug dealers include *a rapaziada* (the guys), and *o pessoal* (the group).

Other terms associated with the drug trade are vague and polysemic. One of the most common terms used to describe the drug dealers was the impersonal noun, *o tráfico* (the traffic), meaning both the drug trade and drug traffickers themselves. Another widely used term was *o movimento*, literally the movement. Both terms evoke impersonal, evanescent, yet omnipresent forces. They partially erase the social identities of particular people, merging them into larger and almost nonhuman forces. A *movimento* is not a person, but can be interpreted as having an ambiguous political reference—a movement for what, organized by whom?—or referring to the physical state of movement itself. *Tráfico* also evokes circulation, movement, and a lack of ties to any one place. Other terms used to describe drug dealing and the drug gang share this abstraction and placelessness. For example, the drug purchasing or stockpiling point in Rio's favelas is known as the *boca de fumo*, literally the mouth of smoke.

Drug trafficking affects not only the lexicon of Rio's favelas, but also how language is used in practice. One crucial aspect of knowing how to live in Caxambu is abiding by the law of silence, which mandates that residents of the neighborhood must not speak to outsiders, and especially not to the police, about the activities of the drug dealers or, more broadly, about any negative aspects of living in Caxambu. Ellen Moodie argues that Salvadorans were often encouraged to "not know" the structural conditions that led to increased crime rates in postwar El Salvador (Moodie 2010). An analogous process took place in Caxambu, but on a more local scale, as residents had to "not know" about local drug dealers. As Dona Carmen once told me: "Here you have to pretend that you're blind, deaf, and dumb. You can't see anything, hear anything, or write anything." Another resident demonstrated how to do this when he told me about how the current drug gang was different than former ones: "Now this *pessoal* (personnel) . . . this *rapaz* (guy) who is here is smarter, more cunning. He doesn't let anyone invade anyone else's house. Do you understand? He doesn't let the *pessoal* . . . because he already has what he wants from the residents, and the residents need him, so we . . . understand? Not that . . . not that I'm in favor. But I'm also not against. I'm neither for nor against. I have . . . I have my own opinion, right?"

This conversation is typical of the use of semantically broad terms—such as *pessoal* (personnel), *rapaz* (guy), and simply *ele* (he)—to talk about particular individuals who are known to both speakers. This semantic ambiguity was not only common in taped interviews but was also a constant feature of everyday talk, and this interview is only unusual for the frankness with which the resident addressed the drug trade's impact on the neighborhood. In the conversation that opened this chapter, for instance, when Dona Carmen referred to me being "friends with everyone," she may have been alluding to the local drug traffickers (or maybe not).

Navigating the law of silence, or knowing how to speak about the unspeakable and understand the unspoken, presents distinct challenges for an ethnographer committed, as I am, to both critiquing oppression and also not violating the trust that my neighbors and friends in Caxambu placed in me. Though this is not a book about the drug trade per se, and it is certainly not an exposé of any hidden secrets, I am aware that speaking openly about the contradictions of daily life and the radical ambivalence produced by violence means violating local social norms. I worry that I risk portraying residents of Caxambu as themselves violent.

At the same time, my friends and neighbors in Caxambu constantly urged me to "tell it like it really is." In the pages that follow, I strive to present both the difficulties and also the creativity, spontaneity, and joy with which the residents of Caxambu lived their lives. It is, of course, tempting to present them as victims of the police or of local drug dealers or, on the contrary, to present a counternarrative of peaceful coexistence. Yet knowing how to live in neighborhoods like Caxambu—and thus the immense daily creativity and skillful social tactics of favela residents—is far more complex. It means navigating the state of (in)security, a social world characterized by both friendship and rivalry, quotidian normalcy and sudden danger, exclusion from formal channels of influence, and yet deep integration into flows of goods and commodities. I hope that presenting the complexities of daily life in Caxambu, and highlighting the perseverance and creativity shown by its residents, allows me to violate the law of silence.

2

"Now You Know
What It's Like"

Ethnography in a
State of (In)security

> Getting caught, or almost caught, in a
> vice raid is perhaps not a very generaliz-
> able recipe for achieving that mysterious
> necessity of anthropological fieldwork,
> rapport, but for me it worked very well.
> —Clifford Geertz (1973, 416)

"Everything Was Dust and Panic"

When I describe how I conducted research in Caxambu, I often tell a story about one of my first encounters with the police. Heavily influenced by Clifford Geertz's archetypal description of fleeing from a police raid, I have often presented this moment as one where I managed to gain an inside view into living in a state of (in)security. As I have reflected more critically on my fieldwork, though, I have realized how my research has been deeply shaped by pervasive representations of favelas as spaces of insecurity and danger. I offer this ethnographic vignette, then, to open a discussion of the conditions that shaped my ethnography. This story also begins a discussion of the "ways of living" adopted by favela residents: their neighborhoods have been so heavily influenced by a discourse that represents them as spaces of danger, insecurity, and violence that favela residents have elaborated a counterdiscourse that challenges these images. The story below shows how I had come to reproduce this discourse. It is followed by a discussion of my own positioning and how I was affected by images of favelas. I then trace a historical genealogy of the discourse that depicts favelas as sites of difference. A final ethnographic vignette contrasts sharply with the first, revealing how conducting an ethnography of (in)security entails attending to silences and ambiguities and attempting to understand the production of ordered disorder.

One day, after I had lived in Caxambu for several months, I was talking to Seu Lázaro at the top of the hill that the neighborhood was built upon. Seu Lázaro was the president of Caxambu's residents' association. Residents' associations were established in many favelas throughout Rio in the 1960s and 1970s, with two main purposes: to represent the interests of favela residents to state officials, especially regarding urban infrastructural needs, and to regulate internal conflicts over land and property (Gay 1994; Santos 1977). Seu Lázaro and I were speaking with two other favela residents about a project that was paving one of the neighborhood's main streets when, quite suddenly, a police car drove up the hill. The car came screeching to a halt and two heavily armed policemen jumped out. One policeman, carrying an automatic rifle, ran down an alleyway while the other, with his hand on a forty-five caliber revolver, walked around the area.

At this point in my research, I had seen searches and even shootouts in the neighborhood, but none from this close up. I was nervous, but I had been told that the worst thing to do when the police came into the neighborhood was to run. Residents said that policemen often believe that anyone who runs away from them is admitting guilt, and regard this as an invitation to shoot at them. The local adage was "se correr o bicho pega," literally "if you run the animal gets you" (the second part of the adage was "se ficar o bicho come," or "if you stay the animal eats you").

Despite my "local knowledge," I had a sudden desire to become invisible or somehow disappear. A few minutes after the police got out of their car, I felt someone behind me patting my lower back, and then reaching around me from behind to feel my front pockets. As this was happening, I noticed that Seu Lázaro, who was facing me and could see what was happening behind me, had not reacted in the slightest. After a moment of confusion—what's happening, who is behind me, why are someone's hands in my pockets, and why isn't Seu Lázaro saying anything?—I realized that I was being searched by one of the policemen. Before I fully understood what was happening, the policeman's attention shifted elsewhere: not finding a gun tucked into my shorts and hidden under my T-shirt, the policeman searched two other people who were standing nearby. He then walked down to a small plaza, a bit further down the street, where the second policeman was searching three young men.

It was only when the police eventually got into their car and drove away and everything was essentially over that I could begin to figure out what had happened, and that the reaction of those around me began to shift. Turning to Seu Lázaro, I said: "Damn, I thought I was being robbed, right here in the *morro* [hillside]," attempting to index my insider status by referring to how local drug dealers, claiming to protect the morro, ensure that crime in the neighborhood is rare. Seu Lázaro responded: "With these policemen you never know, you better make sure that your money's still there." Sergio, who was standing nearby, added: "And you better make sure that they didn't put something else in your pocket that they can then use to arrest you."

Later that day, as I was teaching an English class to a group of adults in the offices of the residents' association, one of the lieutenants of the head drug dealer interrupted my class to ask if I was all right. When I responded that it really wasn't a big deal, he loudly stated: "The police here don't treat anyone with respect, not even foreigners like you, and even Seu Lázaro can't do anything to stop it." When the drug dealer left our classroom, one of my students told me: "See, now you know what it's like."

Geertz famously wrote that his running away from a police raid on a cockfight dramatically altered how Balinese villagers viewed him and his wife (1973, 416). I have often presented the vignette above as an analogous story of how being searched by the police as a serendipitous crossing of a "moral or metaphysical boundary" dramatically shifted my status to that of a "covillager," and allowed me to understand how residents of Caxambu experienced insecurity. Of course the consequences of being searched by the police were far less serious for me than they were for young dark-skinned men in Caxambu. But being searched by the police altered how

I was perceived by residents of Caxambu, including local drug traffickers who had often regarded me with bemused, but somewhat suspicious, indifference. In his ethnography of crack dealers in Harlem, Philippe Bourgois likewise describes being searched by police in New York as a moment when his status in El Barrio shifted (Bourgois 1996, 30). I've often thought of it as a moment when I achieved that mysterious ethnographic goal: rapport.

What I have come to realize, though, is how deeply I had been influenced by a set of discourses and practices centered upon concerns over danger and security that shape how favelas are understood. I offer this chapter, then, as an exploration of the complexities of conducting an ethnography in the midst of a state of (in)security. Several anthropologists who conduct ethnographic research on the police have pointed out that policing so thoroughly saturates many social settings that it sets the conditions of ethnographic inquiry itself (Garriott 2013). An analogous process happened in my case: discourses and practices centered upon competing notions of security or insecurity, crime or safety, so saturated daily life that I myself was caught up in, and often reproduced, some of them.

When I attempted to joke with Seu Lázaro and Sergio about being robbed in the neighborhood, I was participating in a counterdiscourse elaborated by many residents of Caxambu about safety and violence. I was depicting the police as the real source of danger in the neighborhood. Sergio and Seu Lázaro quickly picked up on this, joking back about police corruption and attempts to extort money from favela residents by accusing them of being drug dealers. The implicit contrast that I was constructing was between the police and local drug dealers, who attempted to legitimate themselves by claiming to repress crime in the neighborhood.

My comments drew upon a commonly used contrast between the morro and the surrounding city, depicting them as two separate areas governed by two different codes of security. In the favela, the usual equation between policing, crime, and safety was reversed: I was implying that drug traffickers guaranteed safety while the police were criminals. The second-in-command of the local drug trade did not hesitate to reinforce this understanding of security. By criticizing the police for disrespecting me, he was implying that it was local drug dealers who not only guaranteed that there would be no theft in the morro but who also treated residents with respect. In this way, my reaction to the police raid was connected to a discourse of insecurity that attempted to legitimate the authority that drug traffickers exercised in the neighborhood.

This is the public, acceptable version of what life is like in the morro, a version often presented by residents of Caxambu and other favelas in Rio, and one that I for many years also repeated. In this version, daily life is not dangerous and chaotic, but predictable and safe. Drug dealers are not violent outsiders, but local men (and a few women) who protect favela residents. The perception that outsiders have of what constitutes security is contested and reversed: if the morro is stigmatized by outsiders as a site of danger and disorder, for insiders it's quite the opposite, a place where everyone knows and "respects" everyone else and where crime is uncommon. The police, on the other hand, are the outsiders who disrupt an otherwise peaceful and harmonious (if poor and marginalized) community.

The incident also presented the social tactics of knowing how to live in Caxambu as a matter of learning how to follow the rules composed by these contrasts. The police are a force of chaos and unpredictability, outsiders who intruded upon the morro. Drug dealers, on the other hand, are responsible for safety, insiders who know the particularities of the morro. During normal daytime hours, public spaces in Caxambu were safe, becoming dangerous only when the police appeared. Knowing how to live appears to be a simple matter of avoiding the police while confiding in local drug traffickers for safety.

Yet this depiction of real security should not be taken at face value. It is, itself, a reaction to a much more complex and contradictory social reality and presents an overly simplistic view of my research, and an overly simplistic vision of Caxambu's state of (in)security. It also reproduces—as does the counterdiscourse of security that favela residents rely upon—some of the foundational images of favelas as distinct and different spaces.

While this vignette appears to show how what Geertz calls an "immediate, inside-view grasp" of daily life, Sergio's comments can be seen as pointing to the ambiguity of my status (Geertz 1973, 416). On the one hand, I was a resident of the morro, however temporarily. Talking with me about how I'd been searched by the police was a way for favela residents to point out that despite my lighter skin and greater wealth, I too was vulnerable to police harassment. Yet due to my lighter skin color and assumed greater wealth, I was singled out for different forms of harassment. As Sergio noted, the police often assume that wealthy people in favelas are there to purchase drugs, making them attractive targets for extortion. While being searched by the police showed that I was embedded in a shared context of a criminalized and racialized space, it also marked my difference.[1]

The counterdiscourse of safety is seductive because of how it critiques simplistic stereotypes of the dangerous favela. Like many favela residents, as I lived in Caxambu, I became highly attuned to how stereotypes of the dangerous favela influenced everyday life. In imagining favelas as zones of exception, this discourse, for instance, empowered abusive forms of policing. I felt, on the contrary, a need to present the joy, pride, and happiness of life in Caxambu. I struggled to present the people I knew in Caxambu as distinct individuals, with their quirks, individuality, and sparkle, as well as their faults. I felt driven to critique the simplistic assumption that "favela resident" and "favela" were valid categories of analysis. Perhaps most powerfully, I felt compelled to challenge the rhetoric that depicts favelas as criminalized, socially pathological, and dangerous spaces (and that by contrast represents the rest of Rio as safe and normal).

Yet simply inverting outsider's views of Rio's poor neighborhoods— showing how the apparent disorder of daily life was ordered—normalizes the impact of structures of power on Caxambu's residents. Highlighting the arbitrary nature of policing can naturalize drug-trafficker violence. Viewing the favela as a distinct space ignores the multiple ways that it is tied to the rest of the city. Viewing the police as outside intruders ignores the multiple ways that the state has shaped favelas and has attempted to control and discipline favela residents. Viewing the favela as a space distinct from the rest of the city, governed by a different social code, risks viewing difference as a given rather than the product of structures of marginalization and oppression.

This chapter, like the rest of the book, is animated by the tension produced by these two perspectives: on the one hand, the discourse that residents of Caxambu use to counteract the discrimination and marginalization they face, and their attempt to create a normative system that could help them navigate a fraught social field; on the other hand, the awareness that public presentations of what life in the morro is really like do not map directly onto a complex, contradictory, and unpredictable social and urban landscape. This is a tension that I experienced in my own research and writing—fearing, for instance, that writing about internal conflicts in the favelas, or about the fraught and complex relationships between favela residents and local drug dealers, would only promote stereotypes of the dangerous favela. But I have come to feel that portraying "what it's really like" requires a more critical analysis of how my perspectives have been shaped by images, discourses, and practices that have seen favelas as spaces of alterity, constituted them as a threat to the city, and sought to control or discipline favela residents.

Ethnographic Positioning in a State of (In)security

In his famous analysis of how he came to understand the links between rage and headhunting in the Philippines, Renato Rosaldo emphasizes the need see the ethnographer as a positioned subject. He states: "The ethnographer, as a positioned subject, grasps certain human phenomena better than others. He or she occupies a position or structural location and observes with a particular angle of vision" (1989, 19). The ethnographer's postionality not only affects what he or she observes but also shifts, sometimes quite dramatically, as in Rosaldo's case. For me, the process was more subtle, as I have become more aware of my own embeddedness in a discourse of insecurity that shaped what I saw in Caxambu. As Daniel Goldstein has observed, the concern with security that has become so pervasive throughout Latin America influences not only the people whom anthropologists study, but the very context within which ethnography occurs (Goldstein 2010, 488).

My angle of vision was informed by many factors. As a white American with access to greater resources than most favela residents, I was distinctly an outsider in the morro, no matter how long I lived there or how well I learned the local slang. Yet the experience of having a foreigner living in the morro was not entirely novel. In the 1960s, several Peace Corps volunteers had lived in the neighborhood, and older residents remembered these *estrangeiros* (foreigners) very fondly.[2] Zeca, for instance, spoke about how when he was a boy the neighborhood kids would use any excuse, like a scrapped knee, to seek out the medical care and attention of the Peace Corps volunteers. Older residents told me about a volunteer who they called Seu Antonio who worked with them to dig pit latrines and improve local sanitation.

My race and nationality, though, never went unremarked, and had a large impact upon how residents described their neighborhood to me. Many people I spoke with in Caxambu—not the least of whom were local drug dealers—were adamant about critiquing what they saw as inaccurate images of favelas in the media, so that I could know what it was really like. The fact that I was more light-skinned than most residents of the morro also led many people to compare race relations in Rio to what they knew about racism in the United States. Both residents of Caxambu and other people I came to know in Rio also remarked upon the fact that I chose to live in the morro with my wife.

The social experience of inhabiting a criminalized and stigmatized space, however, was often seen as leveling other differences. More than the dramatic events like police searches, it was dealing with mundane routines of life in the neighborhood that had the largest impact upon how I was perceived by people in Caxambu. When we first moved into Caxambu, for instance, we brought with us a gas-powered stove. I found someone in the neighborhood who sold butane tanks, and after paying him I hoisted the tank onto my shoulder and carried it a few blocks up the hill. By the time I got into my front gate, I was sweating profusely and huffing and puffing. A while later, after I hooked up the tank and went to Seu Anselmo's small bar to buy a soft drink, I noticed a group of people standing together and looking surreptitiously at me. Clara was standing in the group, and when I went over to talk to her, everyone else walked away.

My confusion must have been obvious, and I asked Clara: "o que foi (what happened)"? She told me that people were surprised that I had carried the tank home myself. "Why's that?" I asked. "Well," she said, "they're not used to seeing someone like you get dirty and sweaty." Without realizing it, I had violated the social norm that ties racial difference to forms of labor: wealthier and lighter-skinned people do not usually engage in physical labor. I am not sure whether this was seen as a demonstration of my sense of egalitarianism, or whether people simply assumed that I was foolish for doing such a chore when I could have paid someone else to do it for me. At any rate, sharing in daily chores and routines, most made more difficult because of the lack of decent transportation and shopping options in the hillside, indicated that I was operating outside of the normal and often implicit structures of race and social class.

Even more significant was the fact that my wife worked outside of the morro. Unlike me, she woke up every morning, walked down the steep hillside, and caught a bus in the neighborhood below to go to work downtown. I, on the other hand, spent all day hanging around the morro, chatting with people and occasionally interviewing some, and drinking copious quantities of *cafezinhos* (small, highly sugared cups of coffee) and the occasional beer. No one thought that these activities were "work." Dona Carmen didn't lose the opportunity to make a critical comment. Once when I was buying lunch from her backyard kitchen, she told me: "You're just like all the other men in the morro. Every morning I see your wife get up and go to work while you just sit around and talk with people all day." My explanation that I was "fazendo pesquisa (doing research)" soon became a running joke: *fazendo pesquisa* became a term for hanging out and drinking beer.

I also brought with me to Caxambu assumptions about how to document the social and cultural impact of violence. Prior to becoming an anthropologist, I was a researcher for Human Rights Watch, a major US-based human rights organization. In that capacity, I had written a report on police and death-squad violence in urban Brazil and had made contacts with several organizations active in Rio's favelas (Penglase 1994). This experience provided me with prior understandings of policing and human rights, and also shaped how I thought I would conduct my fieldwork: the human rights methodology of documenting significant exemplary cases of, say, police violence, around which campaigning and activism could be organized led me to look for equally dramatic examples of violence in Caxambu. As Winifred Tate has argued, although this case study approach is an effective campaigning strategy, it is also problematic because it risks separating extreme acts of violence from their larger social context (2007).

Perhaps most fundamentally, I had brought with me a series of assumptions about favelas, one deeply informed by the position that favelas have assumed in discourses about insecurity and violence in urban Brazil. First, driven by my experience as a human rights researcher who had seen a rapid escalation in crime and urban violence in Brazil in the 1980s and 1990s, I assumed that favelas were the natural place to investigate crime and insecurity. I also assumed that the Brazilian state was largely absent from favela communities, that they existed as zones outside of the law. Favelas seemed to be zones of difference and danger, self-contained communities just beyond or in many cases perched above, the "regular" city of Rio. When I lived in Brazil as a child with my family in the late 1970s and early 1980s, we often drove through the favela of Rocinha on our way to school. Favela life seemed both close at hand and yet remote. As zone of mystery and danger, favelas seemed to promise adventure and a glimpse into an authentic Brazilian style of life.

Rosaldo emphasizes that the ethnographer's positionality is not static, but can shift, and that this change in positionality can reveal new understandings. Sometimes, as in Rosaldo's case, this shift can be radical: he states that he was only truly able to understand the links between grief, rage, and headhunting when he had to cope with the accidental death of his wife. My change in positionality was not nearly as dramatic. But as I lived in Caxambu for a longer period of time, my understanding of daily life began to depart dramatically from what was portrayed in my initial story about being searched by the police. Particularly important has been my shift from being an (even part-time) resident of the morro to someone who can look back on this experience from a greater distance, realizing how I too had been caught up in a state of (in)security.

Reflecting back on his fieldwork four decades later, Geertz argues that field research "is not a matter of working free from the cultural baggage you have brought with you so as to enter, without shape and without attachment, into a foreign life" (1995, 94). Rather, fieldwork is an attempt to observe and search out facts while inserted in the midst of political conflict. Large-scale political developments and struggles for hegemony are not external to fieldwork. They are the context that shapes it. As Geertz states: "You may set out to isolate yourself from cosmopolitan concerns. . . . But the concerns follow you. The contexts explode" (95). Understanding my research, then, requires an analysis of the larger context of discourses, policies, and struggles for hegemony that have often taken favelas and favela residents as central objects.

As I have suggested, favelas have been particularly affected by a set of discourses and practices that depict them as zones of exception, as areas where the normal rules do not apply (Agamben 2005). Initially, this difference was twofold: racial and legal. In racial terms, the population of favelas was largely—though not exclusively—composed of the descendants of emancipated slaves, or mixed-race migrants from northeastern Brazil. Early observers saw favelas as pockets of backwardness, and were fairly explicit in tying this perception to racial difference. Legally, favelas were characterized by the fact that people did not own the land that they built their homes on. By the 1980s, favelas continued to be seen as zones of exception, though the two original criteria of difference were complemented by a third, as favelas were closely associated with drug dealing and urban violence. Understanding how this occurred, and what it meant for daily life and for my research, requires placing my research in a larger historical context.

A Genealogy of Favelas and Discourses of Insecurity

Almost from the very first moment that the neighborhoods which came to be called favelas appeared on Rio's hillsides and other vacant plots, they were the subjects of intense scrutiny by outsiders, occupying a distinctive symbolic place in how residents of Rio understood themselves and their city. These images and policies have varied, and I cannot review all of them here, though I want to point out some recurring patterns.[3] These images and policies not only shaped how I conducted my ethnography but also continue to account for the visibility of favelas in images of Rio de Janeiro and deeply influence daily life in Caxambu. As I pointed out in the introduction, it is not by chance that international media reports on Rio de Janeiro's preparations for the 2014 World Cup and the 2016 Olympics have focused so heavily on the state government's efforts to "pacify" the city's poor neighborhoods. Favelas have consistently been seen as prime symbols of difference, as an internal other against which the rest of the city of Rio defines itself. At the same time, favelas have paradoxically been seen as exemplary of Rio, as the real Rio that exemplifies, perhaps magnifying, broader and more pervasive cultural concerns. By the time I conducted my research, urban space was becoming increasingly segregated. Favelas continued to be seen as different, but were increasingly militarized and criminalized. One other paradox also recurs: although favelas have been the object of scrutiny and government intervention for decades, they have consistently been seen as mysterious and unknowable neighborhoods beyond the control of the state, pockets of difference (and often of pathology) located in the heart of the city of Rio.

Though runaway slaves and Rio's poor sometimes occupied the city's hillsides in the nineteenth century, the first neighborhood to be called a favela was built on the Morro da Providência, in downtown Rio in the late 1890s (Abreu 1994, 37; Zylberberg 1992, 52–57).[4] Almost from the start, the Morro da Favela (as it became known as) and other similar shantytowns were regarded by the city's elite and press as an eyesore and a threat. As early as 1902, the Morro da Favela was described as a dangerous place (Abreu 1994, 39). In 1901, Rio's mayor inspected shacks on the Santo Antônio hill, called them "real pig sties," and ordered their immediate destruction.[5] Thus a pattern was set early on, producing what Lícia Valladares has called the "matrix image" of favelas: they were seen as backward, uncivilized, and rural, threats to the city's health and modernity, exotic zones of poverty that few wealthier people dared to enter (Valladares 2005, 36).

Perhaps most important, the people who occupied these downtown hills did not own the land that they built their homes upon. As Boaventura de Sousa Santos has argued, the lack of land title created a broader context of basic insecurity and established a broader pattern of relations with the state (Santos 1977, 91). Because favela residents did not have legal title to their land, they were vulnerable to removal by the state at any minute. On the other hand, this vulnerability was useful to the city's economic and political elite: the economic elite needed a source of labor and yet did not want to pay salaries that could allow their workers to live in more expensive legal residences, while politicians could make use of favela residents as dependent upon their largesse and political patronage.

At the beginning of the twentieth century, favelas spread as emancipated slaves and the rural poor joined with those displaced from downtown tenements in seeking affordable housing. By the mid-1920s, there were an estimated 100,000 people living in favelas (Abreu 1994, 41). This spread of informal neighborhoods paralleled larger transformations, as Brazil shifted from slavery (which was abolished in 1888) to wage labor, and as Rio's elite sought to beautify the city to present it as a modern capital of Brazil's new republic. Setting another pattern, favelas became prime targets for discourses and policies concerned about managing these larger changes.

Not surprisingly, given that Rio's elite were attempting to shed the stigmatizing legacy of slavery, many images of favelas connected them to blackness and primitiveness. Abreu states, for instance, that press reports from the early 1900s made frequent reference to the "persistence of Africa in the midst of civilization" (Abreu 1994, 40). Other images of favelas from this period oscillated between seeing these neighborhoods as threats to the city, centers of disease, poverty, and crime, and as remnants of a more rural and backward, though also simple and honest, Brazil.

A particularly powerful example is a short article written by Benjamim Costallat, a well-known journalist in the 1920s, describing a visit to the Morro da Favela. Costallat wrote: "The favela has no light, no sewers, no water, no hospitals, no schools. It has nothing. . . . But the favela is happy, up there in its hideaway, with the marvelous panorama of the city unfolding at its feet" (1990, 34–35). The favela was defined by what it lacked, but this poverty was combined with positive (and perhaps simple-minded) simplicity and joy. Foreshadowing the dominant image of favelas by the 1980s, Costallat also portrays the favela as existing beyond the reach of the law and as fundamentally violent. Costallat's depiction continues: "In favela the law is made by the strongest and the bravest. . . . It's natural that *valentes* and *malandros* (bullies and hustlers) search out the favela as an ideal residence" (37).

Public policies went hand in hand with these images. In the first years of the twentieth century, a public hygiene campaign sought to eliminate yellow fever and smallpox in the city of Rio. Though favelas were not the specific targets of this campaign, they were singled out, along with other areas housing the poor, as a threat to the city's health. Rio's urban poor regarded the health campaign, and especially the actions of health agents, as an intrusion upon their privacy, and sparked riots that brought Rio to a standstill in 1904 (Carvalho 1997). At the same historical moment, favela residents were also targets of Brazil's vagrancy laws (Huggins 1985). Under the vagrancy laws anyone without a permanent job or fixed address was considered a *vagabundo* and was subject to arrest. Because many favela residents didn't have steady jobs, and because the favelas themselves were considered temporary, the vagrancy laws gave the police a wide berth to arrest favela residents (Abreu 1994, 40–41). This history accounts for what Santos, conducting research in a favela in the 1970s, already saw as a pattern of reciprocal hostility between favela residents and the police (Santos 1977, 42).

These images and campaigns would have a long-lasting impact on Rio's favelas. Almost from the start, favelas were seen as sites of difference and deficiency, whether that was understood in racial terms, with favelas linked to blackness and racial degeneracy; in terms of modernity, with favelas seen as remnants of rural villages; or in class terms, with favelas seen as pockets of poverty and vagrancy. Closely tied to notions of difference were images of illegality, or at least of extralegality, as favelas were seen as beyond the law. These images went hand in hand with campaigns to discipline and control favela residents, whether through public health campaigns or through labor legislation. Favelas were zones of exception, where the regular rules of how the state should interact with its citizens were suspended. Ironically, these persistent attempts by the state to intervene in Rio's poor neighborhoods are repeatedly forgotten, while images of lack persist. But lasting patterns were set in motion as favela residents sought to claim the status of *trabalhador* (worker) to avoid arrest under the vagrancy laws, and as favela residents came to regard the police and agents of the state with deep distrust.[6]

Policies toward favelas—and their prominence in the city's social imaginary—boomed in the 1930s and 1940s during the populist regime of President Getúlio Vargas. Vargas, who assumed the presidency in 1930 after a military-led coup, sought to create mechanisms that could create patronage ties between his government and Brazil's growing working class. Fittingly, the first explicit recognition of favelas by the government was also an attempt to control their growth: the Código de Obras (Construction Code) of 1937 banned the construction of new favelas, and prohibited the construction of new homes in favelas that already existed (Leeds and Leeds 1977, 191–192). This policy was never enforced, and given the explosive growth of favelas at this time it seems hardly enforceable. But favelas came to be seen as areas in need of external control, even at the levels of their built form.

At this time, favelas were also closely associated with samba, a musical form often seen as Brazil's national music.[7] In the 1930s, as the radio and the phonograph facilitated the popularization of samba, songs about favela life came to be seen as indicative of musical and cultural authenticity. With the commercialization of samba, middle-class composers would sometimes claim songs written by favela-based musicians as their own, appropriating a largely Afro-Brazilian and working-class music in a process analogous to what Robin Moore has called nationalizing blackness (1997). This musical development dovetailed nicely with the Vargas regime's nationalism.

The popularization of samba led to a new romantic vision of the favela in popular music. A passage from a popular magazine in 1935 captures this new samba-influenced vision of the favela: "In the morro, music is typical. It's the musical laboratory of Rio, the great workshop of samba, the arsenal of *batucada* (drum beats), the source that Cariocas seek out every year for the sounds that beautify their emotional carnival" (Zylberberg 1992, 97). Although this was a more positive vision of favelas, exoticism still prevailed. The favela came to be associated with the archetypal subjects of samba songs: the free-living and stylish *malandro* (hustler), who disdained regular employment and lived by his wits, and the beautiful *mulata* (mixed-race woman). Here, the mythologized space of the favela is the site where racial and sociopolitical boundary crossing met and were romanticized: the malandro who lived at the margins of the law, not a complete criminal but certainly not a law-abiding worker, being the male complement to the mulata, a woman at the margins of racial stereotypes, not a high-status and therefore unobtainable white woman but also not a socially undesirable black woman.[8]

The Vargas regime's mixture of control and assistance inaugurated a pattern of state-favela relations that persists to this day. When Brazil has experienced more authoritarian forms of government, favelas have been the targets of removal and relocation. During periods of political openness, favela residents have been courted for their votes, and the government has accepted the existence of favelas in the city. In both cases, Brazil's political elite have sought to control favela residents, and have subordinated the needs of these residents to larger goals of economic development and the struggle against communism, or to the narrow interests of partisan political expediency (Abreu 1994, 44; Leeds and Leeds 1977, 188; Valla 1986, 22). Regardless of policy switches, discourses about favelas persistently depicted them as zones of difference and lack, zones that challenged the rest of the city and required outside attention, whether that was assistance or removal.

For instance, with a shift back to democratic politics in the late 1940s, favelas came to be seen as a political challenge. In response, in 1947 the government and the Catholic Church established the Fundação Leão XIII (Leeds and Leeds 1977, 198; Valla 1986, 45). The goal of the Fundação was to preempt the growing popularity of the Communist party by providing favela residents with social centers, schools, and clinics; one of the Fundação Leão XIII's slogans was: "it's necessary to go up the hill before the communists come down" (Leeds and Leeds 1977, 198–199).[9]

With democratization, politicians also began to discuss urbanization, or the consolidation and infrastructural improvement of favelas and their transformation into "regular" neighborhoods. Some of the first steps toward urbanization were undertaken by SERFA (Serviço Especial de Recuperação de Favelas e Habitações Anti-Higiênicas), a state agency that worked in conjunction with favela residents. To ease this cooperation, the government encouraged the establishment of residents' associations, and associations were organized in seventy-five favelas (Leeds and Leeds 1977, 212).

This new policy of urbanization was matched by a view of favelas that saw them as symptoms of Brazil's poverty. A prominent example is a famous samba song entitled "Acender as Velas," or "Light the Candles," composed by Zé Kéti in 1966:

No morro não tem automóvel pra subir
No morro não tem telefone pra chamar
E não tem beleza pra se ver
E a gente morre sem querer morrer

[In the morro there are no cars
In the morro there are no phones
And there's no beauty to be seen
And we die without wanting to die]

When Brazil's military seized political power in the coup of 1964, the federal government no longer had any need to court the favela vote. Some favelas, especially those in the wealthier southern part of the city, occupied valuable real estate and were also seen as an impediment to modernization and development. As a result, removal became the state's main policy: between 1969 and 1972, 80 out of a total of 283 favelas were totally or partially destroyed, most of these located in the wealthier Zona Sul (Valladares 1978, 12).[10]

Democratization and Favelas as Symbols of Urban Disorder

When Brazil returned to democracy in 1985, favelas came to play a major role in debates about the nature of post-dictatorial security and social order. During the public campaign for a return to democracy, a wide variety of people who had previously been socially excluded emerged on the national stage. Indigenous activists, landless rural workers, feminists, and Afro-Brazilian activists all made sure their voices were heard, especially during the drafting of the 1988 constitution. In Rio, same period saw the emergence of a vocal and well-organized favela activist movement.

As in other parts of Latin America, the end of authoritarian rule brought with it an intense debate about the nature of citizenship and about how to restructure the state in a democratic context of the rule of law. In Rio, as throughout Brazil, of the central political questions was what role the state's agents of repression, in particular the police, would play in a new democratic order. At the heart of the issues were competing definitions of security and order, and contrasting notions of transgression. Favelas played a central role in this debate, though they would come to have diametrically different meanings for different political forces. At the same time, the meanings of favelas began to shift, from being seen as racially or economically backward, they came to be seen as challenges to law and legality, as sites of violence and insecurity.

In 1982, Leonel Brizola, a vocal opponent of the dictatorship, became Rio de Janeiro's governor in the first direct elections since the return to democracy. Brizola was a particularly polarizing figure, and did not fit easily into the established political divisions at time. He was not allied with either of the established political parties on the right or left. Instead, Brizola's power base was his own populist political party, the Partido Democrático Trabalhista (PDT). For Brizola, favelas represented both social exclusion and a valuable source of electoral support. During the campaign, Brizola and his populist political party actively courted the favela vote and received key political support from the favela association movement FAFERJ.

Once in office, Brizola and the PDT rewarded this support by carrying out public works in highly visible parts of favelas (Gay 1994, 31). Brizola also felt that democratically elected politicians needed to regain control over the security forces and that policing should be restrained by the rule of law. Significantly, he suspended the police's practices of invading favelas on little or no pretext and harassing favela residents—a persistent demand of favela political leaders (Sento-Sé 1998, 57).

In Brizola's populist vision, favelas were prime symbols and examples of economic inequality and injustice. For him, the police should be subjected to the rule of law, and crime would only end when Brazil's income inequality was diminished. Brizola's rhetoric met substantial opposition, however, and was not matched by thoroughgoing reform or attempts to reform the police (Soares 2000, 110). He was particularly hampered by opposition to his policies by the federal government and stiff resistance within the police force.

Brizola's relaxation of police harassment of favela residents came just at the time when organized drug trafficking was expanding in Rio's favelas. Several high-profile incidents involving drug dealers would eventually lead to Brizola's electoral defeat. In late 1985, the drug dealer Escadinha (José dos Reis Encina) managed to escape from the high-security prison on Ilha Grande by stepping onto a helicopter that had landed on the prison's roof. At this time, the exploits of favela-based drug dealers such as Meio-Quilo, from the favela of Jacarezinho, and Dênis, from Rocinha, were attracting major attention in the media, and these figures were on their way to becoming household names.[11]

Brizola's governorship was significant for two larger reasons. First, Brizola's attempt to limit police actions in favelas inaugurated the belief that drug trafficking in Rio's favelas was the result of the state's absence from these communities. In the minds of many Cariocas (residents of Rio), Brizola's refusal to allow the police to "subir o morro" (invade favelas) allowed drug traffickers to take over favelas. (In a backhanded allusion to this perception, Brizola has become a nickname for cocaine.) During Brizola's governorship, the old association between favelas and crime would be intensified, as favelas were blamed for the expansion of drug trafficking. For example, a respondent to an opinion survey in 1984 said: "Rio de Janeiro must get rid of the favelas, because they are the centers of criminality and are always connected to drugs and drug bosses" (Soares and Carneiro 1996, 37).

Second, during Brizola's governorship a larger discussion about the nature of public order, the role of the police in a democratic state, and about income inequality and social inclusion would largely be replaced by a debate about how best to stop crime, and crime and violence would be tied to Rio's favelas. Brizola's pro–human rights approach to policing and public safety would lead to a dramatic law-and-order backlash by his successor as governor of Rio, Wellington Moreira Franco.

The Territorialization of Drug Trafficking

The territorialization of drug trafficking in Rio's favelas in the late 1970s and early 1980s had a major impact upon how favelas were viewed. I explore the impact of drug trafficking upon daily life in more detail in the chapters that follow, but here I want to show how traffickers both deepened and yet appropriated for themselves the rhetoric of insecurity that depicted favelas as zones beyond the law, marked by crime and danger.

In the 1970s, there was a regionwide expansion of the cocaine trade throughout Latin America, as Colombian traffickers responded to shifts in both US demand for drugs and in patterns of repression. As this was occurring, a criminal organization began to consolidate itself in Rio's prison system. In 1979, prisoners in the maximum security prison on Ilha Grande organized themselves and staged a major prison riot, taking over the prison and killing anyone who refused to join their organization. This group—which came to be called the Comando Vermelho (CV, or Red Command)—then spread throughout the prison system and beyond as members were released from prison or escaped.

In the 1980s the criminal economy in the city of Rio shifted, and members of the CV decided to move into drug trafficking, seeking to monopolize the city's retail trade in cocaine and marijuana. They launched a violent campaign to take over favela-based drug distribution points, killing any favela-based criminals who would not join their organization. By 1984, most of the important *donos*, or "owners" of drug-selling points in favelas, were part of the organization.[12]

While the CV pursued a violent campaign against rival drug dealers, it also cultivated the support of favela residents by carrying out a policy known as *boa vizinhança* (good neighborliness). Many members of the CV were themselves from favelas, and they realized that they could turn the insecurity and the lack of the public provision of safety in favelas to their advantage: if favela residents refused to cooperate with the police, then drug traffickers associated with the CV would provide public safety in favelas, severely repressing robbery, theft, rape, and other criminal activity.

More broadly, traffickers associated with the CV seized upon images that depicted favelas as spaces of deprivation and lack, and promised to institute a form of local authority that would benefit favela residents while advancing their own interests. In a documentary film, Gordo (Carlos Gregório), one of the early leaders of the CV, explained this policy by referring to the CV's motto, "Peace, Justice, and Liberty" (Sales and Lund 1999):

> GORDO: The project was peace, justice and liberty. Peace was to live in peace within the prison. Justice was to do . . . to have social justice. The project was to do everything . . . the Comando Vermelho would enter into every hole ignored by the authorities.
>
> INTERVIEWER: And do what?
>
> GORDO: Everything that the government doesn't do. And liberty, everyone knows what that means: to escape from prison at any cost.

In what came to be known as the *lei do morro* (law of the hillside), leaders of the CV proposed a bargain to favela residents: as long as favela residents turned a blind eye to drug dealing, the CV promised to "respect" favela residents. Unlike the police, traffickers associated with the CV promised to provide public safety, and to not treat favela residents as criminals. As Luke Dowdney has argued, while this was a reciprocal exchange of protection for silence, it was also highly asymmetrical, as drug traffickers could force cooperation though the barrel of a gun. He calls this, in a phrase I will borrow, forced reciprocity (Dowdney 2003).

Like the media and policy makers, favela residents often talked about shifts in drug-dealer strategies in terms of metaphors of violent warfare.

However, the equation between drug dealing and violence was often reversed. For some residents of Caxambu, the expansion of the CV into their neighborhood did not bring violence and danger, but rather greater security and safety. For example, as I walked up and down the steep *ladeira* (stairway) leading from the street up to my house near the top of the hill, I often ran into André, who supplemented his income as a *cobrador* (ticket collector) on a bus by operating a small store from the window of his home. One afternoon I asked André what the neighborhood was like when he was younger:

ANDRÉ: Ah, it was good. But when I was fifteen to twenty there was a climate that was . . . how could I say this? . . . sort of stormy, right? Wars. It was the time of wars in the seventies to eighties. Understand? Drug wars, right? And it wasn't good for the community.

BEN: Of course not.

ANDRÉ: So what happened? No one had peace. But then there was a change in the behavior . . . with a change in the people (*uma mudança no pessoal*) there was a change in behavior. It seems that people started waking up slowly, about what was right and what wasn't. What should be done and what shouldn't. And over time they changed things.

For André, the emergence of the CV brought an end to an earlier period, in the late 1970s and 1980s, when there was an intense citywide conflict over control of sales points of cocaine in Rio's favelas. The "change in people" that he refers to happened as the CV consolidated its control over Caxambu and many other favelas in the 1980s.[13] For André, this did not result in greater violence, but rather in a positive shift in relations between favela residents and local criminal organizations, as new drug dealers thought more systematically about "what should be done and what shouldn't."

In a bitter irony, the CV reproduced depictions that tied favelas to disorder, but presented itself as the authority that could bring order to previously insecure and dangerous neighborhoods. The CV's attempt to institute a different set of rules in favelas also built off of, and deepened, the perception that favelas where distinct and different urban spaces, governed by their own codes. A song by Bezerra da Silva, a former favela resident and chronicler of Rio's poor, takes the perspective of a drug dealer addressing the police, and puts the issue succinctly:

Você manda lá embaixo
Aqui em cima quem manda sou eu
Eu não piso em seu terreno
Nem você não pisa no meu

[You're in charge down there
Up here I'm the boss
I don't step on your property
And you don't step on mine]

As this song indicates, the emergence of the CV and the territorialization of drug trafficking deepened a pattern that depicted the social and physical space of the city of Rio as divided between "up here" (the favela) and "down there" (the "regular" city). These two spaces were now seen as corresponding to two different systems of control: two different bosses, as it were.

Security and Public Safety as Political Merchandise

As organized drug trafficking expanded in Rio's poor neighborhoods, discourses about insecurity became even more prominent, and politicians campaigned on promises that they would implement policies to protect public safety. Security and violence became symbolic political merchandise to be exchanged for votes, and favelas and discourses of transgression were prominent in how public order and security were understood. The association between crime, drug trafficking and favelas, and the discourse that associated favelas with urban difference and insecurity, were cemented in place.

Brizola's successor as governor of Rio, Wellington Moreira Franco, for example, campaigned successfully on the promise that if he were to be elected, he would "end violence in six months." Moreira Franco argued that public safety was best advanced not by redistributive policies, but rather by strictly repressing crime. He told an interviewer: "I see criminality as an issue of urban, social, and public disorder. We need policies to guarantee public order, and the function of the police is to maintain order" (Filho and Filho 2003, 258). If for Brizola police violence represented a rupture of the social order, then for Moreira Franco the equation was reversed: police coercion was necessary to maintain order.

Moreira Franco's response was to lift prohibitions on police actions in favelas: he reestablished the police policy of *pé na porta* (kicking in the door), or unbridled invasions of favela homes and harassment of favela residents (Soares 2000, 111). Though this police tactic seemed to have little effect (rates of crime may have actually risen during Moreira Franco's term), it established a lingering belief that combating crime meant lifting human rights restrictions upon police actions in favelas.[14] Favelas continued to be seen as zones of exception, areas where the normal rules of policing did not apply.

After Moreira Franco's administration, Leonel Brizola was once again elected governor of the state of Rio. Brizola and his vice governor, Nilo Batista, a prominent human rights attorney, attempted once again to shift back to a human rights and redistributive approach.[15] Brizola also named Colonel Carlos Magno Nazareth Cerqueira, an Afro-Brazilian and a reformist, as the commander of the military police. Yet several high-profile incidents during Brizola's second term made a reformist approach to public security impossible, and further deepened the associations between favelas, violence, and a citywide sense of insecurity.

First, after an unseasonably warm weekend in October 1992, newspapers and television screens were plastered with images of a supposed mass mugging carried out on Rio's iconic Zona Sul (southern zone) beaches. Media reports blamed gangs of teenage *funkeiros* (fans of funk music) from the city's favelas and poor suburbs (Penglase 2007; Yúdice 1994). Initial media reports linked these groups to Rio's main favela-based drug-trafficking organizations. The implicit message was clear: favela-based violence, largely carried out by young dark-skinned males, was spreading to the wealthier and whiter southern parts of the city.

As Paul Gilroy has argued in his analysis of media reports on muggings in the UK, anxiety about crime was understood in racial terms, and then came to symbolize a larger national crisis (1987). In this case, the mass mugging was represented largely in geographical and class terms—as residents of favelas and the poorer northern zone invading wealthier beach-front areas—with the racial component left unstated. Letters in the *Jornal do Brasil* newspaper made this clear, explicitly calling for restricting residents of the city's northern zone from access to beach-front neighborhoods during the weekends. The weekend immediately after the muggings, the police stopped buses from the northern zone at Ipanema's Arpoador beach and searched passengers, temporarily detaining youths who did not have identity cards.

Second, a series of incidents in 1993 and 1994 led to the perception that the elected officials of the state of Rio could not control their own police force, and that violence had gotten out of control. In July 1993, a group of off-duty police killed twenty-one residents of the favela of Vigário Geral (Neate and Platt 2010; Penglase and Kass 1993). Among those killed in the shooting were a family of evangelical Protestants, who were seen as innocents having nothing do to with drug dealing. In a second high-profile incident of police violence, thirteen residents of the Nova Brasília favela were killed by the police in October 1994. There was a widespread call for the federal government to assume control over Rio's internal security.[16]

After months of negotiation between Rio's state government and the federal authorities, in November 1994 the army launched Operation Rio (Caldeira 1996; Leite 1998; Resende 1995). The root cause of the federal government's intervention in Rio's internal security was concern about rampant police corruption and the pervasive sense that Rio's authorities had lost control over public security. But Operation Rio quickly narrowed its focus to the city's favelas. The stated goal of the army's operations was to "reestablish reasonable levels of security," with priorities being to arrest members of drug-trafficking groups, disarm the population, and carry out social services in favelas controlled by drug traffickers (Caldeira 1996, 59). To huge media fanfare, the army temporarily occupied five favelas, searching all who entered or exited the neighborhoods and carrying out sweeps to search for drugs and weapons.[17]

Operation Rio resulted in very few arrests and the apprehension of minimal amounts of drugs and weapons. According to media reports, drug dealers in the neighborhoods occupied by the army simply moved their operations elsewhere, though the price of drugs reportedly tripled during the operation. But the official military spokesman for the operations stated that the important impact was psychological: formerly out-of-bounds spaces had come under the authority of the state, manifested through the presence of the army (*Jornal do Brasil*, November 15, 1994).[18] Once again, a state intervention in favelas was depicted as having rescued favelas from a lack of state interventions.

What Operation Rio did, though, was to consolidate a vision of favelas as neighborhoods at war, giving birth to what Márcia Leite has called the war metaphor (2008). Broader anxiety about rising crime, social conflict, and the collapse of the public security apparatus was displaced onto favelas, which were depicted as war zones, distinct and different areas of the city in need of control and pacification. Operation Rio, as João Trajano Sento-Sé argued, "enshrined the ascension of a militarized approach as the only possible alternative to confronting the issue of crime" (1998, 69). Favelas were presented as natural targets for military action. News reports in anticipation of the army's operations (which took months to plan) presented maps of the city showing favelas as black marks set off from the rest of the supposedly peaceful city. Leite argues that media reports at the time were dominated by a metaphor of warfare that presented favelas as threats to the rest of the city. Rio came to be seen as a divided city with prior patterns of interclass sociability between favelas and other neighborhoods replaced by sentiments of fear and insecurity (Leite 1998, 105).

As Operation Rio was occurring, Marcello Alencar took office. Governor Alencar, who was the governor of Rio when I began my research, represented the epitome of a harsh, militarized approach to crime, treating favelas as virtual "free-fire" zones. Alencar and his secretary of public security, General Newton Cerqueira, unleashed the most intense wave of police violence in Rio's history.[19] Cerqueira openly described Rio as experiencing an undeclared war in the city's favelas, and argued that limits to police violence should be removed. He implemented a policy known as the *gratificação faroeste* (Wild West rewards), which rewarded policemen for "acts of bravery." Not surprisingly, police shootings of civilians skyrocketed, as police claiming to have killed criminal suspects in shootouts were given rewards.[20] Alencar was also responsible for privatizing a wide range of state-owned businesses, including the subway system, the BANERJ bank, Rio's electrical company, and the state-owned phone company TELERJ.

At the same time that favelas were being subjected to heavily militarized policing, they were also subjected to a project to alter their urban form. In 1996, the city of Rio de Janeiro's municipal government began a project called Favela-Bairro, partially funded by the Inter-American Development Bank, which sought to integrate favelas into the "official" city. The project's ambitious goals included: improving the basic infrastructure in favelas, regularizing access to essential municipal services, creating and improving public spaces, improving entrance and exit routes, removing homes from dangerous areas, building child-care and job training centers, and regularizing titles to homes. The Favela-Bairro project was based upon explicitly articulated connections between the uniqueness of favelas, crime, and social control. A planner closely associated with the project has stated that one of its goals was to extend regular government services to the favelas to undercut the patronage systems local drug syndicates used to encourage the cooperation of favela residents. The way that favelas occupied urban space was seen as deficient, and this deficiency in turn enabled crime. The solution was for outsiders to eliminate this difference by integrating favelas.

Alencar's heavy-handed approach to public security was altered by Anthony Garotinho, who was elected governor of Rio while I was living in Caxambu. Garotinho, a former radio personality, had campaigned on a technocratic approach to crime and violence. Garotinho saw crime and security as issues of management amenable to technical intervention. He appointed as his secretary of public security an anthropologist, Luiz Eduardo Soares, who was also a well-known human rights activist. Soares's attempt to reform the police, including bringing the civil and military police under a joint command, quickly met stiff opposition. After a stormy five hundred days in office, Soares resigned, claiming that he had been undermined by a *banda podre* (rotten bunch) within the police force. Many speculated that Garotinho feared that the police could harm him electorally by withdrawing from the streets and causing a panic about public safety. Here again, the ability to produce security or insecurity became, quite directly, political leverage that elements of the state could use to advance their agendas.

While Garotinho inaugurated a technocratic approach to policing that has continued to this day—policies such as the UPP "pacification" campaign can be seen as citywide application of community policing efforts begun by Garotinho—he did not alter the association between favelas, crime, and insecurity. Rather, insecurity and crime were seen as objects of knowledge and mastery. Ending violence in favelas required "modern" policing, with favela residents seen as objects to be policed, not citizens whose opinions and demands should be heard.

The UPP policy, which occurred after I conducted my research, systematized this approach. The favela pacification policy was part of a larger reform of the police in the state of Rio. Governor Cabral, who took office in 2007, and his secretary of public security sought a systematic collection of data on crime in various locations, and sought to identify "hot spots" requiring greater policing. They also incentivized policing by basing police salaries and promotions upon hitting preestablished crime reduction goals (Ferreira 2011; Stahlberg 2011). Policing would be carried out according to modern, technology-driven, and "objective" criteria. At the same time, though, favelas were seen as in need of a highly distinctive and militarized approach, as targets of pacification. Unlike the rest of the city, regular city services and citizenship would be conditional upon successful military-style occupation. And the residents of Rio's favelas would have little say in how or when this pacification occurs. Although the UPP policy promises peace, and does appear to have significantly decreased rates of violence, it continues to paint favelas as zones of exception, enemy territory to be retaken.

Clara's Barbecue

It is only as I have reflected critically upon my experiences that I have been able to see that my initial story about what life is "really like" in Caxambu was, while well intentioned, shaped by this larger context of discourses of insecurity that permeate images of Rio's favelas, deeply shaping daily life. The counterdiscourse that I had internalized, one repeated to me by many residents of Caxambu and that I had heard from inhabitants of other favelas, simply reversed the usual equation: favelas were not zones of criminality, they were actually safer than the surrounding city; and local drug dealers did not impose an arbitrary rule of violence upon favela residents, rather, they protected favela residents, while it was the police who were the threat. Order, here, was simply the reversal of what outsiders perceived as disorder. Life in the morro was secure, but this security was produced not by the state, but by local drug dealers.

A different incident, one that occurred after I had lived in Caxambu for almost a year, presents a very different vision of daily life. This story is not particularly traumatic or shocking—it was, in fact, probably as mundane as being searched by the police. But unlike the official version of what daily life is like in Caxambu, this story revolves around jealousy, rivalry, and unresolved conflicts over status and resources. Here the apparently clear dichotomies and social structures that the first story reveals are far murkier and more blurred. And rather than showing how I had mastered how to live in Caxambu, it presents me as an outsider, still unsure of exactly what is occurring underneath the surface. Most important, it shows how alongside a quotidian world of predictability and common identity there was a darker zone of uncertainty, ambiguity, and danger, or a state of (in)security.

As my major period of fieldwork was drawing to a close, Clara invited me to her birthday party. Clara, who is the same age as I am, worked as the secretary for the residents' association and was one of my main informants and best friends in Caxambu. Unlike many people in the morro, Clara had attended college, but dropped out after her family was unable to continue paying her fees. Her educational background, and her position as a gate-keeper for access to resources available through the residents' association, set her apart from many other favela residents. Despite having an extended family who resided in Caxambu (or, as I would eventually learn, perhaps because of this), Clara had tried several times, though unsuccessfully, to move out of the neighborhood. All of these factors made her, to paraphrase Victor Turner, a classic "marginal person" (1967, 145). Since she was both highly critical of many aspects of life in the morro and also deeply connected with many of its residents, she was invaluable for my research. As the secretary of the residents' association, Clara also often had hours of free time, which we often spent chatting and getting to know each other.

When Clara invited me to her birthday party, I felt deeply obligated not only to attend but to reciprocate by helping her pay for the party. The party was a *churrasco* (barbecue) at Clara's house, and so I offered to buy the meat. On the afternoon of the party, I walked down the hill from my house in the morro to the neighborhood butcher shop, in the working-class neighborhood surrounding the morro, with Sergio and Danilo, two friends from Caxambu. After purchasing several pounds of beef, chicken hearts, and spicy *linguiça* sausage, we walked up the road toward Clara's house in the morro. I was carrying two large plastic bags and Danilo another one.

When we came to a main intersection where we had to turn off the road to get to the alley where Clara's house was located, a woman who I had never met before opened up the metal *portão* (gate) of her home and stepped into the street. She called Danilo and Sergio over, and I went with them. Before I knew exactly what was going on, she grabbed the plastic bag of meat out of Danilo's hands, put it inside of her gate, and then came over to me and said: "Give me that!" and grabbed the two bags I was carrying. She then turned around, walked into her gate, and slammed it shut, locking it from the inside. I was flabbergasted. Danilo and Sergio seemed sheepishly embarrassed.

Completely confused, I asked Danilo and Sergio: "What just happened? What was that about?" They replied, not making eye-contact with me: "You'll have to ask her." After I spent a few minutes knocking, and then pounding, on the woman's metal portão, she came to her gate and opened it just enough to talk, with a metal chain keeping the gate ajar. The woman was livid, yelling at me: "It's not right. This doesn't belong to you, you're taking this and taking advantage. We're owed this." I asked her to return my property, and she flatly refused. When I asked why, she said: "You'll have to talk to Clara about that. She knows why."

After few hasty cell phone calls to Clara, and with Sergio serving as a reluctant intermediary with the woman, I began to piece together what had happened. The woman, it turned out, was distantly related to Clara, the cousin of an aunt's husband. This woman's daughter, Valéria, had worked for a few months in the residents' association as Clara's assistant. When the mayor's office failed to come through with its promise to pay for a local day-care center, which was one of the residents' association's main projects and income-earning schemes, Valéria had been fired. Valéria accused the residents' association of failing to pay her back wages and not paying her severance salary. Seu Lázaro, the president of the residents' association, in turn claimed that Valéria had never been a legally registered employee but a part-time hire. Therefore the residents' association was not obliged to pay her anything. Valéria then turned her accusations on Clara: she claimed that Clara was pocketing money that should have gone to her and floated accusations that this was just one of many *trambicos* (shady deals) that the residents' association was involved in.

While these accusations and counter-accusations were flying—Clara, speaking to me on my cell phone, refused to come talk to her "aunt," saying that the accusations were unjustified and that she wouldn't deign to react. Clara's aunt was alternately yelling at me and taunting me to say that I knew that the residents' association was "really a bunch of thieves." Meanwhile, I was trying to figure out how to respond. Ethnographically, the moment was rich with subtexts and unanswered questions about, for instance, how authority, gender, and status were allocated and contested. Personally, I was stuck: I simply wanted to regain the meat, have the party, and figure out what had happened later on. But my possible reactions were few.

I was deeply tempted to simply walk away. Yet this would be a deep breach of local gender norms: a woman had grabbed some of my property and was insulting my friends and my own integrity. Failing to respond would mark me as weak, powerless, not really a man. When I asked Sergio what would happen if I just walked into her house, he said: "Well, you could do that, but I don't know if her *primo* (male cousin) is there." "Who's he?" I asked. "Well," Sergio responded, somewhat evasively, "he's *um da rapaziada* (one of the guys)." Sergio's choice of terms, I realized, could mean two things: either the cousin was simply someone from the neighborhood, or he was one of the local drug dealers.

Feeling stymied here, I thought: I'll call Clara back, and see if she can't find a relative who'll help out. When I reached Clara on the phone, I told her that her aunt was refusing to hand back the meat and had said that one of her cousins might be there. She replied: "Oh yeah, well I'm going to call my *compadre* (the godfather of one of her children)." I knew that Clara was referring to the brother of the father of one of her children, who had recently been released from prison, and who was returning to a position of influence in the local drug-dealing gang.

The situation seemed to be rapidly escalating, and the last thing I wanted was to provoke a violent clash between two of Clara's relatives. I then thought: "OK, I'll call Seu Lázaro, he'll know what to do." This quickly proved to be the wrong response. When I reached Seu Lázaro on his cell phone, and explained what had happened, he said: "Clara's aunt stole something? Well then call the police." After refusing to become personally involved, and reiterating that I should call the police, he hung up.

By refusing to involve himself, Seu Lázaro was following a well-known script. Favela residents' associations claim no jurisdiction over criminal matters (Santos 1977, 41–42). Seu Lázaro refused to involve himself for many of the reasons outlined by Boaventura Sousa Santos in his pioneering research on dispute resolution in Rio's favelas in the 1970s: the residents' association saw its role as local community development, not maintaining social order; attempting to intervene in criminal disputes would be physically dangerous; perhaps most important, the local drug gang had taken the resolution of local crime as its mandate. Yet as the president of the residents' association, Seu Lázaro could not completely ignore the law. Rather, he engaged in what Santos identified as a "ritualistic interaction," in the course of which Seu Lázaro recognized the existence of the police while not following up with any substantial cooperation (Santos 1977, 43).

I was now in another bind. By telling me to call the police, Seu Lázaro shifted responsibility for dealing with this problem off of his shoulders and, once again, onto mine. But he knew, and knew that I knew, that actually cooperating with the police was out of bounds. Not only were the police widely seen as corrupt and abusive but the local drug dealers loudly let it be known that anyone who cooperated with the police would be regarded as an X-9 (informant). I knew what could come from such an accusation: several weeks before, I'd sat with Seu Lázaro on the patio of his home while listening to screams and then whimpers coming over Seu Lázaro's wall from the street beyond as drug dealers beat an accused informant to death.

While I'd been standing in the middle of the road, calling people on my cell phone and trying to get Sergio to help me communicate with various people, I hadn't noticed that Danilo had disappeared. After I finished talking to Seu Lázaro, Danilo reappeared with Sonia, a woman who ran the drug trafficking operation in that part of the morro. She turned to me and said: "I hear you're having a problem here, and we don't want any *bagunça* (hassles) in the neighborhood. Why don't you go over to the bar on the corner and have a beer." I was at wit's end, and had no idea what to do. So Sergio, Danilo and I walked a few blocks away to a little corner bar and shared a beer. Before we'd even finished it, a young man I had never met before walked up with my three plastic bags, handed them to me, and walked off. Danilo and Sergio shrugged, and Sergio said: "All right, let's go to Clara's then." We finished our beer and walked down the alley to Clara's house. When, a little bit later, I tried to bring up the argument with Clara, she said: "Oh forget about it, have a beer and relax."

No one mentioned the argument for the rest of what proved to be a long and festive night, and an afternoon of tension quickly dissolved into a night of joy and celebration. When, many hours later, my wife and I staggered up the road to our house, we passed by a bar where Dona Elsa and Dona Irene, two local women, were drinking a beer and chatting with people walking up the street. Dona Elsa called me over and said: "I heard you had a disagreement, and Sonia had to fix it." As Dona Elsa and Dona Irene had a long and loud laugh at my expense, I sheepishly walked the rest of the way home.

This second moment of crisis paints a more complex picture of the state of (in)security in Caxambu, and depicts me as bumbling, uncomfortable, and distinctly unsure of what do to. It revealed at once both my position as a privileged outsider who could afford several pounds of *picanha* (top-cut sirloin), and yet the limitations and relative vulnerability that comes with such a position, as I became acutely aware that I was unclear about how different people in this conflict were related to the local drug trafficker or the police.

And this is what was important about ethnographic moment: it wasn't an immediate, inside view of a favela mentality, but a glimpse into a gray, obscure field of doubt, secrecy, and intrigue, and potentially fatal confrontations, which even people in the morro were often uncertain about how to navigate. Solving the puzzle of how to regain my stolen meat was not a matter of finding the order underneath the apparent disorder. This moment of crisis does reveal some of the social patterns and themes that structure life in the morro. But it does not render "ordinary, everyday experience comprehensible" (Geertz 1973, 443). Instead, it pointed to the "epistemic murk" (Taussig 1986) that was both the product of, and that enabled, conflict-laden and potentially violent power relations. It reveals how ambiguity and insecurity could be employed at the local level, as Clara's aunt, for instance, deliberately left it unclear whether she had the necessary social connections to back up her threats. Knowing how to live, in this case, meant knowing how to manipulate secrecy and insecurity— leaving unstated and unknown who could call upon which people to intervene on their side—and not appealing to a shared code of norms. But in the end, as Dona Elsa and Dona Irene pointed out to me, the answer was actually pretty simple: by having Sonia fix my situation, I'd shown how I was also vulnerable to the way that local drug traffickers profited from their appropriation of ordered disorder.

Conclusion: Feeling *Estressado* and Not Even Knowing Why

Neither of these two stories about daily life in Caxambu is false, nor is one more real than the other, revealing the hidden truth. Instead, they point to the complexity of living in a neighborhood like Caxambu. One response to the state of (in)security that marks daily life in Caxambu is to attempt to produce narratives, normative codes, or representations that can contain and control unpredictability, producing an illusion of stability. In my first vignette, I did exactly this: I attempted to appeal to the local narrative about who really provides safety. But on the dusty alleys and street corners of neighborhoods like Caxambu, insecurity is also a lived experience, as the forces that shape daily life are often opaque and unclear. Both the official story of Caxambu—that it is in some ways safer than the surrounding neighborhood, and that local residents look after and respect each other— and the daily reality of competition, blurred boundaries, and ambiguity, are equally aspects of daily life.

Describing what life is "really like" in such a neighborhood is not, then, a simple matter of sharing the experience of police harassment and drug-trafficker "protection," and then revealing a code or set of practices that produce stability and predictable social relations. Instead, I am left to won-der if the comment about my knowing what it's "really like" was offered in irony or jest. Did the person who said this mean that I shared in a common reality, or did he mean that "what it's really like" was far less easily deter-mined, perhaps unknowable? Was he signaling that I owed my safety and protection to the drug traffickers, and shouldn't trust the police, and that as long as I abided by local norms I would be OK? Or was he saying that I was now also caught in a situation of doubt and uncertainty, not being able to rely upon the state, yet also vulnerable to the local bandidos and ultimately unsure of my own safety?

Carrying out ethnography in Caxambu meant constantly balancing this doubt, being aware of the uncertainty that lingered in the unspoken, being attuned to what residents told me, yet attentive to what was left out. The thirty-six formal interviews that I conducted with over forty residents of Caxambu provided one essential source of information, and through-out this book I will let their voices be heard. But in order to understand the ordered disorder and disordered order of everyday life in Caxambu, my own experiences of uncertainty and ambiguity are equally important. Conducting research and living in a state of (in)security was, among other things, a lived feeling, an embodied experience. "Knowing what it's like" meant experiencing diffuse feeling of apprehension and uncertainty, when what it's like was not clear at all.

A conversation that I had over lunch one day had with Chico, a mailman and the vice president of the residents' association, illustrates what I mean. That week I had spent a lot of time hanging out in the residents' association and in the small square at the top of the hill, chatting with anyone who was around. It seemed that during that week the police had increased their patrolling in Caxambu. As far as I knew there had been no major incidents of violence in the morro. But there was a new group of policemen who had been assigned to patrol the neighborhood, and because they were stepping up pressure on the local drug dealers, the general atmosphere was tense.

That particular afternoon Chico and I ate in the empty schoolroom that is attached to the residents' association's main offices, watching television while we scooped big spoonfuls of rice and black beans onto our plates. Chico asked me how I was doing, and I said that I was feeling a little tired. He told me that he noticed that I was a bit sad. I said that I thought that it had to do with spending so much time in the morro and hearing everyone's complaints. "Sometimes my wife comes home from work," I told him, "and she tells me that I'm depressed and I don't even know why." He replied, telling me: "You know, that happens to me too. When things are really tense in the morro, it affects the way that everyone behaves. Everyone acts a little differently, on edge. Because you live here, you feel it too. You can end up feeling really *estressado* (stressed out) without even knowing why."

3

A Familiar Hillside and
Dangerous Intimates

This is the *morro* (hillside), man. It's still
the place of blacks. It's where the poor
live. If we were rich, no one would live
up here. . . . If poverty didn't exist, right?
If there were work. That's the way it is.
—Seu Oscar

A *Local Familiar*

In Caxambu, daily life and alternating structures of security and insecurity, danger and safety, are experienced in a particular space, one that
is both a site of marginalization and a place of pride, deeply connected
to residents' identities. When I asked residents of Caxambu what they
thought about their neighborhood, they often responded in either of two
ways. On the one hand, some residents—like Seu Oscar, quoted above—
spoke about overlapping forms of marginalization. Significantly, Seu
Oscar saw the morro as both "the place of blacks" and "where the poor
live," pointing to how patterns of racial discrimination and poverty reinforce each other. Many residents also emphasized how the neighborhood

was subjected to harsh and unfair forms of policing and was stigmatized by outsiders.

But at the same time, residents also often described Caxambu as a large family. Although Seu Oscar emphasized that Caxambu was the product of racism, he also told me of his pride in building a home where he and his wife had raised their children, including an adult son who was a lawyer. Residents of Caxambu often said that the neighborhood was characterized by friendship, social intimacy, and *união* (unity). For example, when I asked Zeca what he liked about Caxambu, he told me:

> ZECA: The people, I like the people, the friendship here, understand? What else . . . the *companheirismo* (companionship or partnership), people here are really friendly, you yourself can see that. Understand? . . . Uh . . . they have their defects. Like we know, no one is perfect, but . . . but I like it here because of that. Because of the *comunhão* (fellowship), the companheirismo, the friendship.
>
> BEN: Yeah, it seems to me that everyone here knows everyone else . . .
>
> ZECA: That's it, it's a family. A *local familiar* (familial place), right? And I really like that. I don't have anything to complain about, and I think that it's really great.

Zeca, who was then thirty-seven years old, lived several houses down the street from me. He was also my research assistant until he got a job as a security guard. Zeca was somewhat unusual because he is a particularly friendly and gregarious person and knew just about everyone in the part of the hillside where I lived, and where he'd grown up. Because Zeca attempted to present himself as an "exemplary Christian"—both to show his evangelical Protestant faith and as a disavowal of his youth as a drug dealer and troublemaker—he was also perhaps more attuned to proper behavior in the neighborhood than other residents.

But in other ways Zeca was typical of the deep roots that many had in the neighborhood: Zeca's mother was born in Caxambu and his father moved there as a small child the 1940s. Several years later, Zeca's mother brought friends, including Dona Elsa, another one of my neighbors, to live near her. Zeca and his brother and sister were all born in the neighborhood (Zeca was the youngest, and was born at a nearby hospital, but his older siblings were born in the neighborhood itself with the help of Vovó Paula, the much-loved local midwife.) Zeca was marrying a woman who lived in a nearby lower-middle-class neighborhood, and toyed with the idea of leaving Caxambu. But instead, he renovated and moved into the home that his parents had lived in and which he and one brother had made into two separate brick homes.

Zeca's description of Caxambu as a *local familiar* was typical. Another phrase that I often heard was that Caxambu was a *morro familiar* (a familiar hillside). In Portuguese, the word *familiar* carries two meanings: it means both intimate, and also belonging to one's family, reflecting that in Brazilian society the family is often the space of greatest intimacy.[1]

The phrases *local familiar* and *morro familiar* indicate how the built space of the neighborhood and its social relations are mutually constituted: the hillside itself was seen as both familiar and also part of the family. As Henri Lefebvre has argued, spaces such as the built environment of Caxambu are social spaces, reflecting the social dynamics of the people who produced and inhabited the neighborhood. Space, Lefebvre argued, "serves as a tool of thought and action" and also as a "means of control, and hence domination" (Lefebvre 1991, 26). But although Lefebvre tends to see built spaces as reinforcing the dominance of structures of oppression, in Caxambu understandings of the neighborhood were tools used for a variety of purposes, some reinforcing domination and others seeking to find small spaces of autonomy or creativity.

In this chapter, I examine how the space of the neighborhood, seen by many residents as a *morro familiar*, mediated daily social interactions, profoundly shaping the experience of a state of (in)security. Residents of Caxambu, I will argue, experienced their neighborhood as a paradoxical space of familiar danger, one that was both deeply intimate and yet often unpredictably violent. In keeping with Lefebvre's analysis of the relationship between space and social processes, the ways that resident of Caxambu experienced their neighborhood reflects and reinforces larger structures of class and racial oppression.

Seu Oscar's comments point us to this larger historical dynamic: like other favelas, Caxambu was the product of how Rio's poor and Afro-Brazilian residents were incorporated into, and yet also excluded from, Brazil's economic and political system. This deep history not only resonates in how Caxambu's residents understand their neighborhood but also sets the stage for more recent developments, such as the rise of drug trafficking and urban violence in the 1980s and 1990s. With the rise of drug trafficking, it became common to see favelas as disconnected from the rest of the city. This perception also reflects a larger analytical viewpoint that often sees neighborhoods that house the poor as islands of poverty, where the poor are effectively "imprisoned" (Wacquant 2008).

However, when we look at the history of Caxambu and how this history shapes local memories and social practices, a far more complex process becomes visible. Rather than seeing favelas as a failure of the state to integrate the city's poor, or as spaces that exist outside of normal state functioning, they should be seen as examples of a particular way that the poor have been incorporated into larger structures, though in informal or extralegal ways. In commenting on the history of poor people's rights in Rio during the first half of the twentieth century, the historian Brodie Fischer points to this larger dynamic:

> Rio's favelas have always been a part of the city's urban fabric, not only because their residents have long been economically, politically, and culturally integrated into the larger city, but also because people from outside their borders have long built wealth and power from them. . . . Their persistence—despite very significant challenges—is explained only by the vested interest in their continued existence that developed among speculators, politicians, local political operators and party entrepreneurs. Extra-legality, in this form, was not a marginal offshoot of urbanization and modernization, but rather a fundamental component of both processes as they played themselves out in a sharply unequal society. (Fischer 2008, 219)

Boaventura de Sousa Santos likewise notes that the Brazilian state has long tolerated settlements it defined as illegal because most occupants did not own the land they built their homes on. Santos argued that this dynamic allowed favela neighborhoods "to acquire a status we may call alegal or extralegal" (Santos 1977, 90). The residents of Caxambu challenge us to understand the nature and effects of this extralegality, of living in a brown zone between exclusion and integration, between poverty and creativity, and, equally, between the formal word of the law and its practical application. It is this space—a space of creativity as much as one of impoverishment—that in the 1980s and 1990s would enable the territorialization of drug trafficking in Rio's favelas. Yet it was also be the crucial space where Caxambu's residents elaborated ways of living to cope with a social universe of extralegality and (in)security.

When they spoke about living in a *morro familiar*, the residents of Caxambu were doing more than describing the neighborhood's history and were not, as Lefebvre might lead us to think, just reproducing dominant socioeconomic structures. At times, their representations of Caxambu were a deliberate attempt to counteract discourses of insecurity that, as was shown in the previous chapter, depicted favelas as sites of violence. This metaphor of a family-based hillside, though, was not simply a response to outsiders' images of favelas. It was also used to shape daily relations on the hillside. Although talk about the neighborhood did not directly challenge larger structures of oppression, it was a way that residents attempted to carve out small spaces of autonomy, and example of what de Certeau calls social tactics (Certeau 1984).

In this sense, local social representations of the neighborhood created a moral map to guide and evaluate social interactions. The image of a *morro familiar* was an attempt to manage unpredictability and danger. Invoking the notion of a family could be used to claim connections to other residents, as a basis for requesting assistance or negotiating over resources, or as a standard by which residents' actions could be evaluated. Talk about a family-based neighborhood can be seen, in J. L. Austin's terms, as a performative utterance, aimed not simply at a describing the neighborhood but also at actively shaping social relations (Austin 1975).

Analyzing how Caxambu's history shaped the way its residents talked about their neighborhood opens up a series of questions: when and why do residents describe their neighborhood as a "family"? What social, historical, and economic processes have shaped this understanding of the neighborhood? What forms of identity does such a rhetoric highlight? How do other social actors—for instance the police, local drug traffickers, politicians, and other agents of the state—appropriate or violate this discourse of familiarity? What forms of power and authority does this language of a "familiar space" legitimate, and what types of jealousies, rivalries, inequalities, and competitions does it disguise?

Feminist scholars have often pointed out that the language of a "family" and ideal notions of the home often disguise inequalities and naturalize oppression. Doreen Massey states that "ways of thinking about space and place are tied up with, both directly and indirectly, particular constructions of gender relations" (1994, 2). It is particularly important, Massey argues, to problematize the widespread association of "home" with "woman," and to challenge the notion that the home is a space of nostalgia and of protection. As she states, "the home may be as much a place of conflict (as well as of work) as of repose" (11). The question, then, is to understand how the language of a *morro familiar* operates and why residents of Caxambu used it, and yet to also pay attention to the fissures and gaps in this moral map.

The rhetoric of familiarity was fraught with contradictions. If residents of the morro often described themselves as a family, sharply contrasting themselves to outsiders, this was a family—like most—that combined mutual help with competition and conflict. The status of local men (and a few women) who were drug dealers was particularly complicated.[2] As part of the family, they were bound to other residents through ties of mutual support. The language of familial respect and obligation also provided a discourse that drug dealers could use to attempt to legitimate their authority over other residents of Caxambu. At the same time, residents of Caxambu knew that the local *bandidos* (drug dealers) were capable of committing acts of violence against them. And as drug dealers appropriated the language of familial respect and obedience, this had a profoundly destabilizing impact on daily life. Particularly significant was how this discourse drew upon, and then disrupted, naturalized assumptions about how authority and legitimate violence were tied to particular places such as the home, and to gender identities.

The image of a *morro familiar* placed drug dealers into the category that I call dangerous intimates. Likewise, while the language of a *local familiar* depicted Caxambu's homes, alleys, and street corners as deeply familiar, literally the product of local hands, residents also knew that the neighborhood was the site of potentially lethal and often unpredictable violence. As a result, the neighborhood was often experienced as a site of "familiar danger." Understanding how to live with the quotidian routine of daily life in a neighborhood where almost everyone knows everyone else yet where the possibility of unpredictable violence by police and local drug dealers is omnipresent, or inhabiting the state of (in)security, constituted a major component of knowing how to live in Caxambu.

Tubarão (the Shark) and Seu Lázaro's Barbecue

An incident from my fieldwork reveals how the language of familiarity influenced daily social life in the morro, and also shows the complexity and contradictions of experience in a "familiar place." It highlights how drug trafficking and urban violence shaped notions of a familiar place, producing a particularly sharp challenge to adult men in the morro who did not participate in drug dealing.

One afternoon shortly before I had moved to Caxambu, I was invited to a Saturday afternoon *churrasco* (barbeque), at the home of Seu Lázaro, the head of the local residents' association. When I arrived at his house, Seu Lázaro's daughter Sônia let me in the front gate. Seu Lázaro was sitting on a metal folding chair on his concrete patio under the shade of a mango tree, drinking beer, and invited me to sit down with him. A short while later a drug dealer nicknamed Tubarão came in through Seu Lázaro's front gate. Tubarão was a wiry black man in his twenties with a clean-shaven head and a twisted broken-tooth sneer, and always wore mirrored sunglasses. His sinister appearance and his eagerness to use violence accounted for his nickname, Tubarão (Shark). Tubarão was respected and feared. He was also often high on cocaine, making him even more erratic.

Seu Lázaro had a large cooler that he kept stocked with beer to sell on hot weekend afternoons. Tubarão sat down next to me and asked if Seu Lázaro had any cold beer to sell. It was a particularly hot day, and Tubarão wasn't wearing a shirt. Strapped to his bare chest was a leather holster that prominently displayed a forty-five-caliber revolver. Seu Lázaro looked over at Tubarão and said, "Sure, but come with me." They walked over near the gate and exchanged a few words, and Tubarão stepped outside.

A few minutes later Tubarão returned. He had draped a white T-shirt over the revolver, though it was obvious that the gun was still there. We chatted a bit about a Mike Tyson boxing match that was going to be shown on television later that evening. After a few minutes Danilo, Seu Lázaro's nephew, came by with two bottles of Skol beer. Tubarão took them and walked out the gate. "You know," Seu Lázaro told me, "I saw that kid grow up. I knew him when he was a little kid, in diapers."

By "hiding" his weapon, Tubarão was being deliberately ironic: he was simultaneously showing his respect for Seu Lázaro, an older adult man who was hosting a guest to the neighborhood, while he was also signaling that his deference to Seu Lázaro was superficial, only T-shirt deep. I was, and still am, instinctively afraid of loaded weapons. I am sure that as hard as I tried, I was unable to look Tubarão in the eye and not stare at his revolver. My discomfort must have been obvious, especially since at that time I hardly knew Tubarão. When he covered his gun with his T-shirt, Tubarão was acting as a "respectful" member of the family, following Seu

Lázaro's wishes that an outsider should not be unduly scared. Yet the larger message was unmistakable: while Tubarão would enact the formal etiquette of respect, he was also signaling to me and Seu Lázaro that he held a form of authority, dramatically symbolized by his revolver, which he would not relinquish.

Tubarão's actions point to the power, and also the contradictions and gaps, in the discourse of familiarity. On the one hand, Tubarão was willing to comply with Seu Lázaro when he could have simply refused to hide his weapon. As a guest to the neighborhood—and by extension to the "family"—I should have been met with friendliness and hospitality. Tubarão was both a part of the family, and also at a remove from it. For Seu Lázaro, the problem of dealing with Tubarão was particularly vexed. On the one hand, Seu Lázaro had, as he noted, literally seen Tubarão grow up. Tubarão was not only deeply familiar but was also a person who, at least in the ideal family, should have been subservient to an elder male relative. Yet Tubarão both complied with, and appropriated for himself, the ideology of the patriarchal head of the family. If he was a social intimate, he was also a dangerous one, and very deliberately so.

Why should Tubarão have made such an ironic gesture of "hiding" his revolver at all? By both "respecting" the discourse of familiarity, yet also twisting it to make a point about who actually held coercive authority, Tubarão was appropriating notions of a "family hillside." The family hillside could provide a tool to deal with a state of (in)security, as it provided Seu Lázaro with a way to try to contain Tubarão's actions. Yet the experience of a space that was both familiar and dangerous was one of the elements that contributed to a context of ambiguity and uncertainty. Why did this understanding of social space have such influence? And what was the effect of all of this on Seu Lázaro and other residents?

Caxambu's Contradictory Foundations

One reason why residents of Caxambu spoke about their neighborhood as a familiar space, and why talk about the neighborhood carried such "illocutionary force" (Austin 1975), capable of at least partially restraining Tubarão, was because of how deeply the neighborhood's history reflected local social relations and shaped local identity. As Keith Basso and other anthropologists have argued, physical space can serve as a powerful mnemonic for local social relations, with particular places evoking memories of past events or of particular people (Basso 1996). Memories of who lived where, and thus of the neighborhood's kinship and social relations, often provide the map that residents use to orient themselves and to describe and designate particular streets or alleys.

This, again, is distinctly ambivalent and contradictory: although the associations between particular people with specific places are a product of Caxambu's dense social ties, they are also the result of the neighborhood's lack of official street signs or addresses. Instead, the streets and alleys at the top of the hill—and throughout Caxambu—carry the names of the neighborhood's residents. For example, in an interview, Dona Madalena described to Pedro and me where the *bicas* (water spigots), used to be located:

> DONA MARGARIDA: There was a spigot near the *escadão* (large stairway up the hill) and another there near Seu Nogueira's house, in front of Aluísio's. The spigot at the top of the hill was Zé Riso's. There was another dry spigot by my house.
>
> BEN: . . . Ah, Dona Elsa told me that there used to be a spigot near her house, below the water tower.
>
> DONA MADALENA: Yes, a spigot near . . . on Isaura's avenue. On Vieira's street.
>
> PEDRO: Almost in front of Seu Nogueira there.
>
> DONA MADALENA: Yes. We called that Vieira's street. [Addressing me:] You don't live near Vieira, you live on Dona Alda (*você mora na Dona Alda*).
>
> PEDRO: On Dona Alda, you live on Dona Alda.

Not only were these names not the official names of the neighborhood's streets and alleys (according to city maps, I lived not "on Dona Alda" but on the Rua Barão de Muritiba), but I found that Dona Alda and Isaura had long ago passed away. In addition, Dona Madalena and Pedro did not say that I lived "on Dona Alda's street," but used the more direct, "you live on Dona Alda." In this way, memories of those who lived in the Caixinha area—those who, as people sometimes said in a revealing turn of phrase, had "moved to the top floor"—lived on in the mental maps that residents used to orient themselves on a daily basis.

Connections between social identity and the space of the hillside reflected Caxambu's history of occupation. And many residents saw this history as deeply ambivalent. On the one hand, residents often tied their family's occupation of the hillside to stories of displacement brought about by the abolition of slavery, rural migration, and the eviction of the poor from downtown Rio. At the same time, they saw this occupation as one characterized by strong local social ties and institutions of mutual help.

Some residents of Caxambu traced their family's presence on the hillside to the abolition of slavery in 1888. Other early settlers of Caxambu came to the hillside at the beginning of the twentieth century, when they were displaced from their homes in downtown Rio. Dona Joana's family history most clearly exemplifies this pattern. When Zeca and I asked her how her family came to Caxambu, she told us:

DONA JOANA: My father first lived over in . . . near the Praça Quinze [a downtown square], on a hill that was there. He lived there. They wanted everyone to leave the hill, because they wanted to tear it down, but the people didn't want to go. So they set fire to some of the shacks at the bottom of the hill, and those above also caught on fire.

BEN: Oh yeah, there used to be a hill there in the downtown, that they removed.

DONA JOANA: In the downtown, near the Praça Quinze . . . they wanted to tear it down, level it, and showed up there with guns.

ZECA: The residents didn't want to leave . . .

DONA JOANA: So my father lived there, along with the late Seu Domingo. They lived there. They lost their homes, and went looking for new ones. And they found them here. There was a shack here, another one over there. So they bought them.

BEN: There were already shacks up here when they came?

DONA JOANA: There were. My father came to live here and his *compadre* lived next door. Later, the disease came, what they called the Spanish, and my father's wife died.[3] He was left alone . . . with four small children. Then he met my mother. . . . My father met her and needed someone to help with the kids. There were lots of kids. My mother came to help and ended up staying, ended up living with him. Then all my brothers and sisters grew up and my mother stayed here with my father. My mother had several children, but all of them died. I was the only one who escaped.

Dona Joana's story reveals the large-scale forces of marginalization, forced displacement, child mortality, and disease that had an impact on the early residents of Caxambu. Dona Joana's father probably lived on either the Morro do Castelo or the Morro de Santo Antônio, both hillsides near the center of the city. The Morro do Castelo was razed in October 1921 (Abreu 1987, 76; Meade 1997, 171–174), displacing families from one of the oldest and poorest neighborhoods in downtown Rio. Homes on the Morro de Santo Antônio, one of the first hillsides to be occupied, were demolished in 1910 and again in 1916 (Abreu 1994, 45). Abreu notes that in 1916, after residents secured a judicial stay of their eviction, a fire, which he describes as "certainly of a criminal nature," destroyed most of the homes on the hillside. This might be the fire that Dona Joana refers to.

At the same time, though, Dona Joana's story reveals that alongside the marginalization and displacement of the urban poor was a pattern of unofficial tolerance of squatter neighborhoods. Abreu states that after the forced demolition of shacks on Morro de Santo Antônio, those expelled from their homes were given official approval to build homes on the Morro do Telégrafo, further away from downtown Rio and very close to Caxambu (Abreu 1994, 46). The journalist Sérgio Cabral also notes that while the city authorities were tearing down tenements in the late 1890s, the evicted residents were allowed to take the wooden frames from the demolished buildings, presumably to build new homes on the hillsides or in more distant areas (1996, 31). Similarly, in 1903, when mayor Pereira Passos demolished entire blocks of the city where the poor lived, he signed the following decree: "crude shacks are prohibited, regardless of any pretext put forward for their licensing, with the exception of the hillsides which have not yet been occupied and with appropriate licenses." As Jaime Benchimol argues (1990, 265), what could have been the justification for this decree except for its tacit approval of favelas?

The lack of solid legal tenure for the land that they lived on generated a basic insecurity. As Santos argues, though the state officially tolerated favelas, the lack of legal title to land also meant that this tolerance could change into a policy of removal at any moment. "This harsh fact," Santos argued, "is never forgotten by . . . any favelado and accounts for the basic insecurity that characterizes squatter settlements" (1977, 91). It also set an early pattern of an ambiguous relationship with the formal mechanisms of the state: according to José Murilo de Carvalho, the inhabitants of Rio's favelas "lived on the tenuous frontiers between legality and illegality, sometimes participating simultaneously in both" (1997, 17).

Caxambu's first occupants may have moved onto the hillside in 1920s or perhaps even earlier.[4] But the neighborhood grew very rapidly in the 1940s and 1950s, a period which coincided with a larger citywide expansion of favelas, as Rio's industrial growth accelerated and the surrounding region's agricultural economy declined. Favelas grew most quickly in the northern zone of Rio, where Caxambu is located, accompanying the expansion of train lines, the creation of the Avenida Brasil highway, and the growth of new factories. Favelas also become more common in the wealthier southern zone, as this rapidly expanding upper-class area generated a demand for service-sector and construction jobs. A key factor for the location of favelas was proximity to jobs: the 1948 census revealed that 77 percent of the favela residents in downtown and 79 percent of favela residents in the southern zone worked in the same area that they resided (Abreu 1987, 106).

Caxambu would have been an attractive option for the displaced poor, either those moving from the countryside or evicted from homes close to downtown. The hillside was close to the ports, and hence to jobs. In the early 1900s, the area where Caxambu is located was shifting from a residential neighborhood to a center of small-scale industry, and thus there were jobs nearby. The neighborhood below Caxambu was well served by mass transportation—first by *bondes* (trolleys), later by buses and the metro—and was relatively close to downtown.

Social scientists who have analyzed favela development have debated how to assess these neighborhoods. Some observers, most prominently Janice Perlman, have argued that favelas are the product of a process of marginalization (1976; also Pino 1997). Although early industrialization in the city of Rio benefited from a cheap workforce, the urban poor were excluded from the formal city. Others have argued that favelas represent, in fact, a "solution" that the urban poor developed to their poverty; rather than seeing favela residents and the powerless victims of marginalization, this perspective shows them as agents, building their own homes and neighborhoods (Valla 1986). The residents of Caxambu whom I interviewed tended to combine these perspectives, seeing the neighborhood as both the product of exclusion and yet also as an answer to their problems.

While residents I talked to were clearly aware that poverty and the lack of affordable housing options led them and their relatives to move to Caxambu, they also emphasized the advantages of living in Caxambu. Older residents often emphasized how they had seen the neighborhood improve, and that the neighborhood's history of development meant that many of their children and relatives lived close by. They also often commented upon how the neighborhood's status as a favela meant that they had hilltop views that would have been unaffordable in a "legal" neighborhood. In a conversation with Zeca and me, Seu Oscar said:

> SEU OSCAR: I was born here. If you try to take me away from here, I'd die. It's true. For me it's like having a million dollars in my pocket. If you put me in an apartment, I'd die.
>
> ZECA: He wouldn't be able to adapt.
>
> SEU OSCAR: Of course not. You've seen this [pointing over the wall of his patio to the view of the Maracanã soccer stadium and the distant hills beyond]. You've got to like this. This here was a *barranco* (ravine), full of rats and animals. Now I've got grandchildren here. For me that's real wealth. You could live in an apartment, and your window would look into someone else's home, and your neighbor would be looking into yours. That's what's great about the morro. In rich neighborhoods, homes on hillsides are more expensive. But here we've got that wealth.

A Space of Struggle and Violence

Reflecting this contradictory social history of occupation, where the official marginalization was met with unofficial incorporation, and stories of poverty and racism intersected with family histories of survival and self-sufficiency, was an equally contradictory understanding of local space. Whereas the streets at the top of the hill reflected this process of social occupation, and were mapped according to former residents, the same streets were also often associated with memories of suffering and violence. For instance Zeca told me:

> I'll never forget this . . . you know how one time I was telling you about respecting my parents, and how they raised me? Well, I'll never forget that one day, when I was pretty young—I don't know, I must have been about eight or nine—well, sometimes people, you know, people who are involved with drugs, are killed at night. And in the morning their bodies are still there in the street for everyone to see. Well one time my father took me and my brothers and showed us the body of someone who had been killed. He made us look at the body, lying there all bloody, and he said: "See, I want you to see what happens to *marginais* (criminals), I want you to see what happens to people who take

the wrong path (*que vão pelo caminho errado*). For a while they might do well, but this is what happens to them."

Although parts of the hillside carried memories of suffering and violence, these experiences were often interpreted to focus on the common struggle to overcome hardship. Living in Caxambu meant sharing the experience of inhabiting a neighborhood marked by exclusion, one that lacked regular urban infrastructure such as piped water or sewage. But this experience was seen not as one of passive victimhood. Instead, what residents emphasized was the determination with which they faced such obstacles and what they saw as the improvements that they had brought to the neighborhood. For many people, two aspects of the neighborhood were particularly important: the dense and multistranded connections that many residents had with each other, and the common experience of struggling to overcome hardship. What marked a person as pseudo (if not actual) kin, as being part of the "family," was sharing in the *luta do dia a dia* (daily struggle).

For instance, in their recollections of what Caxambu used to be like, older residents would often remember having to walk up muddy streets and steep paths, and carrying water to their homes from the few spigots on the hillside. Most prominent in these memories was *barro*, meaning clay or mud, which was often mentioned as a symbol of poverty and discrimination. For example, one day I asked Seu Anselmo what the morro was like when he first built his house at the top of the hill in the early 1960s, he told me: "The morro was all dirt, man. This was all dirt, *barro*, there was nothing. There was only water until a certain time in the morning, then it stopped. At night, or in the afternoon, there was no more water."

Here barro was associated with backwardness, with lack of progress, and with lack itself. Streets of dirt and barro, in Seu Anselmo's words, were signs that the morro had nothing. Seu Anselmo also linked his recollection with one of the other main hardships that people in the morro singled out: the lack of a reliable source of water. Barro and a lack of water are the two main symbols that the morro was different—was more difficult to live in—than the surrounding "official" neighborhood.

Memories of barro were always tied to memories of traversing the space of the morro, especially embodied memories linked to work and daily domestic chores. Older residents would often talk about the difficulties of getting up and down the morro in the old days, worrying about slipping and falling, and having to worry about getting mud on their shoes when they had to walk down the hill on rainy days. When I interviewed Seu Jânio, an elderly man who owned a store at the top of the hill, I told him that I was interested in the history of the morro. He replied by talking to me about how access to the hill was difficult in his youth:

> When I was a kid it was difficult here (*era sacrificado*, literally it was a sacrifice). It was hard to bring merchandise to the morro. . . . At the age of eight I was already working, for a family, the Nogueira family. It was really difficult to get things up the hill. We had to carry it on our backs. . . . The access to the hillside was terrible. When it rained it was terrible. We had to go down the hill to go to work, and when it rained there was so much mud that we'd go down with a wet rag in our hands so that when we got down below we could clean our shoes. It was a lot of mud. Understand?

Similar responses were not given just by the older residents. Even younger residents of the morro, who could not have had much direct experience with unpaved streets, as the major ones were paved in the 1970s, would answer the same way. For example, Moacir, a thirty-one-year-old man who I often talked to after he dropped off his children at a day-care center next to my home, associated his childhood memories of playing pranks in the morro with the fact that the streets were mud and that there was little water. The sign of how the morro had improved, the symbol of progress, was cement pavement. Moacir told me: "I was born here, I was raised here. It was pure mud here, right? *Barro puro* (pure mud), I mean. A long time ago the water tower actually worked, but . . . since I was a boy it hasn't supplied any water. . . . I think that now it's gotten much better. Because now everything is paved. . . . Now when it rains there isn't that mud."

By contrasting what the morro was like in the past—a place marked by lack, and by the hardship and potential for discrimination associated with muddy streets—with its current state, the residents of Caxambu were emphasizing two things. First, they were pointing out that Caxambu was becoming a "regular" neighborhood. If in the past the morro was a symbol of poverty, and perhaps something to be ashamed of, with its current streets of concrete and homes of brick, it was no longer. But second, the residents of Caxambu were also highlighting how they themselves were strong and resourceful people for having been able to endure such hardships. If outsiders saw having muddy feet as a symbol of poverty and lower social status, the morro's residents viewed having endured and overcome this hardship as a marker of their greater resiliency and strength.

In the discourse of the familiar hillside, suffering and overcoming hardship were positively valued as signs of being a respected part of the family. Seu Lázaro was one of the paragons of being a hard-working, "suffering" resident: not only had he endured the morro's past of dirty and muddy streets, working ever since he was a teenager to support his family, but as the president of the residents' association, he lobbied hard for improvements to the neighborhood. As he and other older residents of Caxambu often repeated to me, the improvements that younger people like Tubarão took for granted—like paved streets and electricity—were won only with hard work and persistent effort. This made interactions between adults like Seu Lázaro and young men involved in the drug trade like Tubarão particularly complex: because Seu Lázaro had helped to build and care for both local families and the shape of the hillside itself, younger people like Tubarão owed him a debt of gratitude. Yet Tubarão, someone whom Seu Lázaro had seen "in diapers," also represented larger uncontrollable forces that were reshaping the neighborhood.

The Hillside and the Asphalt

Describing Caxambu as a large family was informed by two contrasts that played an important role in daily interactions: first, the contrast between *moradores* (residents) and nonresidents (often called *pessoas de fora*, literally people from outside); and second, the contrast between the *morro* (hillside) and the *asfalto* (asphalt, the local term for the surrounding "official" city). Bomba, for instance, often tied the neighborhood's history to local patterns of sociability, and contrasted the morro with more prosperous neighborhoods. In the following excerpt from an interview, Bomba articulates this common feeling with a heavy dose of nostalgia, complaining that the morro is losing some of its "family" atmosphere:

BOMBA: Our situation was a good one. It was a situation of brotherhood. Because we lived in clans. For example, if my mother went to work, then . . . then Zeca's mother would wash my mother's clothes and take care of me. And when Zeca's mother went, my mother would take care of Zeca, understand? If I made some mischief, Zeca's mom would punish me, she'd spank me. No one was envious, everyone helped each other. For example, if Zeca was at my house, ah . . . he'd eat at my house. . . . Down below [outside of the favela] no one eats lunch in anyone else's home.

BEN: Of course not . . .

BOMBA: They close the door on you. Not here. Here everyone pulls together. If someone is sick, someone else washes their dishes or cleans their clothes. That's changing now, it's not like it used to be. It's becoming very individualistic, understand? Here if someone was given some clothes—back then people often got clothes from their bosses, from rich people—then everyone would share it with their neighbors. See? Now there are buildings down there [outside the favela] where the person in 101 doesn't know their neighbor in 102.

BEN: Yeah, when I lived in Catete [a middle-class area] I didn't know anyone.

BOMBA: See? Not here. Here everyone knows everyone, without exception . . .

For Bomba, the hillside's pattern of occupation meant that daily social life was, or should be, guided by a spirit of generalized reciprocity, where every member of the family looked out for others and residents shared resources. Reciprocity and mutual assistance, though, occurred within a context of duties and obligations, and did not imply equality. For Bomba, the context of brotherhood structured who could legitimately exercise authority: elder residents (like Zeca's mother) could legitimately punish him if he misbehaved.

The contrast between the morro and the working-class neighborhood below Caxambu was often articulated along these two contrasting registers: while the surrounding asfalto had amenities and an urban infrastructure that Caxambu lacked, the morro possessed a sense of sociability lacking in wealthier areas, which were described as characterized by individualism and anonymity. For instance, when I asked Seu Anselmo about the differences between the morro and the surrounding neighborhood, he told me: "There's a lot of difference. . . . You see, people who live in the morro have this thing: if you pass by and don't say anything, they'll complain: 'Damn, so-and-so passed by and didn't say hello!' Down below, people root for you to pass by without saying anything."

Residents often pointed to the friendliness of the neighborhood and to the rules that governed how you could use its space. For instance, in the afternoon, Dona Lucia, a seventy-four-year-old woman who lived across the small alleyway behind my house, would leave her door and windows open. She would sit at her window alternately reminding her great grand-daughter not to play too far away and greeting passers-by. In her raspy voice she would call out to people passing by who greeted her in a traditional manner by asking for her blessing, saying: "A bênção, Tia Lucia? (A blessing, Auntie Lucia?)." They would perhaps stop and ask about the health of her husband, or listen to her complain about how the Favela-Bairro construction project changed the flow of rainwater down the hill's alleys, flooding her home. Others would merely pass by with a "Tudo bem? (Everything OK?)" or a "Boa tarde (Good afternoon)." Regardless, Dona Lucia would laugh and smile, and call out a response.

Although people in Caxambu drew sharp distinctions between mora-dores and outsiders, they also sometimes distinguished between people within the morro. Significantly, these distinctions rarely referred to race or economic class. Caxambu's residents were poorer and darker-skinned than the average resident of Rio.[5] But there was considerable income and phenotypical variation within the neighborhood. Few families were impoverished, but there were some where no adult or working-age child held a full-time job, and so they were worse off than most moradores. On the other hand, there were families with a lower middle-class income by Brazilian standards. For example, Seu Oscar's adult son, who lived with him and contributed to his family's income, was a lawyer, and Seu Lázaro's adult daughter Sônia was an office manager. So although residents of the morro talked about themselves as *pobres* (poor people), this was a term that encompassed a rather wide range of incomes.

Race was also hardly ever used as a category to distinguish between residents. In the terms used by Livio Sansone, the morro could be thought of as a "soft area" of color relations, where conflicts or tensions were rarely explicitly articulated in terms of racial differences (2003, 51–55). The majority of the residents of Caxambu were black or Afro-Brazilian, though this is hard to say with any degree of certainty, as statistical studies of Caxambu—and of the city's other favelas—have not compiled data on racial identity. Skin color was a probable marker of belonging, as a darker-skinned person was seen as perhaps more likely to live in the morro than a lighter-skinned one.

But race was rarely an explicit marker of difference, as black, brown, and white-skinned residents lived next door to each other, often socialized together, and not rarely intermarried. Zeca, who proudly identified himself as a *negão* (a big black guy) and said that everyone should be proud of the skin color that God gave them, insisted to me that there was no racism at all in the morro.[6] Other residents shared this opinion, and a major point of pride about the neighborhood was that, as Pedro (a white-skinned descendent of Portuguese immigrants married to a brown-skinned Northeasterner) told me: "We all get along here. It doesn't matter if you're white, black, yellow, or green."

This is not to say that race—or more precisely, reference to color—was absent from everyday conversations. Quite the contrary: skin color, as well as other physical attributes that were seen as linked to race—most notably hair texture and facial features—were constant topics of conversation and were often used to identify particular people. For example, Dê, the head of the local drug gang, was often referred to as the *negão*, and particular people would be described as *aquela moreninha* (that brown woman) or *aquele branco* (that white guy). Racial attributes were also often parts of nicknames. One of the lighter-skinned children of Dona Carmen and Seu Jaime was called Branquinha (Whitey), a popular bar owner who had red hair and very pale skin was called Russo (Russian), and a young man who worked in one of the stores at the top of the hill was called Nêgo (Black).[7] But race was never used as the basis of collective identities.

Religious affiliation was also rarely used to distinguish between residents of Caxambu and those of the surrounding city, and the morro was marked by a diversity of religious affiliations. Pentecostal Protestant churches were popular and highly influential, as they are in many poor communities in Brazil (Burdick 1993; Chestnut 1997). In Caxambu, the two churches that most Protestants belonged to were the Assembleia de Deus (Assembly of God) and the Igreja Universal do Reino de Deus (Universal Church of the Kingdom of God).[8] But other smaller denominations, such as Deus é Amor (God Is Love), were also popular, and there was quite a bit of movement of individuals from one evangelical church to another. Other moradores—perhaps the majority—were Catholics, and some also participated in Afro-Brazilian religions such as Candomblé, Macumba, and Spiritismo. Movement among these religions was also common, especially since evangelical Protestants made strenuous efforts to convert those who participated in Afro-Brazilian religions, whom they viewed as involved in devil worship.

The *Cria do Morro*

Rather than differences of race or religion, what was of overriding importance was a relationship to the place itself: it was the shared experience of inhabiting the morro that was the most relevant criterion in local senses of identity and difference. When residents did distinguish among themselves, the central contrast was between those who were born in the morro, often called *cria*, and those who moved there after birth. For instance, when I asked Russo, a bar owner, what he liked about Caxambu, he joked about the fact that I'd recently appeared on a television show about non-Brazilians who carried out projects in Rio's favelas. Russo then told me: "I like . . . I like the people here, because we're all really united, understand man? I like the place. Because I moved here, I'm not a cria. But I've always been treated well, and I treat other people well too. I mean, I don't have any complaints. Understand? And every day more good people arrive here, like you, a famous television personality."

In wider usage, a *cria* (short for *filho de criação*) is a foster child: someone who is informally adopted and is raised in a foster household (Cardoso 1984; Fonseca 1986). Usually this happens with orphans or with poor children who are raised in the homes of the wealthy, becoming both pseudo kin and a source of unpaid labor. Claudia Fonseca notes that in favelas and other lower-class communities there is a "general acceptance of fosterage" (1986, 17–19). Several elderly residents of the morro had grown up under these arrangements, and had bitter stories to relate about how they were mistreated and abused in their adopted households. Seu Anselmo, for instance, told me that when he was a boy he was "given" by his father to a wealthy family, and lived with this family until he ran away to find his mother, who lived in Caxambu. Similarly, a wealthy woman took in Dona Madalena when she was only eight, and Dona Madalena told me she was forced to sleep in the kitchen next to the stove.

In resignifying *cria*, the residents of the morro are reclaiming a word, altering its connotation from negative, meaning an adopted but significantly inferior member of a household, to positive, as a cria comes to mean a person of status and privilege. But the term means more than just this. In traditional use, a cria is adopted and raised by a household. A cria do morro, then, is a child adopted by the hillside itself. It is the morro—the neighborhood as a whole—which takes in and raises the cria.

Michael Jackson has argued that metaphors condense social, individual, physical, and material realms into a single powerful rhetorical construction. Jackson states that metaphors are not instances of dualistic thinking; they are not "a way of saying something 'in terms of' or 'by way of' something else." Instead, metaphor "reveals not the 'thisness of a that' but that 'this *is* that'" (1989, 142). The use of the term *cria* simultaneously ties together relationships to a social community (the residents of the morro), biology (being born), and relationships to the space of the morro itself. As Jackson points out, is not just that all these aspects of a metaphor "stand in for" each other. Rather, all are seen as being equivalent: one is born on the hill, raised by the neighborhood, and generated by the hill itself. It is hard to imagine a concept that would more powerfully tie together residence, neighborhood, the materiality of place, and identity.

Becoming a Morador

The importance of shared occupation of the space of Caxambu in local social identities was brought home to me several times when I was included in the category of morador. In public meetings about the neighborhood, people often mentioned their status as residents as empowering them to participate in discussions. For instance Clara, the secretary of the residents' association, would almost always preface discussions about whatever issue was under discussion with: "I, as someone who works for the residents' association but also as a moradora, think . . .". When I would attend meetings in the morro, I was often reticent to voice my opinion. Clara asked me one day why I was always so quiet, and I told her that I felt that I didn't really have the right to speak up, since I was an *estrangeiro* (foreigner). "But you live here," she told me. "You're a morador, and so you can participate too."

Another time I was walking down the hillside when I passed by Nêgo, who was sitting on a chair on the sidewalk in front of the store where he worked. At this point I didn't know him very well, but said hello as I passed by. The Favela-Bairro construction project was in the process of paving the bottom part of the street where it sloped down from Nêgo's store to Russo's bar. So I stopped and asked Nêgo what he thought about the construction. He began to complain about it, saying that while they were paving the road the construction workers kept bursting the plastic PVC water pipes that residents had hooked up to the main water line in order to supply their homes. This had been causing major problems throughout the hillside, flooding some homes and depriving others of water.

As he complained about the project, Nêgo shifted, as many residents often did, to complaining about the residents' association, saying that they were doing a bad job of representing the residents' interests, and hinting that money must be exchanging hands to keep Seu Lázaro, the residents' association's president, so quiet. I asked Nêgo whether the association had ever thought about appointing people from the neighborhood to oversee the project in different parts of the hillside. He said no, that he had heard about this happening in other morros, but not in Caxambu. As I got ready to leave, Nêgo told me: "You know, you should really be the president of the residents' association." I laughed at this, and replied that I thought that it would be better to have "someone from the morro" in that position. "But you live here," he replied, "so you could do it too." I told him that I appreciated his vote, but that I wasn't sure that I wanted so many headaches, and we chuckled as I walked away.

Workers and Bandidos

The young men in Caxambu who worked as drug dealers occupied a particularly complicated position in local understandings and experiences of the "familiar hillside." On the one hand, they were tied to other resident through relations of kinship, friendship, and long-term propinquity. Seu Lázaro made this clear in his comments about Tubarão, when he said that he had known Tubarão since the drug dealer was a baby. On the other hand, people in Caxambu made a pervasive distinction between residents who were involved in drug dealing and the vast majority who were not. If drug dealers were social intimates, they were also seen as a source of danger that was never completely domesticated. Just as the space of the morro was fraught with contradictions, a source of pride and of discrimination, a space of familiar danger, so were local drug dealers seen as both pseudo kin and radically other, as dangerous intimates.

Like people who live in other favelas and poor communities in Rio, many residents of Caxambu divide their local social universe into two categories: *bandidos* (drug dealers) and *trabalhadores* (workers) (see Alvito 2001; Zaluar 1985). Residents emphasized that the two are distinct and should be kept apart: the vast majority of the hillside's residents, everyone hastened to add, are trabalhadores. They "aren't involved," and are said to keep separate from the bandidos. For instance, one day Dona Carmen was telling me about one of her cousins, and described him this way: "He's really cool (*maneiro*), polite, a good person. He doesn't mix! He never mixed. Just like my son, he doesn't mix, neither he nor my other boy. The girls yes, they mix. But the boys, my oldest daughter . . . and him! No way! They don't mix."

The local definition of who is a trabalhador was quite broad. To fall into this category one must be neither a drug dealer nor a *viciado* (addict).[9] But a person could be a trabalhador without actually being employed. Zeca, for instance, told me that he and four other trabalhadores were arrested by the police one weekday afternoon as they were playing cards in front of a small bar at the top of the hill. The police, Zeca complained, assumed that any man on the hillside was a drug dealer, and carted him and his friends off to jail only to release them the following day. "But we were all trabalhadores," Zeca complained, leaving unexplained how it was that five workers were spending their afternoon drinking beer and playing cards.

Local discourse depicted bandidos as people who had once been familiar social intimates, members of the "family," but became radically other. They were often described as having "gone to the other side." Their criminal activities were often referred to as "the life of crime," as if it were not an activity that they occasionally engaged in, but a self-contained universe. Just as the local social world was divided into two categories, workers and bandits, so were there two opposing ethical orientations, "this world" and "the other side." Boys who became drug traffickers are spoken of as having had their "heads turned to the other side" and having entered a different world, bound by different codes and obligations.

This understanding of drug dealers has clear parallels with the phenomenon of spirit possession, which is common in Afro-Brazilian religion, including Candomblé. Candomblé initiates sometimes refer to the *orixás* (deities) that possess them as the "owners of their heads" (Wafer 1991, 16). In this way, "having your head turned" can be seen as analogous to describing the act of being possessed. The use of these metaphors might reflect the influence that Pentecostal Protestantism has on local discourses that attempt to understand the source of evil. Some Brazilian Pentecostal Protestants reappropriate the metaphors of Candomblé, but understand spirit possession not as serving the gods, but as demonic possession (Chestnut 1997).

In analogous terms, the residents of the Caxambu often describe involvement in the drug trade by resorting to tropes that describe people being possessed by evil. In this way of speaking, bandidos were seen as local boys who live in a parallel and contiguous, but nonetheless radically other, social world. For instance Zeca, who used and sold drugs until he converted to the neo-Pentecostal Igreja Universal do Reino de Deus church, offered the following explanation: "We know . . . that when children use drugs, they enter into the *submundo* (underworld) of crime, why? Because of a lack of occupation. They don't have anything. . . . So they go to the *lado errado* (wrong side)."

The residents of the morro believed that being a bandido included obedience to a different social code, one with its own privileges and obligations. Central to this world is violence: entering the "world of crime" meant that the bandidos were both committed to resorting to violence as a means of resolving disputes and had accepted that violence would be visited upon them. This is the *condomínio do Diabo* (bargain with the devil) that Alba Zaluar has described: the "world of crime" might mean easy money and the privilege, or even obligation, of being able to employ violence against others (Zaluar 1994). But it also means that one accepts becoming a target of violence. Zeca, for instance, once told me: "It's terrible when bad things happen to people who aren't involved. Because those who are involved in drug dealing are ready for it, right? They know what they're in for." It was also common to comment on the short average lifespans of drug dealers, as they lived intense, but brief lives, ending in prison or death.[10]

Residents of Caxambu who had friends or relatives involved in the drug trade knew the heavy price that it exacted. A friend told me, for instance, that her cousin has chronic bronchitis from standing in the rain on cold nights when he worked as an *olheiro* (lookout). For many, the life of crime meant the certainty of imprisonment, shakedowns and beatings at the hands of the police, and the constant possibility of a violent death. For instance, a teenage girl told me: "I've seen lots of people get beaten up because of selling drugs. . . . I think this: to be a bandido you need to have the *disposição* (willingness) to get beaten up by the police, to get beaten and not talk . . . because, you know, if you *cagüetar* (rat) to the police, when you get out of jail you're going to die."

This willingness to both commit violence and to have violence visited upon oneself was central to the alterity of bandidos. It was a sign that they might be "in this world," but were in some ways transitory, leading lives of intense but brief material profit. Bandidos themselves recognized this status. Some would comment, in a tone deliberately designed to display their machismo and disregard for the conventions that tied *otários* (suckers) to minimum-wage toil, that they were "marked for death." One drug dealer who I knew, since he often bought his lunch from Dona Carmen where I also often ate, told everyone that he carried a grenade around with him at all times. When Dona Carmen told him he was crazy, he said: "When the time comes I want to take out as many policemen as possible before they kill me."

At the same time, though, dealing drugs was also seen as a prosaic fact of life: drug dealing was often seen as a job, and involvement in the *tráfico* (drug trade) was often spoken of as work. When describing what they do, drug dealers would often say "eu trabalho no tráfico" (I work in the drug trade) or would be described by others as "ele trabalha na boca" (he works at the "mouth"—the drug-selling point). The brutally explicit logic of accumulation and purely economic considerations were never far from the surface. One afternoon I had a long discussion with two teenage drug traffickers about how much people in different professions in the United States earn. After they calculated what the minimum wage in the United States would be for a *faxineiro* (janitor), perhaps the lowest job imaginable for these boys in terms of respect, one of the drug dealers blurted out: "Damn, if I lived in the US I'd be a janitor, not a bandido."[11]

The perception of drug dealing as a job was brought home for me one evening as I was leaving an English class which I taught as a volunteer in a favela in the Tijuca neighborhood. This favela had a particularly complex security situation, since one *comando* (drug-dealing organization) controlled the bottom part of the hillside and a rival group controlled the top. The English class that I taught for adults was located in a church in the middle of the hill, just below the "border" between the two rival groups, and classes were occasionally interrupted by the sound of bullets. Whenever I finished teaching class, one of my students, most often Rosinha, would wait with me while I caught a *kombi* (mini-bus) down the steep hillside. One evening I said goodbye to Rosinha and got onto the minibus as usual. As the driver began to pull away, I heard someone yelling behind us in the street. I looked back to see a teenager armed with an AK-47 running toward the kombi. I could also make out a wide-eyed look of fear on Rosinha's face, as the kombi stopped and the drug dealer pulled open the side door. Panicking, I was convinced that the drug dealer was going to yank me out of the kombi. Instead, he jumped onto the seat next to me, looked at me without any apparent surprise, and turned to the driver saying: "Hit it man, I'm late for my shift."

The boys and men (and occasional women) who were involved in the world of crime, who were bandidos, were also linked to the other residents of the morro by ties of kinship, friendship, and joint neighborhood residence. Although local discourse drew sharp distinctions between bandidos and trabalhadores, residents of the morro also emphasized that the bandidos were "from here," were "local boys." When drug dealers were spoken about as kin, very different understandings of bandidos and crime came to the fore.

One day, for instance, Zeca and I were talking to Dona Joana, a woman in her eighties. One of the older people in the neighborhood, and the daughter of an emancipated slave, Dona Joana was widely respected as representing the "roots" of Caxambu and for her long life of hard work, self-sacrifice, and sobriety. As she told me in an interview: "I don't drink or smoke, thank God. But I worked for forty years in a beverage factory, working sixteen hours a day." Zeca asked Dona Joana how her family was doing, and she said that everyone was fine. (Dona Joana herself had no children, but her sister, who also lived in Caxambu, had twelve children, many of whom had children of their own.) Zeca asked: "What about Zezinho?" Dona Joana replied: "Oh, Zezinho. Yeah, he's still in prison. I don't understand why they put him there. All he was doing was selling that stuff, and if people want it what's wrong with that?"

The insistence that the bandidos were distinct from the trabalhadores contradicted the language of Caxambu being a "family morro," and in such a tightly knit and crowded neighborhood, the rule of not mixing was often violated. For example, Danilo and Sergio once told me about the importance of not mixing with bandidos while we sat at a bar where two drug dealers were also drinking. Here we can see how this symbolic separation is often performative: Danilo and Sergio were, no doubt, signaling to the bandidos that they didn't want to interfere with their business and, just as important, were showing the bandidos that they were warning me to keep away.

As these comments indicate, the disjunction between bandidos and workers was mediated by local residence and shared social ties. For some residents of Caxambu, the fact that they shared kinship ties with the local bandidos meant that they could avoid being the target of harassment and violence. Nêgo put this point across forcefully when he told me: "It could be that someone here in the community, one of the *malandros* (hustlers, or drug dealers), is doing his business and treats you poorly. You can to talk to whoever is responsible for that person and they'll make sure it stops. . . . If you look at it closely you'll see, I know that guy. They're all from here. It could be your grandfather, your cousin, you know? If you stop and think, and talk, you'll see: 'Oh, I'll go talk to him, he's from here.' They're cria. They're *fundamento* (locals). Everyone's from here, it's all a family. Everyone knows everyone else."

Dangerous Intimacy and the Ambivalence of the Familiar

While local drug dealers were seen as cria and fundamento, the most local of local, they were also seen with a considerable degree of ambivalence and distrust. Younger men who had once been friends with boys who became drug dealers had particularly complex attitudes about these dangerous intimates. For instance, I often spoke with Rogério, a man in his late twenties who taught computer literacy classes at the residents' association, where I also taught English. One day he told me: "I like the friendships that I've made here, OK? They're not a lot, right, because I had lots of friends when I was a kid who, unfortunately, *debandaram pelo lado do tráfico* (fell into the tráfico). So, when people do that you have to choose: either you're with them or you're not. So we have a friendship as colleagues. It's . . . friendships are difficult, right? A friend is someone who when you need him he's there to help you."

For Rogério, although drug dealers were friends you grow up with, they were no longer someone you could trust. His unstated message was that their loyalties—and just as importantly their demands—were no longer ones based solely upon friendship and generalized reciprocity. Instead, friendship ties with drug dealers were sometimes seen as dangerous, as the demands made by drug dealers upon their friends could put men like Rogério in compromising situations. Friendships with drug traffickers were also seen as a main reason why young boys became involved in crime. As Nêgo told me when we were talking about things that he would like to see to improve the neighborhood: "There have to be more projects for kids in the community. Because if you analyze it, like I just said, here we're . . . we're all like . . . we all know one another. I know his cousin, his father, understand? So . . . what happens? . . . With that ease of knowing each other, right, that familiarity . . . because he's already a cousin, it can turn your head to the other side (*vai se virando a cabeça pro outro lado*) [that is, can convince you to become a drug dealer]. Because he's a brother-in-law, you might turn to that side."

Nêgo's coments are particularly interesting. On the one hand, he saw kinship ties with drug dealers as a good thing. The fact that drug dealers were "all from here," meant that they treated residents with respect. At the same time, though, such connections were potentially dangerous. Familiarity with drug dealers opened a door to a dangerous but seductive world, turning boys' heads to the "other side."

Other residents of Caxambu saw the presence of armed drug dealers in the neighborhood as linked to a larger pattern of discrimination faced by residents who did not participate in the drug trade. For some residents, the presence of armed drug dealers in Caxambu was a primary factor that distinguished it from the "regular" neighborhood below the hill. For example, one day I asked Moacir if there was any difference between "up here" (meaning Caxambu), and "down there" (the working-class neighborhood below the hill). Chuckling to himself, he said:

MOACIR: Sure . . . there's a difference . . . there's a difference because . . . uh. It's different because down there is lower, right? [Starts laughing]

BEN: . . . and up here it's higher. [We all laugh]

MOACIR: Yeah, it's higher, that's a difference. Also there . . . another difference is that down there it's harder to see . . . like . . . guys walking around with guns. It's rare, but not impossible. It could be that a guy from here is down there and he's armed. So that's another difference. It's harder to see that. Those are the differences. Now in terms of . . . in terms of humanity, of human to human, it's the same.

It was common to hear the complaint that the blanket criminalization of the morro because of the actions of a few was unfair. Ursinho, a twenty-seven-year-old man, put the point succinctly. I asked him whether he thought that there was any difference between the morro and the regular city, and he told me:

No. In my opinion, not just because I live here in the morro, there's no difference. There could be some difference on the part of some people, right? Because the morro was always discriminated. Lots of people think that because we live in the morro that we're all *bandidos* and *marginais* (criminals). Lots of people think that only bandidos and marginais live in the morro. But really, and you're here to prove this, really there are lots of good people in the morro. Lots of good people live in the morro because of necessity.

Residents of Caxambu usually blamed the media and the police for the criminalization of their neighborhood, a process I explore in more detail in Chapter 5, and complained that it was deeply unfair. But they were clear about how it negatively impacted their lives. For instance, Pedro told me:

PEDRO: If I want to buy a television I have to say that I don't live here. If I want a good job, I have to give a different address. And if you say that you're from the morro, you won't be able to buy anything on credit. People are . . . you can't buy a telephone. Why? Because of the bad image. That's discrimination against people who live in the morro. Out of . . . let's say 90 . . . no 99 percent . . . if you look for a job . . . a job in the state, the city, the federal government, you're discriminated against if you live in the morro.

BEN: Are people discriminated against just because they live here, or . . .

PEDRO: Because people live . . . because they're poor. Because they live in the morro. Because they think that everyone who lives in the morro is a criminal. . . . If you say Caxambu, you're eliminated, you're scratched off the map.

Pedro went on from here, stating that where a person lived determined radically diverging forms of political subjectivity. He stated: "Here's an example, for you to understand. People ask you: 'Where do you live?' You answer: 'Boston.' People think, wow, Ben is a *pessoa cidadão* (citizen). If you'd answered, 'I live in Brooklyn,' the response would be: 'Oh God, get out of here.' You think that I'm joking, but I'm serious."

Pedro's initially quite commonplace observation—that favela residents are discriminated against because of where they live—was thus connected to both a transnational comparison of the discrimination faced by poor and African-descended people (though Pedro himself is white), and to a political critique. Since I lived in Boston, Pedro argued, I'm a citizen, a *pessoa cidadão*. In contrast, he implied that residents of Brooklyn (and of Rio's favelas) are not treated as citizens. In this way Pedro argued that political status is based upon place of residence: just as Caxambu is "scratched from the map," so residents of favelas are eliminated from the category of full citizenship.

The blanket criminalization of the neighborhood not only affected employment possibilities but also carried other economic and social costs. I asked Anacleto if he thought that the Favela-Bairro construction project going on in the morro would result in increased investment in local homes. His response shows not only how violence is linked to media portrayals of favelas (and how the local law of silence operates), but also how residents of Caxambu are aware of the ways in which media portrayals of favelas affect them.

> The majority of houses here are made of brick. If you have a brick house, you've already invested in it. . . . But that's where the location enters in. It's a morro, it's a favela. So then there's a *discriminaçãozinha* (little discrimination) even in terms of money. There are big houses here in the morro that would be worth one hundred down below, but here you can only get thirty. . . . Why does that happen? The houses in the morro will only increase in value if the security situation improves. And it doesn't count if the security only improves here. Because a guy from down below . . . he just won't look here. He'll see morro. And the morros in Rio de Janeiro are completely unsafe, there's no security at all. . . . And I'm not saying that Caxambu is like that. . . . Is there a danger? There is. Caxambu is a morro like all the others. But in terms of criminality it's different. . . . You don't see Caxambu in the newspaper, on television. You might say: "But I saw it." Sure, but it's not every day. It's maybe every six months, it's a big difference.

Anacleto's comments capture part of the paradox of depicting Caxambu as a *morro familiar*. On the one hand, Anacleto was clear that living in a stigmatized neighborhood meant that investment in homes was undervalued. He also clearly attributed this "little discrimination" to a general lack of security. On the other hand, though, he quickly back-pedaled: while Caxambu is a "morro like all the others," it was safer, different.

Although residents rarely invoked racial criteria to distinguish among themselves, they often complained about how racial prejudice interacted with fear of criminality to stigmatize them and their neighborhood. The morro itself may have been a space of "soft" racial relations. But residents of Caxambu clearly understand that people who do not live in the morro often see them as simultaneously black, poor, and dangerous, and they often point this out. One morning, for instance, I was walking up the hill after having gone for a run in a park near the morro. Bomba, who was sitting in the shade of a neighbor's wall at the top of the hill, as he often did at that time of the morning, saw me walking up and called me over to talk. "You know," he told me, "the next time you go for a run in the park, you should make sure to wear a T-shirt that says Caxambu on it. That way no one will rob you. They'll think: 'Damn, he lives in the morro and he's *white*. He must really be tough.'"

Although the morro was often understood and experienced as a "familiar hillside," residents also knew that some members of their family were capable of committing acts of violence against them, and that living in such a neighborhood exposed them to multiple forms of violence and mistreatment, from lower wages to the possibility of being shot by policemen or gang members. The issue, as Nêgo's contradictory comments to me reveal, was how to manage to be both close enough to these dangerous intimates to avoid their violence, or perhaps even secure some of their assistance, and yet distant enough to avoid becoming entangled in their violence.

Nêgo's case was particularly illustrative of how complex it was to "know how to live" in the midst of these contradictions. Like many other young men in the morro, Nêgo based much of his identity, and quite a bit of his livelihood, upon his ability to be *esperto* (smart or cunning) and not an *otário* (a sucker).[12] Being able to claim "close relations" with the local drug dealers allowed him to see himself as someone who partook in their daring transgression of the established legal economy. Yet Nêgo also had to distance himself from local drug dealers. Since he did not possess the official licenses necessary to operate a business, the police could—and sometimes did—force Nêgo to shut down his bar. If he was perceived as being close to traffickers, Nêgo would also be a target for police extortion. On the other hand, since they often had extra money, the local drug dealers were some of Nêgo's best customers.

Nêgo's ambivalent attitude toward drug traffickers reveals some of the complexities inherent in Brazilian kinship structures, especially in poor families. In much of Brazilian society, a network of extended family ties (a *parentela*) is often an important resource (Wagley 1964). Yet in poor communities, the same network is also regarded warily, as the needs of extended kin may have a negative impact on one's own immediate family (Kottak 1967; Woortman 1982). For instance, Clara, a close friend in Caxambu, relied upon extended kin and yet worried about the impact this had upon her financial situation. She often told me that her sister and brother, who did not work and lived at her mother's home, were a drain upon her financial situation, since they often asked for "loans" that she knew would never be repaid. Yet Clara also appealed to her family in times of need: Clara's sister often took care of her children, and Clara cultivated her ties with a maternal aunt who lived outside of the morro.

Some people who lived in Caxambu also argued that although family ties are important, the demands of families and friends could often drag down attempts at personal improvement. Vagner, a man in his twenties studying to be a nurse's aide, revealed to me this hidden side of familiarity, a sense of distrust and concern about people who he saw as falsely claiming to be friends. Vagner told me: "I think that there's lots of *falsidade* (deception), that's the truth. Falseness. Some people say that they're your friend, but they betray you behind your back. There's lots of falseness in the morro. It's hard to make real friends. They say they're your friend, but it's each person for themselves. They don't like to see people move up in life. They step on you." Dona Elsa likewise told me that sometimes when she had made some extra money washing clothes or doing an errand, she made sure to hide away the extra food that she could buy. "Otherwise," she told me, "my sons, who never come to visit, suddenly show up with their women and all their kids."

This ambivalent attitude toward families—seen at once as an essential source of protection and assistance and yet also regarded warily for the demands that an extended family could put upon scarce resources—was even more pronounced when the "family" included individuals involved in drug dealing. Part of why Clara regarded her brother's appeals for help with suspicion was because he said he was trying to extricate himself from the drug trade after having been shot in the leg for failing to repay debts that he owed. Clara worried that he was actually using the money to buy drugs. Clara also had several male cousins who were drug dealers, and her son's *padrinho* (godfather) was at one point the head of drug trafficking in the morro. This connection helped guarantee my safety during one period of my fieldwork, and Clara sometimes took advantage of this relationship. But Clara worried that her son Martinho's admiration of his influential padrinho might lead him, like many other boys his age, into full-time involvement in the drug trade. As a result she tried to carefully monitor how much time Martinho spent with his padrinho. Claudia had to negotiate the paradox of dangerous intimates: while kinship and quasi-kinship connections allowed Clara access to resources, she worried that these same connections to drug dealers could expose her family to violence.

If local drug dealers were seen as dangerous intimates, the spaces of the hillside were also contradictory: both spaces of social intimacy and friendship, and yet spaces of potential danger. Particularly persistent was the idea that the street was both familiar and dangerous, and that excessive time spent hanging out in the streets was a main reason why boys became involved in the drug trade. Boundaries between the "dangerous" street and the "safe" space of the morro, and between regular workers and the dangerous bandidos, were constantly blurred in practice, even while local rhetoric insisted on their separation. As a result, people often took precautions to avoid letting their children spend too much time on the street. They did this not because the street was an unknown and anonymous space but, on the contrary, because its intimacy was potentially dangerous. Clara, for instance constantly worried about Martinho, her oldest son, who would often find ways to sneak out of the house without her permission to play soccer in the street. Clara struggled to discipline him, telling me that she was worried about his future because he was at the age when boys start to smoke marijuana and get involved in trouble, and she knew that some of his friends were no good. She was particularly adamant about not having him spend time "on the street."

Men and Women Confronting Dangerous Intimates

Clara's concern about Martinho reveals once again the fissures and contradictions embedded in the image of a "familiar hillside." Clara was well aware, as most inhabitants of Caxambu were, that familiarity can cut both ways: although Caxambu's streets were spaces where most people knew each other, and where drug dealers could be appealed to on the basis of kinship ties, such family ties were also often dangerous. I explore the gendered component of urban violence and drug trafficking in the chapter that follows. Here I want to point out how the difficulties of dealing with dangerous intimates like local drug dealers differed for men and women in Caxambu.

In my fieldwork I did not collect information on domestic abuse or gender violence, both because I wanted to examine the more public and visible forms of violence in Caxambu and because I felt that as a man it would be difficult for me to gain the trust needed to gather such information. Understanding the social dynamics between residents, drug dealers, and the police, I felt, was challenging enough. Fortunately, substantial research on gender violence in poor communities in Brazil can help us to see how discourses about a "familiar hillside" connect with gender violence.

One crucial point is that men and women have different resources for dealing with violent intimates. For women, the experience of having to deal with dangerous social intimates—especially violent husbands and abusive uncles or stepfathers—was unfortunately all too common. As a result, there are culturally acceptable strategies that women can resort to. For instance, women would often look to other male kin, such as brothers or elder sons, for protection against violent husbands or lovers (Fonseca 1991, 151). Female children facing violence at the hands of stepfathers are often sent to live with other relatives (143; Goldstein 2003).

For men in Caxambu, though, the experience of dealing with dangerous intimates was more complex. Of course for many lower-class men, having to accept the authority of other men was hardly a new experience. Young boys were expected to submit to the authority of their fathers and elder male kin, and in the workplace submission to the *chefe* (boss) was expected. But these experiences were sharply mediated by hierarchies of age, race, and class. As a younger generation of drug-dealing men—such as Tubarão—appropriated for themselves authority over other men, the ties between masculine power, familiar spaces, and vulnerability to violence produced novel and anxiety-filled experiences. Tubarão, for instance, referred to Seu Lázaro using the honorific *Seu* (Mr.), while Seu Lázaro referred to the drug dealer only by his nickname. But Tubarão could enter Seu Lázaro's home, disrupt Seu Lázaro's visit with a guest, and then defiantly "comply" with Seu Lázaro's request by pretending to hide his pistol under his T-shirt. Men in Caxambu would often speak of being humiliated and mistreated by the police or other more powerful outsiders. But incidents when local men faced harassment or violence at the hands of local drug dealers were often shrouded in silence.

Conclusion: Keeping Your Head Up
While Not *Batendo de Frente*

The history of Caxambu's occupation of space, and the meanings attached to the neighborhood, mediated social relations to create an experience of daily life that was deeply contradictory. On the one hand, the morro and those who lived in it all knew each other intimately. As the neighborhood was built over generations, it was deeply inflected by local memories, becoming deeply familiar. On the other hand, the neighborhood was also seen as a space of exclusion and danger. What appeared to be predictable and safe spaces, trustworthy friends or helpful kin, could all sometimes be unpredictably dangerous. Although residents of Caxambu struggled to understand why some young men might become drug dealers, and were attuned to how a police raid or conflict between drug dealers might transform a peaceful street corner into a dangerous shooting gallery, ultimately these patterns were often beyond their understanding. Men like Seu Lázaro sought to place drug dealers like Tubarão within a kinship network where they could exercise some influence over their behavior, yet knew that this influence was only partial, at best.

The challenge, as Seu Lázaro's daughter told me, was to lead one's life without *batendo de frente*, or "hitting head on" with the more powerful, while also "holding your head up high." I'd gotten similar advice from Seu Lázaro: "There are certain things that you can't hit straight on (*não pode bater de frente*). You have to respect certain people, even if you don't always agree with what they do. You have to pass by and say 'Hi, how's it going?' Smile, and be friendly. Because small dogs don't pick fights with big dogs." It is this tactical approach to social relations, what Certeau calls surreptitious creativities (1984, 96), that best exemplifies the complexities and difficulties of knowing how to live in Caxambu. For the residents of Caxambu, dealing with the paradoxes of dangerous intimates and spaces of familiar danger, meant knowing how to lead their daily lives while balancing on the thin line that separated safety and intimacy from danger and violence.

Yet violence can never be entirely contained in a stable system of signification and meaning. It always overflows, always resists stability. What most preoccupied the residents of Caxambu was not the problem of violence per se (though they did, of course, worry about this), but the unpredictability of daily social life, or what Jackson has called the "problem of the aleatory"

(1989, 66) The violence associated with the drug trade made the challenge of unpredictability particularly acute: unpredictability and chance become, literally, matters of life and death, and facing a social world where well-known people can commit acts of violence, without having recourse to any way of predicting why this might happen or understanding why this occurs, could be paralyzing.

In attempting to deal with this state of (in)security, the residents of the morro often turned to a metaphysical realm. Here, if they could not actively control what was happening to their lives, they could at least construct a place where things do not happen for merely random and unpredictable reasons. This might have no direct impact upon their lives. It could not help them to confront the drug dealers or the police, nor could it help to mobilize Caxambu's residents to challenge the many other structural types of violence that impacted the neighborhood. But it could provide them with some sense of certainty, of trust in a larger plan, with a brief clarity that explains why people do what they do and, perhaps more important, what this all means.

This aspect of daily life in Caxambu was brought home to me one afternoon as I ate lunch in Dona Carmen's backyard. Dona Carmen was watching television and commenting freely on the show. It was a talk show featuring an evangelical Protestant minister and various guests who claimed to have had miraculous cures after prayer sessions. One man, though, called in to complain that despite going to church every day and having his congregation hold a special prayer chain for his wife, her health continued to deteriorate.

"See, he doesn't really believe," Dona Carmen told me with disdain.

He's doubting the power of Jesus, and he'll always live in fear. He wants Jesus to help, but he doesn't really believe. Because, you know, our fate is in God's hands. Only He knows our path. At any minute you might die. You have to have the faith to deal with that so that you'll take the right path. If at the hour of your death you haven't accepted Jesus, it's too late. Because no one understands life. A few weeks ago Claudio came to see me. Do you know Claudio? Probably not, because he'd been in prison for a long time. Well he had just gotten out of prison and came to the morro to see his family and his child. He came to talk to me, to ask me and my husband for our blessing, and asked me to make him some lunch. We talked for a long time, and then he paid for the lunch and walked out of the gate. Just like that, just walked out. The next day we heard that they'd found his body down below, at the entrance to the morro. They stuck a tire over him and set him on fire. You see, you never know. There he was one day, talking to me and happy to see his child and be out of prison. The next day he was dead.

4

Tubarão and
Seu Lázaro's Dog

Drug Traffickers and
Abnormalization

> We've got lots of security here. You'll
> never see any robberies. That doesn't hap-
> pen. The only risk we have is that because
> it's a favela, there's drug dealing. And
> when there's drug dealing, there's police,
> and sometimes the two can *bater de frente*
> (clash), right? That can happen. It almost
> never does. But you can't say that it won't.
> So you have to watch out for that.
> —Rogério

Drug-Trafficker Authority, Shadow Economies, and Strategies of Abnormalization

Daily interactions between residents of Caxambu and drug dealers were
shaped by local factors, such as joint social ties and the shared experience of
living in a neighborhood that is both deeply familiar and often dangerous.

In addition, residents of Caxambu had to navigate a citywide structure of authority constructed by a network that reaches far beyond Rio's poor neighborhoods. The drug gangs in Rio's favelas are part of what Carolyn Nordstrom calls a shadow economy. The shadow economy, Nordstrom argues, can be thought of as "complex sets of cross-state economic and political linkages that move outside formally recognized state-based channels" (2004, 107).

Several of the components of the shadow economy characterize drug trafficking in Rio. First, in Caxambu and Rio's other favelas drug trafficking occurs in a context of "not-war-not-peace" (Nordstrom 2004, 166). The city of Rio is not at war. Yet the city's favelas register levels of homicide comparable to those of countries experiencing civil war. In this context of not-war-not-peace, the police carry out counterinsurgency operations aimed at "liberating" favelas from drug traffickers, sometimes with the participation of the army. Second, while I focus on how the drug trade affects Caxambu, this is just the visible tip of a much more complex network that links Caxambu to far-away production and processing zones, and that moves through legal and illegal, state and nonstate, spheres.

Third, and most important, Nordstrom points out that shadow economies are not governed solely by the cold economic logic of profit and loss, but are social phenomena, shaped by and in turn producing forms of culture. Shadow economies, she argues, "fashion economic possibilities, they broker political power, and, importantly, they constitute cultures" (2004, 107). In doing so, they create new forms of authority: "In these conditions the complexities of power become apparent, as old and new forms of authority coalesce into hybrid and unexpected forms of government" (145).

In this chapter, I pursue Nordstrom's line of questioning, asking, given that drug trafficking in Caxambu and Rio's other favelas occurs in a space that is both deeply local and yet the product of larger-scale forces, and given that drug traffickers and the other residents of Caxambu are not strangers but social intimates tied together in complex and contradictory ways, what cultures and forms of power do drug traffickers create? How do drug traffickers draw upon, and refashion, local ideologies, identities, and ways of being? What challenges does the drug trade present for residents of Caxambu who do not participate in it, and what sorts of social tactics does one need to know in order to live in such a world?

Most of the analysis of drug-trafficker authority in Rio has focused on what favela residents and outside observers alike have called the *lei do*

morro (law of the hillside). As I discussed in Chapter 2, when drug traffickers sought to use favelas as bases for the citywide distribution of cocaine,
they made an offer to favela residents: if favela residents would refuse to
cooperate with the police and "respect" drug dealers by turning a blind eye
to their activities, then drug traffickers would in turn provide security and
safety in favelas. This arrangement has been interpreted in two ways.

Some observers, especially Rio's police and policy makers, have argued
that the so-called law of the hillside simply disguises the reality of harsh,
violent domination. In 2008, for example, the Rio state government began
the "pacification" policy of establishing UPP police posts in Rio's favelas,
carrying out combined police and army operations to permanently occupy
various favelas. These operations were described by news reporters, police
officials, and local politicians as freeing favela residents from the *domínio
do tráfico* (domination of the drug trade). Favelas were described as enemy
territory, subjected to the whims of drug traffickers who wielded arbitrary
violence and kept favela residents as virtual hostages. In this understanding, which I call the domination of drug traffickers model, violence is seen
as instrumental, a tool disconnected to any other social forces or structures
of meaning.

A contrasting understanding of drug-trafficker power, most often articulated by social scientists, argues that drug traffickers often have the acquiescence of favela residents, though not necessarily their full acceptance and
support. This model emphasizes the larger context of the state's neglect
of favela residents, in particular how the police have failed to provide residents with safety from crime, and how the judicial system has failed to
resolve local disputes. Drug traffickers, this perspective argues, have taken
advantage the state's neglect of poor neighborhoods by providing residents
with security and a framework for resolving conflicts. In exchange, favela
residents promise not to cooperate with the police and come to see drug
traffickers as legitimate local authorities. This is a highly asymmetrical bargain, with drug traffickers able to coerce cooperation through violence.
Nonetheless, interactions between favela residents and drug traffickers are
portrayed as an exchange, even if it is characterized by what Luke Dowdney has perceptively called forced reciprocity (2003, 52). Arguing along
these lines, Teresa Caldeira (2000) has argued that the absence of the rule
of law has led poor people to accept, or even encourage, violence committed by policemen or local death squads as long as the violence is seen as
"punishing criminals." I will call this approach the asymmetrical exchange

model, as it depicts favela residents as supporting drug-trafficker violence in exchange for security.

Both of these models have their merits: it is just as dangerous to downplay the willingness of drug traffickers to use violence as it is problematic to ignore the larger context of poverty and marginalization. Yet when interactions between drug traffickers and favela residents are examined more closely, a more complex picture emerges. The law of the hillside appears to be a normative system that legitimates violent actions by drug traffickers, normalizing their power. But it would be wrong to take the metaphor of the law of the hillside at face value and think of drug dealers as instituting a local form of government in Rio's favelas. Unlike favela-based residents' associations in the 1970s, drug dealers in Caxambu did not create any formal mechanisms, with regularized procedures and normative standards, to adjudicate conflict (Santos 1977). There was no drug-dealer court. Rather, when drug dealers did intervene in local conflicts, they often based their decisions on personal connections, and with an overriding concern for what was best for their own business (Arias and Rodrigues 2006). Even more important, drug dealers often violated their own rules, suspending what is "normal." Drug traffickers, I will argue, pursued a strategy of abnormalization: although they claimed to provide safety and security, they also often deliberately disrupted daily life.

When drug dealers committed acts of violence, this was not purely instrumental or devoid of any kind of social logic. In seeking to legitimate themselves, drug traffickers drew upon, as they also disrupted, local ideologies about the legitimate use of force and the ability of adult men to protect their dependents and command respect. As I argued earlier, residents of Caxambu often thought of themselves as a large family. In this understanding, drug traffickers were ambiguously positioned as dangerous intimates. Drug traffickers sometimes claimed to be part of the "family" of Caxambu, appropriating the role of the provider and protector, yet at times highlighted their difference. When incidents of violence are viewed ethnographically, in the context of these aspects of daily life, they emerge as neither completely disruptive of local structures of meaning nor as completely normalized and accepted as the cost of safety. Rather, residents of Caxambu constantly struggled over how to make sense of violent actions by drug traffickers, sometimes operating within drug-trafficker codes of acceptable violence, and yet at other times questioning such characterizations.

The issue is not whether favela residents simply accepted drug-trafficker violence or were forced to submit to it. It is also too simplistic to argue that favela residents accepted, or even encouraged, violence committed against members of the own communities (Caldeira and Holston 1999; Goldstein 2003). Instead, the more important question is: when and why did favela residents agree with drug-trafficker attempts to legitimate their authority? When did these attempts fail? What violent actions did favela residents see as justified, and which did they condemn? Likewise, rather than assuming that either the police or drug traffickers provided order, a more fruitful approach is to ask how various social actors in favelas attempted to produce either security or insecurity. How did favela residents understand and experience the effects of drug trafficking and police violence, and how was this understanding tied to broader notions of safety or danger, predictability or unpredictability? In what ways did drug traffickers disrupt the everyday lives of favela resident? And were there at the same time elements of drug-trafficker authority that favela residents could attempt to use to their advantage?

An incident from my fieldwork can open this discussion by revealing the complex relationship between the law of the hillside and daily experiences of (in)security. One day, a drug dealer shot a neighborhood man and also killed a dog that belonged to the family of Seu Lázaro, the president of the residents' association. The shooting shows how drug traffickers attempt to legitimate their authority by pursuing a strategy of abnormalization, alternately imposing and suspending the rules that govern security and "normal" interactions.

Tubarão and Seu Lázaro's Dog

One Thursday morning, the *morro* was abuzz with talk about a shooting that happened the previous afternoon. When I walked out the front gate of my house that morning, I came across Seu Lázaro and Clara, the association's secretary. They were having an intense conversation in the doorway of the association. From what I could piece together, someone had shot and killed one of Seu Lázaro's dogs. After talking with Clara, Seu Lázaro had to rush off to a meeting at the mayor's office, and I couldn't ask him more about what had happened. But as the morning wore on, various people passed by the association and added their comments about what had occurred.

The previous afternoon, a man known in the neighborhood for being a *viciado* (addict), appeared in the morro. He was very drunk and said something that Tubarão, one of the soldiers of the local drug gang, took as an insult. The man who insulted Tubarão no longer lived in the morro. As someone told me later, he was notorious for *fazendo besteira* (screwing up, or causing problems): I was told that he had an uncontrollable cocaine addiction and had had an affair with an older woman. After moving in with her, he sold all her possessions to buy more coke. The final straw came when he got the woman pregnant and then refused to accept responsibility for the baby. He had so antagonized his neighbors, and had run up such large debts, that the drug dealers had expelled him from the neighborhood.

When the man reappeared this particular April afternoon, perhaps attempting to settle his debts, he had already incurred the animosity of both the drug dealers and many people in the neighborhood. It took little to set off Tubarão's anger, and he took the man's sudden presence in the neighborhood, challenging his expulsion, as a personal insult. Tubarão wanted to kill the man on the spot, but some of the other drug dealers who were there restrained him. The bandidos (drug dealers) told the addict to run away, and fired some gunshots at the ground to scare him off. As the addict began to run down the hill, Tubarão shot him, hitting him in the hip. Just then, Tubarão also shot and killed one of Seu Lázaro's dogs, a large black mutt. After the shooting, the drug dealers grabbed the addict's body and dumped him, still alive, on a street at the edge of the morro. The man was eventually taken to the hospital, but died the following day.

In the following days, stories about the shooting spread throughout the neighborhood, becoming the main topic of *fofoca* (gossip). Although people were concerned that Tubarão had killed someone—and were especially worried about how the police would react—the fact that he had killed a dog belonging to Seu Lázaro's family was the center of conversation. People also wondered how Dê, at that time the man in charge of the drug dealing in the neighborhood, would respond to Tubarão's actions. Tubarão was, in fact, "disciplined" by Dê, and was not allowed to sell drugs for several days.

The day after the shooting, I was chatting with Clara when Dona Elsa came and sat down with us. She was dismayed that someone had been killed, and blamed the drug dealers for not taking Tubarão's gun away earlier. I asked her why he had shot the dog, and she said that he'd been snorting a lot of coke, and was *doidão* (crazy). Others had told me that

Tubarão felt that the dog was about to attack him, and so had opened fire. Dona Elsa was upset that someone would kill another person, and she also blamed the bandidos for not controlling Tubarão. "It was the middle of the afternoon," she said. "What if Tubarão had shot a child?" This was a very real fear. In the late afternoon the morro's streets became busier than usual as children returned from the afternoon session of school, and those who attended school in the morning took advantage of the cooler temperatures to transform the streets into makeshift soccer pitches.

Interpreting the Law of the Hillside

For many Brazilian politicians, police officers, and policy makers, the law of the hillside is nothing but an ideological smokescreen that disguises the harsh reality of arbitrarily violent drug traffickers. In this way of interpreting drug-trafficker authority, Tubarão's actions reveal the "truth" that drug traffickers act in an authoritarian fashion. Not only do they decide who can or cannot enter the morro—Tubarão, in this case, shot the addict for defying his expulsion—but they also frequently endanger the safety of the favela residents whom they purport to "protect." In this view, drug-trafficker violence is a tool—albeit a harsh one—that they use to impose their will upon favela residents. Violent actions by drug traffickers are seen as disruptive of everyday life, and they are seen as an occupying force, sharing little in common with favela residents.

Media reports about violence in Rio's favelas often emphasize this view of drug traffickers as acting like a despotic government, and depict favelas as radically cut off from the rest of the city, subjected to different "laws." For example, an article in the *Jornal do Brasil* newspaper entitled "Tráfico dita lei na favela" or "The Drug Trade Dictates the Law in the Favela," begins, in an apocalyptic tone:

> A million people are living according to rules imposed by drug traffickers in the 602 favelas of Rio. It's a whole world of people, even in a city of 5.5 million residents. Nothing less than one-fifth of the population of the city is squeezed into a territory of twenty-six square kilometers where survival depends on respecting the three commandments of the modern times in the favela: not seeing anything, not hearing anything and, principally, not saying anything. (April 30, 2000)

Although this understanding highlights the coercive power that drug traffickers possess, it views their actions as disembedded from any larger context. Drug traffickers might occupy favela spaces, and might be related to favela dwellers, but their actions are disconnected from local systems of meaning. As Alba Zaluar points out, however, drug traffickers possess an ethic that draws upon the moral vision of favela residents, even while drug traffickers disrupt local social relations (1994, 19–26). In the aftermath of the shooting, there was widespread discussion in Caxambu (even if much of it was quietly whispered), about what had occurred and why. If drug traffickers simply ruled through violent power, there would be no need to try to interpret and make sense of their actions. Dê, the head of the drug dealing operation in Caxambu, did not hesitate to take action, disciplining Tubarão. Why would Dê have taken this action unless he was operating according to an ethic that distinguished acceptable forms of violence from unacceptable ones?

Clearly, drug traffickers in Caxambu built a structure of authority that was based upon more than coercive power. How, then, should we understand Tubarão's actions and the effects of drug dealer violence on everyday life? The approach favored by social scientists—the asymmetrical exchange model—offers a window into understanding these dynamics. In a pioneering article, Elizabeth Leeds has argued that rise of drug-trafficking syndicates was intimately connected to the state's failure to provide services and to its repressive role in favelas. A pattern of abusive policing of favela residents, the lack of provision of public safety by the state, and a widespread distrust of the formal legal system generated the context within which drug-trafficking organizations emerged (1996). In her insightful ethnography of gender in a favela in northern Rio, Donna Goldstein also argues that favela residents felt insecurity since they saw the police and judicial system as corrupt and abusive (2003).

Organized drug trafficking groups must be placed within this larger context of marginalization and vulnerability. Leeds states: "The perception by favela residents—indeed, by most of the working class—that the formal justice system does not work for them has led a portion of the population to accept an alternative justice system" (1996, 62). As it sought to take over drug-selling points from other criminal groups, the Comando Vermelho's strategy was to offer this alternative. In exchange for their silence and acquiescence toward criminal activities, the CV offered favela residents protection against crime and the resolution of local conflicts. Goldstein agrees with Leeds's assessment, stating: "In the brown zones of Rio de Janeiro, the local gangs provide a parallel state structure and alternative rule of law.... Local gangs are seen as necessary—they protect the favela from outsiders, they offer housing and employment and help in times of trouble, they do what the police cannot do—but they, too, are viewed with a great deal of ambivalence" (2003, 200).

Goldstein and Leeds both highlight that this relationship between favela residents and drug groups is fraught with tensions and ambivalence. Leeds notes that although most favela-based drug dealers occupy relatively low-paying and highly vulnerable positions in the citywide trade in cocaine, they are extremely visible within favelas. She states: "They are either revered or grudgingly respected or feared. Their presence is never neutral" (1996, 58). She also notes that interactions between favela residents and drug groups are "determined by the personality, leadership style, and personal philosophy of the drug leader" and that "favela residents are usually uneasy about such forced cooperation" (60–61). Goldstein concurs, stating: "Because the code of justice is dependent on the personalities and caprice of the leaders and gang members of the moment, there can be no predictability or continuity to the way affairs will be solved. Often, situations are likely to be resolved by brute force or murder" (2003, 190).

Although this perspective is useful, Leeds and Goldstein share several problematic underlying assumptions. First, the forced exchange between drug traffickers and favela residents is described as creating a relatively stable normative system, a set of rules or perhaps even an "alternative rule of law." Second, they argue that this exchange is based on the ability of drug traffickers to provide safety and security. Favela-based drug gangs, Goldstein states, "are called upon to right the wrongs of everyday life, and in this role they are tolerated and sometimes venerated" (2003, 200).

Other analysts of favela-based drug traffickers focus on how drug-trafficking organizations have built upon preexisting networks which link favela residents to state actors. Desmond Arias has examined how traffickers have consolidated their control over favelas by constructing flexible and horizontal networks that link them to local social movements, politicians, and state institutions, and global flows of illegal commodities (2006). In a similar vein, Michel Misse has argued that Rio's drug trafficking groups drew upon a pattern of "dangerous liaisons" that connected criminals to agents of the state (2006, 179–210). Misse emphasizes, in particular, the relationship between markets in illegal goods (such as the illegal lottery) and markets in political goods offered by agents of the state (such as protection or selective enforcement of the law). He argues that the gap between the criminalization of drugs, on the one hand, and demand for this illegal market, on the other, creates an important political-economic space. The gap between criminalization and demand allows corrupt police to sell selective enforcement, and politicians can use their ability to encourage or discourage crackdowns on crime as political merchandise for electoral support.

Arias and Misse both emphasize that the networks and linkages between criminal organizations and the state are dynamic, conflicted, and unstable. Ties between traffickers and politicians, or between traffickers and favela residents, Arias argues, are based on opportunistic political calculation by the parties involved, and are always open to renegotiation or collapse. Arias and Corinne Rodrigues also show how traffickers often exercise power arbitrarily, favoring more influential favela residents or those with whom they have stronger social ties. But this strategy has its limits: when traffickers undertake actions that are "consistently seen as an abuse of power that affects protected groups of residents . . . traffickers risk losing their limited legitimacy" (2006, 74). Misse likewise argues that ties between criminals and state agents are "dangerous" because they are subject to constant renegotiation, often through violence.

Misse and Arias develop clientelistic and network-driven models that usefully emphasize the links between the state and criminal organizations, while Leeds and Goldstein are more attuned to how local contexts shape understandings of legitimate violence. Yet all of these approaches share a central underlying assumption. The forms of governance constructed by drug traffickers in Rio's favelas are seen as relatively stable normative systems that govern the legitimate use of force. Dennis Rodgers has made a similar argument about drug-dealing gangs in poor neighborhoods in Nicaragua, arguing that they "establish localized regimes of order in wider conditions of social and state breakdown, constrained economic circumstances and uncertainty" (2006, 291).

In these discussions, drug-trafficking organizations appear to be statelike entities that claim the monopoly over the legitimate use of force within a given territory. By this argument, favela residents accept, or perhaps acquiesce to, drug traffickers as long as the violence used by traffickers generates stability and safety. But as we have seen in the case of Tubarão, this is hardly the case: the "protection" offered by drug traffickers often goes hand in hand with arbitrary violence, and the legitimacy of their actions is by no means completely accepted.

Everyday Emergencies and Public Secrets

In conceptualizing the relationship between violence and stability, the asymmetrical exchange and the drug-trafficker domination models actually mirror each other. Rio's policy makers often assume that violence by drug traffickers is completely disruptive of the everyday lives of favela residents, and that only the state, through permanent police occupation, can and should provide the basis for order. The asymmetrical exchange model simply reverses the equation. In this view, it is the state—especially the police—that disrupts the daily lives of favela residents either by failing to make itself present or by arbitrarily violent police raids. Violence by drug traffickers, on the other hand, is tolerated as long as it brings a sense of safety and order to favela communities. In both approaches one set of actors is seen as violently disruptive, while the authority of the other is seen as producing order. Violence—whether by the police or drug traffickers—is conceptualized as either barbaric or as the necessarily precondition for stability.

Both approaches fail to capture the complexity of everyday life in neighborhoods like Caxambu. In doing so, they risk portraying favela residents as either helpless victims deprived of any agency, or as the (perhaps unwitting) accomplices of criminals. Also problematic is how they depict the relationship between violence and social order. As Kay Warren has warned, it is important not to see violence as a threat to an otherwise "normal" social order (2002). Doing so naturalizes existing political structures, drawing attention away from how stability is often built upon exclusion, violence, and inequality. Assuming that either the state or drug traffickers provide security runs the risk of taking those institutions' rhetoric at face value. But as Michael Taussig has pointed out, political regimes often cultivate instability, uncertainty, and terror to control the lives of people that they seek to govern (1992).

Tubarão's actions show how drug gangs deliberately arrogate to themselves the power not only to institute normative systems but also to violate the systems that they themselves create. Likewise, this authority is not founded on open discussion and consensus, but on the deliberate construction and manipulation of secrecy and ambiguity. Drug traffickers do not simply trade protection for silence, with favela residents seeing this use of force as normal, but neither do they operate in complete disregard for local ethics.

Clearly a different interpretation is needed in order to understand how a state of (in)security is constructed, reproduced, and experienced. The challenge, once again, is to see the order in the disorder, and the disorder in the order. To accomplish this, I borrow several analytical tools. In examining drug-trafficker authority, I will draw upon Giorgio Agamben's notion of a state of exception (2005). Drug traffickers impose a set of rules upon favela residents, yet often disregard these rules and act in an arbitrarily violent fashion. Agamben's work can be used to show how these are not mutually contradictory processes. Instead, the ability to produce order and disorder, to shift from what is "normal" to a state of emergency where the rules are suspended, is constitutive of drug-trafficker power.

In order to examine the effects of this "permanent state of emergency" (Benjamin 1978) upon the lives of favela residents, I will also borrow Michael Taussig's notion of "public secrets" and "active unknowing" (1999). Just as Agamben complicates simple dichotomies of order or disorder, emergency or normality, Taussig complicates notions of truth and dissimulation, transgression and conformity. Residents of Caxambu know that even though drug traffickers claim to provide safety, they often act in an arbitrarily violent fashion. They know that the rules that drug traffickers institute are just as often violated as they are enforced. They also know that they have to be seen as not knowing this, publicly performing the act of hiding what is common knowledge.

Recall once again the advice that Dona Carmen, one of my neighbors, gave me one day while I was buying a plate of rice and beans from the café she ran in her back-yard kitchen. "In order to live here," she told me, "you can't see anything, hear anything, or say anything. You have to pretend you're deaf, blind, and mute." At one level, Dona Carmen seemed to be warning me to avoid any interactions with criminals. As I discussed earlier, although residents of Caxambu consistently attempted to symbolically separate themselves from drug traffickers, such lines were often blurred and required careful management. But Dona Carmen was also saying that I needed to learn how to pretend not to hear and see what I inevitably heard and saw. Rather than simply telling me to obey the drug dealers, Dona Carmen was instructing me on how to take part in the morro's public secret.

The First Order Is Respect: Being
Responsa and Not Being a *Vacilão*

When residents of Caxambu talked about their interactions with drug traffickers, they rarely spoke about a normative set of rules. Instead, they emphasized that interactions with the local *malandros* (hustlers) were anchored in three conditions: reciprocal respect; the provision of safety and the resolution of disputes; and an overarching code of silence. Although this seems fairly straightforward, actual daily interactions—as the story of Tubarão shooting Seu Lázaro's dog reveals—show that knowledge of the "rules" was only one aspect of knowing how to live. Far more challenging was navigating the space between the rules and the complexities of daily life. A song by favela-based rapper MV Bill called "Como sobreviver na favela" (How to Survive in the Favela) describes the challenges of living under drug trafficker authority.[1] The first comandment that favela residents must follow is that of respect:

A primeira ordem: não pode ser Judas
Tem que ser irmão se não leva tiro na bunda
Tem que respeitar toda a malandragem
Se não pro inferno vão te dar sua passagem

[The first order: you can't be a Judas
Be a brother or you'll be shot in the ass
You have to respect the hustlers
Or they'll buy you a ticket straight to hell.]

Sergio, who worked as a neighborhood garbage collector, once gave me a piece of advice as we sat chatting at Seu Jonas's bar at the bottom of Caxambu's main stairway. He told me that he always feels *tranquilo* (calm) in any morro that he goes to, and that if I followed his suggestions I'd be fine in any favela that I cared to visit. First, he said, I had to be *considerado*, someone whom people in the neighborhood know and hold in good regard. Second, I had to be *responsa*. When I asked him what this meant, he said I had to honor my promises, follow through with my decisions, and not be a *vacilão*, someone who can't be depended upon and always causes *besteira* (foolishness). *Vacilão* is a common term for someone who can't act decisively and who doesn't live up to his promises. By contrast, someone who is responsa doesn't hesitate to live up to his commitments. These terms also carry clearly gendered and masculinist tones: a person who is responsa can act decisively and impose himself upon a situation, and is not someone who is dominated by others or by his own weakness.

The contrast between being responsa and being a vacilão helps reveal the main components of respect. Roberto Da Matta has argued that many aspects of social organization in Brazil follow a pattern of complementary opposition within a structure of hierarchical inclusion. For Da Matta, the family is the prime example of such organization: parents are seen as different from children, men from women, and older siblings from younger ones. Yet all of these people complement each other within a larger structure of hierarchy, where each person knows his place (Da Matta 1991 [1979]). In this sense, being responsa means knowing where one fits within a larger hierarchical structure, and acting accordingly.

Here it is possible to see how the law of the hillside draws from larger notions of gender and kinship. As MV Bill's song highlights, respect is understood through the metaphor of kinship: to avoid drug-trafficker violence, you have to "be a brother." While drug dealers are spoken of as distinct and different, this opposition exists within a larger context of shared social ties and shared occupation of the hillside. Residents of Caxambu would often point out that the drug dealers were born and raised in the neighborhood. As Nêgo once told me, when speaking about the local drug dealers: "If you look at it closely you'll see, I know that guy. They're all from here. People from here. It could be your grandfather, your cousin, you know?"

Brazilians, as is the case with people in any complex, cosmopolitan, and highly unequal society, have multiple different and sometimes contradictory ways to understand kinship, gender, and sexuality (Parker 1991, 27). These ideologies are also dynamic, contested, and set within larger contexts. Nonetheless, in my conversations with favela residents, it was clear that traditionally patriarchal and heteronormative ideas about gender and were dominant. These understandings, Richard Parker points out, "continue to exert profound influence over the flow of daily life, constituting a kind of cultural grammar that continues to organize important aspects of experience" (1991, 29).

As anthropologists have long pointed out, notions of gender and kinship often "stratify the allocation of legal rights and social privileges" (di Leonardo and Lancaster 1997, 2). The cultural grammar of respect is clearly located within the traditional understanding of how power and authority are allocated in a patriarchal family. In a society heavily marked by the legacy of slavery, the patriarch was responsible for protecting his family, dependents, and slaves. These dependents, in turn, owed the patriarch respect and obedience. As several analysts have pointed out, violence plays a central role in constituting masculine gender identities: the patriarch, and by extension the "ideal" man, can respond appropriately to challenges to him or his family (Da Matta 1997; Freyre 1945; Parker 1991). Alternatively, being vulnerable to violence, especially being vulnerable to the physical imposition of someone else upon one's body, is a marker of femininity.

Yet the language of respect, rooted in underlying notions of gender and kinship, barely conceals tensions and anxieties. As Matthew Gutmann has pointed out, it is important to distinguish between idealized gender norms and actual lived experiences of gender (2003, 3–4). Anxieties about masculine status are nothing new; in poor communities, especially, it is often difficult for men to demonstrate their masculinity through economic support for their families. Claudia Fonseca notes that the "inferior status and limited economic opportunities of unskilled manual laborers exacerbate the fear of female betrayal" (2002, 68).

Linda Rebhun argues that because gender norms are increasingly at odds with lived experiences, gender ideologies among poor and working-class people in Brazil should be seen not as "blueprints for practices" but as "symbolic vocabularies through which to judge status" (1999, 112). People in Caxambu would often comment upon how boys were drawn to drug trafficking not simply because of the money they could earn but also because of the status that they thought this gave them. The money from drugs that they could spend and their ability to display guns and other symbols of power were seen as a quick path to adult male status (see also Athayde et al. 2005, 224–232; Zaluar 1994). When I asked a group of teenage girls in Caxambu why boys became drug dealers, Andreia referred explicitly to connections between the drug trade, money, and adult male authority. "Boys today, they're like this: boys don't want to be workers like their fathers. They want to be men, to be *homenzinhos* (little men). They want to be in charge of themselves. To be able to buy things that their moms can't afford . . . and they hear how much money drug dealers are making, and they want it too."

As Andreia points out, the way that drug traffickers appropriate the symbolic vocabulary of status is distinctly double-edged. On the one hand, the image of the man who can protect himself, provide for his family, and "be in charge of himself" is deeply enticing for young, dark-skinned men who experience humiliation and vulnerability in their daily lives. It also provides a common cultural code—that of the man who protects his family—through which drug traffickers can attempt to legitimate their power. Yet it poses radical challenges to older men and to men who do not participate in the drug trade.

Tubarão's shooting of the dog reveals this dynamic: just as idealized images of the patriarchal family mask inequality and rivalry, so too alongside the language of respect there often lie more complicated relationships of suspicion, competition, and anxiety. The way that drug traffickers appropriated traditional discourses of masculinity powerfully shaped perceptions of how violence could be legitimately exercised. The man whom Tubarão shot was not just a vacilão who failed to show respect, but had broken many of the neighborhood's standards of "decent" morality. He disobeyed the drug traffickers' orders to leave the neighborhood, took advantage of an older woman's affections in order to fuel his addiction, and then failed to take responsibility when she became pregnant with their child. When I spoke with them about the shooting, Dona Elsa and Clara told me that they were upset that the *viciado*, as they called him, had been killed. "No one deserves that that kind of ending," Dona Elsa told me. But neither Dona Elsa nor Clara seemed particularly surprised.

Two other aspects of the shooting, though, seemed to worry Dona Elsa much more. First, she was upset that the other drug dealers had failed to control Tubarão, who shot the man after they had let him go. She was worried that innocent children and other people—people who had done nothing to disrespect the drug dealers—might have been harmed. This seemed to reveal the frightening possibility that Dê's control over his own drug dealers was more fragile than it appeared. If Dê could not effectively impose discipline within his own organization, then how could he really protect the neighborhood? If Dê's authority was nothing but a show, then how could the decent residents of Caxambu feel secure as they went about their daily lives?

In fact, the shooting angered Dê, who prided himself on his ability to control his men, and so Tubarão was disciplined for what he had done. Dê suspended Tubarão for a week, ordering him to hand over his gun and refusing to let him sell drugs. According to local commentary this was serious punishment, as Tubarão would earn no money during this time.

Tubarão disappeared from sight for a day or two, and then spent much of the rest of the week sitting on a stoop off of one of the main staircases, drinking beer.

It was the shooting of Seu Lázaro's dog, though, that generated the most concern and speculation. As everyone who lived in that part of the neighborhood knew, Seu Lázaro had watched Tubarão grow up. Dona Elsa often told me that in the morro, older people often assumed responsibility for disciplining young children, even those who were not their own kin. Not only was Seu Lázaro an older man, to whom Tubarão should have owed respect, but Seu Lázaro was the head of the residents' association. Tubarão's violence against Seu Lázaro's dependents, and Seu Lázaro's apparent inability to reprimand the younger man, deeply challenged the older man's authority.

Alba Zaluar has pointed out that drug gangs in Rio's favelas have "provoked a *reviravolta* (about-face) in the internal relations of power in favelas, especially those governed by generational hierarchy" (1994, 27). As men like Tubarão can tap into the resources made available through the shadow economy of the drug trade, they are able to claim the authority often denied to older men. As Andreia pointed out, they no longer want to be like their fathers. But their claims to authority are not simply accepted, as Andreia inferred by calling boys who sell drugs *homenzinhos* (little men).

There was actually quite a bit of tension between the residents' association and local drug dealers. Dê, the main drug dealer in Caxambu, wanted to have little to do with some of the most common sources of conflict in the neighborhood, those over property sales, access to water, and boundaries between neighbors. He was happy to leave mediation on these issues, which are usually seen as falling under the jurisdiction of residents' associations, to Seu Lázaro. Seu Lázaro, in turn, struggled hard to preserve the appearance of the residents' association's independence and neutrality. Yet, as Boaventura de Sousa Santos pointed out in his pioneering analysis of dispute resolution by a residents' association in the 1970s, in order to encourage residents to respect their authority, residents' associations must present at least the threat of coercion. In the 1970s, Santos argues, this entailed a complex relationship between residents' associations, the formal legal system, and the police (1977). To encourage participation in dispute mediation, residents' associations would threaten to send a conflict to the formal legal system or threaten to call the police, though this threat was almost never carried out.

As favela-based drug dealers stepped in to repress crime in Rio's favelas and prohibited cooperation between favela residents and the police, they disrupted this dynamic. Seu Lázaro could not use the threat of police action to bolster his authority, since cooperation with the police would directly violate the drug dealers' authority and place Seu Lázaro in danger. Neither, though, could he present himself as simply the puppet of local drug dealers, since this would make it difficult for him in his other dealings with city authorities and would damage his internal credibility in the morro. Rather, he sought to avoid situations where he had to invoke possible coercive power, instead issuing vague comments about how it was "in everyone's best interests" to get along. But everyone in Caxambu knew, though they also tried not to know, that the only coercive power that Seu Lázaro could appeal to was that of the drug traffickers. Aware of this influence, the local drug dealers often attempted to pressure Seu Lázaro into doing favors for them such as serving as an intermediary with the police or securing permits for Saturday night baile funk parties, all-night dance parties held on the concrete soccer field at the top of the hill, which were often hosted by local drug dealers.

As a result, when Tubarão shot Seu Lázaro's dog, there was rampant speculation about what this might signal about relations between the residents' association and the local traficantes. Some residents of Caxambu who thought that Seu Lázaro was "in the pocket" of the local bandidos wondered if the shooting indicated a breakdown in relations. For others, it showed how powerless Seu Lázaro really was. Residents speculated wildly about what the true nature of the relationship between Seu Lázaro and Tubarão might be, as if knowing some supposed secret about this relationship might entitle the knower to a sense of certainty about how the drug traffickers might act.

When Seu Lázaro related the shooting to me a few days later, he said that when it happened he was working inside the residents' association, repairing a room where a new computer center was going to be installed. He hadn't heard the gunshots, and was shocked to come outside and find that his dog was dead. Talking with Clara and me, Seu Lázaro said: "Tubarão will have to answer to the saints." I didn't understand this comment, thinking at first that Seu Lázaro was appealing to a higher authority, arguing that Tubarão would not escape unpunished by God.

But talking to Clara later, I found out that Seu Lázaro was being much more specific. She told me that Seu Lázaro's dog was a family pet and a religious obligation of his wife, Dona Paula. At that time Dona Paula was deeply involved in Afro-Brazilian religion, frequenting a Candomblé temple in the northern suburbs of Rio (though she soon converted to Protestantism and joined an evangelical church). Dona Paula was a devotee of Oxóssi, the *orixá* (deity) who is the god of the hunt and is fond of green plants and dogs. To demonstrate her devotion, Dona Paula carried out actions to please Oxóssi, and was keeping the dog in the orixá's honor.

Killing the dog was also a major transgression of the rules of mutual respect for other reasons. Although I often saw pets treated with almost criminal negligence, in this case the dog was well cared for. Shooting the dog was almost like shooting a member of Seu Lázaro's family. Not only this, but in a sense the dog belonged not to Seu Lázaro or Dona Paula, but to Oxóssi. Tubarão had not only failed to show Seu Lázaro respect but he had also angered much higher and more powerful authorities. The sentiment shared by Dona Elsa, Clara, and others seemed to be: if even Seu Lázaro's dog, a dog promised to Oxóssi, isn't protected, then who is?

The Second Order: The Provision of Safety

Another key component of relations between drug traffickers and residents of Caxambu is the idea that drug traffickers provide safety in the neighborhood by suppressing crime and providing rough, but quick, justice. MV Bill's second rule about how to survive in the favela is:

> A segunda ordem: roubo na favela
> Se os caras te pegarem, vai dar merda
> Já roubou uma vez, rouba duas, rouba três
> Vai cair pra trás porque tá na bola da vez
> Antes de cair vai falar com o sangue bom
> Que vigia a favela e não quer vacilação
> Tarado quando não morre
> perde o pau e perde a mão.

> [The second order: theft in the favela.
> If the guys find out, you're in deep shit.
> You stole once, twice, three times
> You're going down, your number's up

Before being shot down, you'll talk to the Man[2]
Who guards the favela and doesn't allow screw-ups
Perverts in the favela when they aren't killed
Lose their dick and their hand.]

Residents of Caxambu often stressed this aspect of life in the morro, telling me that they felt safer in Caxambu than in the areas that were not under the control of the local drug gang, and that they trusted the traffickers more than the police. For instance, Pedro told me: "Everyone here likes you and your wife. Everyone here receives you with open arms. You can walk around at will, can leave that tape-recorder right here—'Oh, it's Ben's'—and no one will touch it. Do you understand? Because . . . the Man here [the head of the drug gang] respects people, and doesn't want anyone to mess with anyone else. You see sometimes . . . I even leave the door of my house open. . . . I trust them more than I trust the police." Dennis Rodgers has noted a similar pattern in Nicaragua, where inhabitants of a poor neighborhood would critique *pandillas* (street gangs) in general, and yet felt that the local gang "looks after the neighborhood" (2006, 277).

Although Pedro and others in Caxambu attributed their safety to the local traficantes, they were particularly fearful that the morro might be "invaded" and taken over by rival drug gangs, who might not be locals and who might not respect residents. The residents of Caxambu followed news reports about wars between rival gangs and splits within the CV with keen interest, as they worried that rivalries in the drug trade might intensify violence in their neighborhood. For instance, on May 22, 1999, during my period of fieldwork, a leader of the Comando Vermelho and his son were killed in prison. The killing became a major topic of conversation in Caxambu. Some residents openly worried that the killings might disrupt the balance of power and lead to increased conflict as different factions fought for ascendancy.

Anxieties about drug-gang rivalry often went hand in hand with fears of violent and corrupt police: the rise of the drug trade in the late 1970s and early 1980s fed off patterns of corruption and illegality in the police and justice system. Corrupt members of the police force realized that they could turn rivalries within Rio's drug groups to their advantage. Corrupt policemen often supplemented their income by extorting payments from detained traffickers, sometimes threatening to turn dealers or seized weapons over to rival gangs. It was even widely speculated that certain battalions of Rio's military police provided assistance to one or another of the rival drug groups.

A former resident of the favela of Dona Marta, for instance, told me that a major police operation in November 2010 to occupy and "pacify" the favela of Morro do Alemão was not actually aimed at improving the city's safety. Instead, he claimed, the police were allied with a drug gang that was a major rival of the CV, the gang that controlled Alemão. The police took over this favela, he claimed, as part of a bargain whereby the CV's rivals would limit their violence if the police helped them take control over control of the drug trade. I have no way of knowing whether this story is true. The point, though, is the assumption, on the part of many favela residents, that the police and rival drug gangs often work hand in hand.

Another major public secret in the morro was that although the drug traffickers and the police were supposed to be rivals, and favela residents should never speak with the police, people knew that the police and drug traffickers often worked together, though not necessarily with the best interests of favela residents in mind. The prohibition on speaking with the police was thus matched by the knowledge that traffickers often, in fact, had close relationships with policemen. This common knowledge that this taboo was transgressed resulted in a figure of anxiety and mistrust: the corrupt policeman. I noticed, for instance, that every few weeks a relatively well-dressed man would drive up to the top of the hillside and spend a few hours talking with the drug traffickers in front of the main *boca* (drug-selling point). Whenever this happened—often in the middle of the afternoon—people quickly vacated the surrounding streets and alleys. Finally I asked Seu Lázaro what was going on, and he told me that the man was an off-duty policeman, there to negotiate the *arrego* (fix) between the police and drug dealers. "He's a nasty guy," Seu Lázaro told me, "someone you really don't want to deal with."

Not only did residents of Caxambu know that their "safety" was in the hands of constantly up-for-grabs negotiations between drug dealers and the police—and they took great pains to "not know" this—but they also personalized their relative safety, seeing it as dependent upon Dê's leadership. Security in the neighborhood was not the product of a set of rules, but was contingent upon one person's leadership. By thinking of safety in these terms, residents were often reminded of how fragile and potentially fleeting peace was, as they knew that Dê could be shot or arrested at any moment. For instance, I asked Anacleto if he thought that situation in

Caxambu could change in the next few years, and told me: "Tomorrow, it could change tomorrow. Who knows if tomorrow it'll be so stable?"

Traffickers not merely provided a sense of stability and safety where the state was unable or unwilling to; they also relied on a strategy of abnormalization, producing and encouraging anxieties and fears, which they could then use to legitimate their control. Without the twin threats of rival gangs and abusive police, for instance, the bargain that residents made with traffickers would have nothing behind it except brute force. For favela residents, on the other hand, public statements about the "time of peace" in Caxambu went hand in hand with everyday experiences of police harassment, arbitrary trafficker violence, and a larger fear that the current situation of stability might collapse unpredictably.

For many favela men, seeing their safety as contingent upon Dê's authority meant placing themselves in the vulnerable position of being dependent upon other, often younger, men for their status and security. For example, Dona Carmen's husband, Seu Jaime, was a retired police officer. Although they relied upon his pension for part of their income, Dona Carmen never hesitated to browbeat her husband, accusing him of being lazy while she worked cooking food in her backyard café. One afternoon I asked Dona Carmen and Seu Jaime if they thought that Caxambu was dangerous. Dona Carmen didn't hesitate to answer, saying:

> No, it's not dangerous. I can't complain about that. . . . You're proof of that, because you live here with us and you know, right? . . . For example: if someone were to mess with you, go to your house, break down your door and steal your things. If you go and complain, ah, your things are going to have to appear. There's no doubt about that. If someone here robs your wife, they'll want to find out who it is. No way, that doesn't happen here! I mean, my kitchen is all open, right? My fridge is out here, the gas for my stove, and no one steals anything. Thank God, right? That sort of security we have. Not just with God, but with the guys who look after things.

In her response, Dona Carmen quickly connected safety to personal possessions, domestic space, and to a man's ability to protect his wife. My safety, my possessions, and my wife's safety were all guaranteed, she said, by "them," meaning the local drug dealers. Her own domestic space, she said, was open, but she was not afraid because she could trust in "the guys." Unspoken in all these comments was her failure to mention Seu Jaime, her husband and a former policeman, as a source of protection. The implication escaped no one: as Dona Carmen made her comments, Seu Jaime simply smiled sheepishly.

The Third Order: Silence

Underpinning relations between drug traffickers and residents of Caxambu was the so-called law of silence: residents of the morro were prohibited from speaking to the police about the activities of local drug dealers. Seu Lázaro, for example, could not call the police after Tubarão shot his dog. MV Bill describes the law of silence as follows:

> A terceira ordem é boca fechada
> Que não entra mosca e também não entra bala
> Caguete na favela você sabe que não pode
> Se a língua bater nos dentes você leve um sacode
> Nem pense em falar mal de um bandido
> Para a polícia, se não você está perdido.

> [The third rule is keep a closed mouth
> Because flies won't get in, nor will bullets[3]
> Informants aren't allowed in the favela
> Open your mouth, and you'll get beat down
> Don't even think of talking about a bandido
> To the police, if you do you're lost.]

Márcia Leite and Luiz Antonio Machado da Silva have convincingly argued that the silence of favela residents should not be seen as a sign that they are complicit with drug dealing. Instead, the inability or unwillingness of favela residents to speak about the coercion and violence that traffickers exert within their communities is a defense mechanism (*dispositivo de defensa*) (2007, 67). Ethnographically, though, the picture is even more complex: the defense is not simply remaining silent, but rather knowing how to hide information about drug trafficking that is often actually widely known.

In Caxambu, the law of silence functioned as a public secret: everyone knew that it was prohibited to speak about the activities of drug traffickers, even though everyone knew about the activities of drug traffickers. Particularly revealing is how favela residents used indirection in comments that seemed to be talking about no one in particular, but which were, in fact, describing drug traffickers. The local head of the drug trafficking organization was referred to by his direct name only in utterances where there were no other clear indications that he was, in fact, the head of the local drug gang. In all other cases, he was referred to simply as *o homem* (the Man), or *o dono* (the owner). In other words, the use of secrecy ("hiding" Dê's name), presumed that the listener actually shared in the secret knowledge. In this case, the purpose of hiding knowledge that was openly known was not to avoid revealing a secret, but to actively create a community of people who know what they shouldn't know. Participating in knowing the "truth" of the secret was a way of marking oneself as an insider, part of a metaphorical family who could, it was hoped, count on the protection of drug traffickers. But as Taussig points out, concealing that which is known also creates a space of ambiguity and epistemic murk (1986).

To some residents of Caxambu, the ironies of hiding what everyone knew were sometimes the source of humor. For example, a group of teenage girls once gleefully told me a story about what happened one afternoon when the police stopped João. One of the better-known characters on the hillside, João was a mentally ill and emaciated man who between bouts of hard drinking barely sustained himself and his senile mother by running errands in exchange for food or money. The girls told me that after the police hit João and threatened to arrest him, they asked him: "Where's the boca?" In Rio's favelas, the place where drugs are sold is known as the *boca de fumo*, literally the mouth of smoke. Unlike the American terms "crack house" or "shooting gallery," it is not a term for a specific place, but is semantically much vaguer. The word *boca* (mouth) is also replete with ambiguous significance: the mouth symbolizes both sustenance (because of its role in eating) and destruction (as in the *boca do inferno* or mouth of hell). Eating is also a common Brazilian metaphor for sex (Parker 1991). João seemed to be aware of these metaphorical entanglements. The girls told me, giggling to themselves: "João told the police 'right here,' and pointed to his mouth." João's answer was almost Zen-like in its simultaneous simplicity and complexity: by answering the police he was both obeying them, yet also following the law of silence by refusing to provide them with information. By pointing to his mouth, he was successfully manipulating the semantic ambiguity that is such a common aspect of terms associated with the drug trade. Finally, he was pointing out the obvious: you'd have to be pretty stupid to not know where the boca is.

Living in a State of (In)security

If the power that drug traffickers wielded in Caxambu is seen as enacted within and then reshaping a rhetorical and social terrain, then we can ask: what tactics can moradores use not in opposition to, but *within* this terrain? If traffickers appropriate a language of patriarchal power, then why do favela residents recognize themselves in this discourse? How does this act of interpellation function, and what effects does it have? Drug traffickers both imposed rules and violated them, generating a state of (in)security, a zone of ambiguity and contradictions. How did this zone of ambiguity present favela residents with both challenges and opportunities? Broadly, there were two strategies that residents used: they either appealed to trafficker rhetoric about how things should be in order to shape how they were; or they attempted to channel the public secret, using ambiguity and secrecy to their advantage.

The strategy of appealing to the basic components of drug trafficker rhetoric was fairly common. Drug traffickers attempted to legitimate their authority by using the rhetoric of kinship, manipulating pride in local place, and by providing at least the semblance of an intelligible order to justify what counts as legitimate or illegitimate violence. All of these elements of the *lei do morro* could be and often were used by residents of Caxambu.

For instance, when Dona Elsa and Clara, and other residents of Caxambu, talked about the man whom Tubarão shot and killed, they called him *o viciado*. In such a tight-knit neighborhood, he also was, of course, someone's brother, uncle, and son. Yet the identity that was highlighted was the label applied to a person who had violated the "appropriate" rules of conduct. One of Dona Elsa's main worries, after the shooting, was not simply that Tubarão killed someone, but that in the process he might have also shot people who she called *gente inocente* (innocent people). By classifying the man who was shot as a viciado, Dona Elsa was placing herself and her family in the category of good people. In this way, drug-trafficker rhetoric shaped how residents of Caxambu understood deserving and undeserving victims of violence: the viciado, it was implied, was not innocent and should have known that his actions would displease the drug dealers.

Although his death was lamented, it was not seen as particularly surprising: unlike the innocent, he had violated the rules of respect.

The way that the residents of Caxambu spoke about some victims of drug-trafficker violence has very close parallels with how victims of domestic violence are often spoken about. In her ethnography of domestic violence in a poor neighborhood in Bahia, in northeastern Brazil, Sarah Hautzinger presents a nuanced interpretation of how women understand domestic violence. Hautzinger states that for some of her informants, "the roles of men and women were distinct and complementary, requiring compliance on both parts. If the woman failed to fulfill expectations, she effectively forfeited adulthood, and then it became appropriate for her male partner to resort to authoritarian measures" (Hautzinger 2007, 71). Hautzinger observed a lack of sympathy for chronically battered women who violated established gender norms. Like a woman who did not perform the culturally appropriate roles of mother, lover, or household contributor, the viciado was seen as someone against whom violence could be legitimately used.

On the other hand, Hautzinger notes that women's vulnerability to violence, and the ways in which violence against them is understood, varied according to their social positioning. Not only did women's various positioning with respect to men—such as mothers, sisters, or lovers—matter, but so did women's positioning with respect to other women. For example, while one woman was seen as "weak" for failing to stand up to her abusive husband, or as even perhaps "wanting" to be beaten, an older woman who suffered abuse as a young woman was able "to cast herself as a slow, patient winner" (Hautzinger 2007, 90).

In a similar way, attitudes about victims of drug-trafficker violence depend not only on relations between the victim and drug traffickers, but perhaps even more on the relations that the victim had with other people in the neighborhood. The man shot by Tubarão, for example, had consistently antagonized his neighbors and relatives by stealing and scamming them to find money to buy cocaine. Seu Lázaro, on the other hand, was an exemplar of the proper older man who had maintained his household, taken care of his wife and children, and worked with little complaint as a truck driver.

The way that people in Caxambu talked about who deserved violence, though, should be seen as more than just the passive acceptance of trafficker authority. Residents of Caxambu also used these categories performatively, using understandings of deserving and undeserving victims of drug-trafficker violence to their advantage. Highlighting the viciado's faults was a way of simultaneously emphasizing their own respect for the drug dealers. Performing this respectability, in turn, was a way of trying to ensure their safety. Seen this way, the apparent acceptance of violence by residents of poor communities emerges as something far more complex. Instead of a passive acquiescence to drug-trafficker authority, or the extralegal violence of police death squads, the acceptance of violence might hide a much more complicated social tactic. Favela residents are rarely in a position to challenge the authority of drug traffickers or violent policemen openly. Instead, they attempt to operate within this system of authority, trying to preempt violence by highlighting aspects of a victim's behavior that contrasts with their own respectful actions.

The way that drug trafficking drew upon kinship relations provided another resource with Caxambu's residents could attempt to use to their advantage. On the one hand, invoking ties of kinship or friendship with drug traffickers—and thus hoping for a greater degree of respect—was a common tactic. Yet at the same time, residents of Caxambu often felt deeply ambivalent about personal connections with drug dealers. One woman, for instance, put it to me this way: "Nobody wants their son to be a traficante. But lots of people want the drug dealer on the corner with a gun in his hand to be their best friend's son."

Thus, another aspect of knowing how to live in Caxambu was not simply knowing what sorts of kinship or friendship connections one could draw upon in dealing with the local drug dealers. Instead, the social dynamics of invoking—and yet at the same time fearing—close social ties to such dangerous intimates was a far more complex and difficult social process. Clara, for example, worried that her family ties to drug dealers might induce her son Martinho, who was twelve at the time of my research, to abandon school and become a trafficker. Yet she also utilized her connections to the drug traffickers when necessary. Her son's *padrinho* (godfather) was at one point the head of drug trafficking in the morro. This connection helped guarantee my safety during one period of my fieldwork, when I had returned to Brazil from an extended time in the United States, and the leadership of the tráfico had changed. When I revisited Caxambu in 2001, Martinho walked with me up the hill on my first day back in the morro in order to help me find some old friends. Martinho's padrinho had recently been released from prison, and had assumed control of the drug-selling operations in Caxambu. Martinho's swagger and confidence in walking around the hill, knowing that he was the godson of "the Man," was almost palpable.

Clara also sometimes took advantage of this relationship. For instance, just a week before the Caxambu's samba school was due to parade in the annual carnival, Clara had still not purchased her costume, which is often a major expense for favela residents. My wife and I had spent quite a bit of time and money buying our costumes, and I was very surprised at Clara's blasé attitude, even while she talked enthusiastically about how she wanted to participate in the parade. Two days before the parade, I told her that maybe she needed to get a costume before it was too late, and asked her if she needed help to pay for it. Clara laughed at me and said: "Oh, I'm not worried, my *compadre* will make sure I get a free one." The day of the parade my wife and I met up with Clara, and sure enough, she had gotten a free carnival costume.

While residents can sometimes attempt to structure their relations with drug dealers to their advantage in such a way—by essentially working within the rules—another strategy is to manipulate ambiguity and secrecy, to use the public secret. This strategy reveals the ambiguity and uncertainty that were the flipside of the order provided by drug traffickers.

One of the main commandments of the law of the hillside is that favela residents must refuse to cooperate with the police. The most dangerous accusation that could be leveled at someone in the morro was to accuse that person of being an X-9 (informant).[4] Yet one of the public secrets was that this rule was not always obeyed: the police sometimes coerced information out of residents through harassment, torture, or extortion; residents who had incurred the hostility of local drug dealers, often because of unpaid drug debts, were sometimes tempted to turn informant for revenge; and there was a constant concern that rivalries within the drug group might lead traffickers to use the police to usurp power for themselves.

As a result, alongside the public truth of noncooperation with the police was the secret knowledge that transgression of this rule sometimes occurred. This produced a widespread anxiety about who might be, or might be accused of being, an informant. Brandishing the accusation of being an X-9 (or, more dangerously, intimating that one had information about drug dealing that the authorities or rival gangs might want) could thus be a powerful weapon that residents could use. Accusing a neighbor of being an X-9, for instance, was in some ways tantamount to calling for that person's death.[5] And the fear of informants—much like anxiety about infidelity within patriarchal families—revealed the unsteady foundation of drug-trafficker power. Becoming an informant, or threatening to be one—like a wife committing adultery—was a weapon of last resort that could be used against the local drug dealers, though one that carried with it the very serious possibility of death.

In a much more mundane way, the fact that so many people in Caxambu were related to each other, and hence to the (albeit small number) of men and women involved in the drug trade, also produced uncertainty and ambiguity that residents could use to their advantage. For example, in my conflict with Clara's aunt that I discussed in the introduction, one of the unknown factors was whether or not Clara's aunt's son, who was a drug dealer, was at her home when I was arguing with her. Many people in Caxambu were related, in one way or another, to someone who was a drug trafficker. Because of rivalries and competition within the drug-trade, this meant that some people were related to drug dealers who were rivals of the group that controlled the favela at the moment. As a result, in daily conflicts and arguments, both among favela residents and between favela residents and drug traffickers, these ties could be appealed to or simply implied. A resident could allude to his connections to someone in the drug trade, to suggest to a neighbor that the resident had potential connections that could be drawn upon in a potential conflict. Alternatively, a resident could mention someone's connections to a now-disgraced drug dealer. Once again, the questions is not whether favela residents support violence against their own community, but how they attempt to marshal, manipulate, and exert whatever influence they might have over more powerful social actors.

Gender Differences in Dealing with Dangerous Intimates

Men and women in Caxambu possessed very different resources for dealing with drug traffickers, in particular for negotiating the difficult position of being dependent upon more powerful men, yet also vulnerable to their violence. For women, the situation of having to deal with dangerous social intimates was often familiar. For many women, domestic spaces are all too often spaces of danger and potential violence. As a result, women in favelas, as throughout the world, have had to develop various culturally elaborated discourses and practices for dealing with dangerous social intimates, especially violent husbands and abusive uncles and stepfathers.

Depending upon their social positioning, women sometimes had access to spaces where they could critique, if not necessarily openly challenge, drug-trafficker authority. Dona Carmen, for example, was fearless in her public condemnation of the local drug dealers who, nonetheless, would buy lunch from her kitchen and laugh at her comments. One afternoon as I was eating lunch in her yard, Piolho, a teenage drug dealer with a penchant for joking and making mischief, came to buy lunch. Dona Carmen launched into a tirade, saying that he should realize that he wasn't going to live long in his line of work. "That's right," he replied chuckling and sneering, "I'm marked for death." She then turned to me and said, "Benjamin, what you think, coming all the way from the United States to sit here and eat lunch with bandidos? No, not bandidos, *vagabundos* (bums). That's what you are, vagabundos." Piolho simply laughed.

Because of her gender, social ties, and religious affiliations, Dona Carmen could openly make such comments. As a married woman in her fifties who had raised several children and who helped to sustain her family by working as a domestic and then in her own backyard kitchen, Dona Carmen was an exemplar of the proper female. Further, the television in her kitchen was constantly tuned into talk shows on the Rede Record television channel, owned by the Universal Church of the Kingdom of God. This was only one way that Dona Carmen displayed her identity as a proud *crente* (evangelical Christian). Because she was an older woman and an evangelical, the drug dealers did not see Dona Carmen as a serious challenge to their authority. Dona Carmen also had some less visible connections with local drug dealers through her daughters, who had on-and-off relations with several members of the local drug-dealing organization.

For men, though, the experience of being vulnerable to violence by male social intimates was profoundly disorienting. While women could look to brothers and sons for help, and had socially acceptable strategies for dealing with changes in masculine authority, men did not have these alternatives. Not only were men not used to having to submit to the authority of other men, but adult masculinity was partially defined through the ability to challenge threats to one's consanguineal family (Woortmann 1982, 123). As a result, men only rarely voiced criticism of drug dealers, and when they did it was often couched in exceedingly vague terms.

For example, one afternoon I interviewed Seu Anselmo as he sat in the shade drinking a beer. I had known him for quite a long time because he lived across the street from me and I would often stop at his small store to buy a *guaraná* (a Brazilian soft drink) or a beer for dinner. In the interview he began to tell me about his life in a way that, at the time, made little sense:

> SEU ANSELMO: . . . I think of myself as a man who knows things but on a practical level. It was life that taught me everything that I know. Understand? I don't . . . no one brainwashed me (*foi ninguem que fez a minha cabeça não*) . . .
>
> BEN: Sure, that's important [a little unsure of where he's going with this] . . .
>
> SEU ANSELMO: . . . I might even obey, sometimes a person might tell me: "It's like this, it has to be this way." I have to accept. But it's the following: I accept in a way that I don't carry it out because I don't agree (*eu aceito de uma forma que não posso levar pra frente porque não concordo*). Right? . . . A person might tell you something, and you . . . you accept, but you don't carry it out because you don't agree. Because that's not the way to be, it's not how you see your life.

Unlike Dona Carmen, Seu Anselmo felt that he could not openly criticize the person who tells him "it has to be this way." For a man to openly disagree with the authority of the drug traffickers would constitute a major breach of the gendered structure of respect that undergirds drug trafficker power: not only would it be a violation of drug-trafficker authority but it would also be seen as a challenge to the patriarchal model that drug traffickers draw upon. Seu Anselmo was clearly aware of this, knowing that he had to accept the orders of other men. Yet this acceptance put Seu Anselmo in a difficult, inferior, and metaphorically emasculated position. His response to this quandary—of how to maintain his masculine self-respect while publicly being submissive to the orders of other men—was to place himself in the impossible position of accepting but not accepting, obeying but not being controlled.

Conclusion: The Saint's Revenge

Cynthia Sarti argues that the ideology of a patriarchal family contains a "model of authority" that the urban poor often invoke to order and make sense of their own, often contradictory and tension-filled, lives (1992, 38). The cultural grammar of a large family should not be seen as some sort of traditional survival of archaic gender roles in poor communities. Instead, as Eunice Durham argues, lower-class Brazilians' attachment to kinship and gender ideologies, "results . . . from an adequate appreciation, within the vision and limits of the given situation, of the actual conditions of workers' lives" (1980, 209–210).

As drug traffickers appropriate gender and kinship norms, they present residents of Caxambu with a culturally familiar framework that residents of Caxambu can attempt to use to their advantage. But as they do so, they also destabilize local structures of authority. Caxambu's drug trade allows some young men to tap into the shadow economy's flow of resources and claim a new mantle of authority. Yet this claim to be the authority that provides order is contingent upon the ability to create disorder. This strategy of abnormalization, then, reshapes local ideologies of authority, masculinity, and legitimate violence.

It remains to be seen how the police pacification policy that began in Rio's favelas in 2008 will reshape the forms of governance that Rio's drug gangs have established. As the police occupy Rio's favelas, providing public security and preventing crime, they undercut one of the drug gang's main claims to legitimacy. Ironically, though, it appears that in some "pacified" favelas, although homicides and shootouts have decreased, favela residents actually perceive an increase in theft and petty crime. To explain why this may be so, Monique Carvalho argues that residents of the pacified favela of Dona Marta still fear the police, and fear that if they do turn to the police the local drug dealers who remain in the neighborhood might see them as police accomplices (2013, 300). The police commander in charge of the UPP in Mangueira, a favela neighboring Caxambu, also noted that the local drug traffickers had such deep kinship ties to residents that many inhabitants of the pacified favela still refused to cooperate with the police. For many favela residents, the kinship relations and model of patriarchal power that drug dealers rely upon may be more convincing than either a state that has proven to be fickle in its commitments to favela residents or the rhetoric of the rule of law, which favela residents know has often been used against them.

In a dramatic example of the lingering power of drug gangs, even after Caxambu was occupied, when a local drug dealer was killed, local businesses obeyed orders from drug dealers to shut down in symbolic mourning. Uncertainty about who is really in charge, and about what forces really shape daily life and can exact punishment for wrongdoing, appears to persist, even as the state of (in)security takes new forms. In some ways, insecurity may have simply gotten more complex: although the police in pacified favelas now appear to be the visible force instituting order, favela residents know that the tráfico remains in the neighborhood, as a less visible role, and worry that police occupation may not last after Rio hosts the Olympic Games in 2016. In such a context, knowing how to live in a state of (in)security entails hedging one's bets, obeying both the visible and invisible authorities.

In the case of Tubarão shooting Seu Lázaro's dog, it turns out that Seu Lázaro was right and the saints did have their revenge. Several months after Tubarão shot the man and Seu Lázaro's dog, I was chatting with Tubarão's father. He said that Tubarão was in the hospital. I asked what had happened, and Tia Naná, who was sitting with Tubarão's father sharing a beer, said simply that it was because of a *brincadeira* (game) with guns. Two drug dealers had gotten into an argument, and Tubarão had tried to break it up, pulling out his gun. During the subsequent shoving match, Tubarão shot himself in the face with his own gun. Tubarão's father said that Tubarão was in the hospital and was recovering. I asked if he would be permanently injured, and he said no, the bullet had entered the bottom of his chin and had come out below his eye. Tubarão was unable to speak, but the doctors said that he would eventually get his voice back.

A few weeks after this conversation Tubarão was back in the morro, parading around with a large bandage covering the lower part of his face. One afternoon as I was chatting with Seu Lázaro, Tubarão was standing in the small plaza at the top of the hill, trying to yell to someone below but was only able to make a high-pitched, raspy noise. Seu Lázaro laughed a satisfied chuckle, saying: "Now that's funny. Tubarão has become a little girl."

5

"The Men Are in the Area"

Police, Race, and Place

> Because it's not white, my phenotype is
> often confused with that of a criminal.
> —comedian Hélio de la Peña (Harazim
> 1994)

Police Invasions and the Co-Production of Disorder

Drug dealers were not the only group that abnormalized daily life in Caxambu. The strategy that drug traffickers used to build their authority—instituting the rules that governed "normality" while simultaneously violating these rules—was founded upon local distrust of the police. Though the police were not a common presence in the morro—when the police entered the neighborhood this was commonly called an *invasão* (invasion)—they exerted a pervasive impact on daily life. This chapter examines police practices in Caxambu by focusing on the mundane, everyday interactions between the police and residents of Caxambu. I argue that the police and local drug traffickers together co-produced disorder, as they fought against each other, but also sometimes cooperated, and their actions sometimes complemented each other.

Prior analysis of policing in Brazil's large cities has largely examined extreme forms of police violence, especially police shootings. An ethnographic focus on the mundane, everyday forms of policing opens up a new window into understanding how the police affect the daily lives of favela residents. It has often been assumed that the police are rarely present in favelas, and that when they do appear, the effects of policing are largely negative, creating animosity, distrust, and fear. Research on policing in urban settings like Rio that are characterized by extreme inequality also often argues that the police seek to cordon off the neighborhoods of the poor from those of the wealthy.

An ethnographic focus on policing, though, shows how *productive* policing is, though perhaps in unintended ways. As they destabilize daily life, the police attempt to assign new meanings to places and people, creating structures of meaning and emotion that last long after they have left. However, the police do not succeed in producing a docile population that accepts the power of the state, nor do they simply divide the poor from the wealthy. Instead, their actions permeate the lives of favela residents as they actively disorder daily life.

Particularly important is how favela residents—especially young dark-skinned men, the main targets of policing—understand policing and experiences of racial exclusion and other forms of marginalization. Policing, I will argue, produces new understandings of difference, creating forms of marginalization that draw upon older ideologies of race but deploy these ideologies in new ways, combining racial difference with other markers of inferiority. As the police pursue favela-based *bandidos* (criminals) and *traficantes* (drug dealers), they tie together place, assumptions about criminality, ideologies of race, and notions of types of persons.

Over fifty years of research has conclusively demonstrated the existence of racism in Brazil, a society that has prided itself on not having the same sort of explicit racial segregation as the United States. Scholars have shown that black and mixed-race (*pardo*) Brazilians suffer from a pervasive racial prejudice that is deeply woven into Brazilian society (Andrews 1991; Fontaine 1985; Hanchard 1994; Hasenbalg and Silva 1999; Lovell 1994; Reichman 1999; Silva 1985, 1999). Racial prejudice is particularly clear in the Brazilian criminal justice system (Adorno 1999; Cano 2010; Mitchell and Wood 1999). For example, in a study of the judicial system in São Paulo,

Sergio Adorno found that compared to white defendants, black defendants were more vulnerable to police abuse, were more often pursued by the police, were less likely to exercise their constitutional right to legal protection, and had a greater probability of being punished than white defendants (1999, 137).

But this approach tends to assume that race is fairly stable and static, rather than dynamic and discursive, shaped by and reshaping other forms of difference. Brodie Fischer has observed that "many recent scholars have focused so intently on proving that racial discrimination exists as an autonomous social force that they have generally not emphasized the ways in which social and racial prejudices interact" (2004, 33). An alternative approach, Howard Winant argues, focuses on the social processes of racial formation, processes that are inherently variable, conflictive, and discursive (1992, 183–4).

Each interaction between the police and favela residents in Caxambu presents a "moment of crisis" where it is possible to see how social and racial prejudices interact. When residents of Caxambu spoke about interactions with the police, they consistently complained of racial discrimination. This is clearly part of a larger pattern: Silvia Ramos and Leonarda Musumeci found that when young, nonwhite men were asked if they had experienced discrimination, they most often referred to mistreatment by the police (2004). Following Winant and Fischer, I am led to ask: is race at least partially a *product of* policing? Are experiences of racial exclusion increasingly built out of social phenomena other than—or in addition to—appearance? As they abnormalized daily life in Caxambu, how did the police reshape the way that people understood their neighborhood, their daily lives, and their own identities?

A Conversation with Zeca and Nêgo

One afternoon I was talking with Zeca and Nêgo. Zeca was one of my best friends in Caxambu, and worked for a while as my research assistant. Nêgo, a dark-skinned man in his early twenties, worked at a *tendinha* (small store) located just down the street from where I lived.[1] As we were talking, we sat on metal folding chairs on the sidewalk opposite Nêgo's store, in the scant shade provided by a low concrete wall. We knew that the police were in the morro because earlier a group of teenagers, some of whom were drug dealers, had walked past us on their way down the hill. Nêgo asked one of the young men where he was going. "To the beach," he replied. "After all, *os homi tão na área* (the men are in the area)." When two police cars drove by, we could see the barrels of their automatic rifles sticking out of the windows of their cars. They drove by slowly, staring at the three of us, and our conversation momentarily ground to a halt as Nêgo and Zeca stared back. After a moment it continued:

> ZECA: So he's asking you what . . . what is a favela? What does favela mean?
>
> NÊGO: For me a favela is discrimination. When you go down below, if you live up here, you're already being discriminated against. Even more so if you're dark-skinned and such (*sendo da cor escuro e tal*), then you're discriminated against even more. You feel . . . even the police if they come here, if they come here and see us here, they won't treat us like they treat people below. They'll treat us differently. Humiliating people for no reason, just because they're sitting here.
>
> BEN: Is that because people live here, or because of the color of their skin?
>
> NÊGO: Of course, because of their color, their color. The two things. We're discriminated against. People like us who live in a poor community, like Caxambu, or other communities, we're really discriminated against. Not everyone who lives in a morro is a traficante.

In his comments, Nêgo did something that nonwhite Brazilians supposedly rarely do: he openly critiqued racism, and identified himself as a victim of racial discrimination. As I have noted earlier, race was rarely used in the morro as an explicit marker of difference. In her ethnography of race in a favela in Rio, Robin Sheriff also argued that "references to race and color are highly circumscribed—hemmed in, in fact, by a universally understood and conscientiously practiced etiquette" (2001, 50).

Livio Sansone has perceptively argued that in some Brazilian social contexts race, or more precisely color (*cor*), is important for organizing systems of power and inequality, whereas in other situations it is less relevant (2003, 51–55). In what Sansone calls soft areas of race relations, such as spaces of leisure or interaction with social peers, being black does not hinder social interaction and can often bring prestige. He observes that many of these soft spaces, like Caxambu, are often "implicitly black spaces" (53). In the "hard" areas of race relations, such as employment, differences of skin color significantly allocate prestige and status.

In his comments about the police, Nêgo clearly violates the etiquette that discourages discussions of racial difference. Nêgo's comments also reveal how the police can shift how racial dynamics map onto the space of the hillside, in the process transforming perceptions of identity. The police change Caxambu from a soft space of racial relations, a largely though not exclusively black space where differences in skin color were rarely relevant, to a hard space, were differences in skin color were tied to differential treatment. It is important to notice, though, that Nêgo identified more than just race as a criterion for discrimination: in his comments he tied together race, place, income inequality, and assumptions about crime. The police, he said, treat everyone who lives in Caxambu as poor, black, and a potential criminal.

One way to understand how policing shapes perceptions of racial difference is to draw upon Oracy Nogueira's classic analysis of race in Brazil. Nogueira explained the distinctiveness of racial dynamics in Brazil by comparing two contrasting systems of racial classification: systems based on what he called the "prejudice of origin" and those based on the "prejudice of mark or color" (2006 [1954]). Racial systems based on the prejudice of origin, Nogueira argued, classify people according to ancestry. The notorious "one-drop" rule in the United States was the emblematic case of the prejudice of origin. Under this system of classification, a person with a black ancestor was classified as black, sometimes regardless of that person's appearance. Systems of racial classification based upon the prejudice of mark, he argued, operate differently, classifying a person according to appearance. This system, he felt, best described Brazilian racial classification systems, where a person can be classified as *branco* (white), *negro* (black), or by any number of intermediary terms (most often *moreno*), regardless of the race of that person's parents. For example, Clara, one of my friends in Caxambu, described her youngest daughter, who she said was more *clarinha* (light-skinned), as *morena*, and called her older twin daughters *negras* (black).

Perhaps what Nêgo and other young men in Rio's favelas are pointing out is a third system of classification, one based upon the "prejudice of crime," or more accurately, the "prejudice of criminalized space." For Nêgo, simply living in a "poor community" like Caxambu marks someone as different, and they are treated differently when they "go down below" to the working-class neighborhood adjacent to Caxambu. The stigma attached to living in a favela is, then, compounded by racial difference—or "being dark-skinned and such"—and confirmed by the police, who sew together socioeconomic, racial, and spatial markers of difference. It's clear that policing is an arena where reference to phenotype—in Nogueira's terms, the prejudice of mark—is explicit. It is tempting to draw the line there, and simply see the police as enforcing racist domination, a moment when the reality of racism in Brazil makes itself visible. But I think that young dark-skinned favela residents are pointing to something more complex, showing how multiple systems of social discrimination can operate, with skin color becoming most socially relevant when it is tied to the prejudice of crime. A teenager from Caxambu expressed it this way in a funk song called the "Rap do Racismo":

> Mais uma coisa eu vi que me abalou
> Foi lá no shopping que alguém robou
> Naquela confusão branco saiu voado
> O coitado do preto que foi culpado . . .
> Se um preto está todo arrumado
> Dizem logo que é advogado
> Mas se não está é esculachado,
> É ladrão ou é tarado . . .

> [Another thing that I saw that shocked me
> At the mall someone stole something
> During the chaos a white guy took off
> A poor black person was blamed . . .
> If a black person is well dressed,
> They say he's a lawyer
> But if he's not he's insulted,
> He's a thief or a pervert . . .]

Analyzing Policing: From Deadly Force to Everyday Violence

As I noted in the Introduction, Rio's police force is notoriously lethal, and police shootings are also clearly concentrated in poor neighborhoods such as Caxambu. For example, between 1993 and 1996, the majority of police killings of civilians occurred in favelas, though the favela population is less than 25 percent of the city's total (ISER 1997). The way that the police act is also deeply shaped by practices and discourses that imagine policing favelas as engaging in warfare, an issue that I discuss further below. This highly militarized and all-too-often lethal form of policing—often modeled on counterinsurgency and not crime prevention—has in turn shaped how some analysts have understood the impact of policing in deeply divided urban spaces such as Rio de Janeiro.

Some analysts have seen high levels of police violence as indicative of the Brazilian government's failure to control its own police force. As Philip Parnell has pointed out, when examining policing it is important not to make the common mistake of believing that seeking social order and applying the force of law are synonymous (Parnell and Kane 2003, 6). For the Brazilian police force, this is abundantly clear: the police often operate outside of the rule of law, and segments of the police sometimes operate autonomously, disregarding their commanders. To a certain extent, Rio's police can be seen as "war machines" (Mbembe 2003), segments of the state that act semiautonomously, pursuing their own goals through their ability to mobilize resources for violence. Several structural and historical factors account for this.

Brazil's police forces are composed of two state-level forces—the military police and the civil police—and a small federal police force. The military police are in charge of day-to-day patrolling, whereas the civil police investigate crimes after they occur. The two units have separate command structures and hierarchies, do not always have overlapping jurisdictions, and are often rivals. Both are under the command of the secretary of public security who, in turn, is appointed by the state's elected governor. The separation between the military and civil police often generates rivalry and competition, and makes it difficult for the two forces to share information or resources. It also creates two separate command and control structures. This complicates decision-making structures, while creating two parallel structures of authority and channels of influence that higher-level police officers are loath to relinquish.

Antagonism between the police and poor Cariocas (residents of Rio) also has deep historical roots, going back at least to the early twentieth century (Bretas 1997; Carvalho 1997). Rio's police force was established while slavery was still legal. The historian Thomas Holloway has argued that the mission of the police was to protect public order (1993). In a city where a sizeable number of people were enslaved, upholding public order meant primarily ensuring that some people remained the property of others, not ensuring public safety of all.[2]

Brazil's military dictatorship, which lasted from 1964 until 1985, deepened a pattern of impunity for policemen who commit acts of violence against civilians. During the dictatorship, the military police were put under the control of the army.[3] The military police, along with specialized army units, were one of the main components of the repressive apparatus that the dictatorship used against those who challenged its power. Policemen were given free rein to act violently against those who challenged military rule. Military policemen accused of crimes were not tried in the regular civilian court system, but in special military tribunals, where few were convicted. In 1979, as Brazil's military rule drew to a close, a blanket amnesty was decreed by the military government. This amnesty pardoned opponents of the dictatorship and allowed political exiles to return without fear of legal prosecution, but it also ensured that soldiers and policemen who had committed crimes that were seen as politically motivated, such as torture or summary executions, would not be prosecuted.

By the time I did my fieldwork in Caxambu, the public security policies of Rio's governors had swung back and forth between repressive policing and reformist attempts to bring the police under the greater control of elected officials. Rio's governor when I began my research in Caxambu was Marcello Alencar. As I described in Chapter 2, Alencar unleashed the most intense wave of police violence in Rio's history by tying police promotions and salaries to "acts of bravery" in pursuit of alleged criminals. Less often noted is how Alencar's policies affected relationships between drug traffickers and the police. Because the police could be monetarily rewarded for armed confrontations with drug traffickers, they had less of a financial incentive to accept bribes from traffickers. Relations of bribery, which had ensured a certain stability, quickly fell apart. At the same time, many favela-based drug traffickers were killed or imprisoned, destabilizing drug-trafficking operations as a younger generation of drug dealers came to power.

While I was living in Caxambu, Anthony Garotinho was elected governor of Rio. Garotinho's record on public security was decidedly mixed. On the one hand, his secretary of public security, Luiz Eduardo Soares, proposed a throughgoing reform of the police, including bringing the civil and military police under a joint command. When Soares's attempts at reform met with stiff opposition from within the police, though, Garotinho backed down. Soares's dismissal was a dramatic example of how the police could successfully defy attempts to limit their actions.

The historical pattern of impunity for violent policemen, along with a pattern of substantial autonomy and a lack of effective control, meant that when I conducted my research, policing in Rio took an unusual form. On the one hand, policing in favelas, which is usually carried out by the military police, was more akin to the armed intervention of the army than the patrolling of a beat cop. Here the police, as a component of the state, would appear at their most hierarchical and centralized. At the same time, though, segments of the force often sold their ability to use violence, privatizing the state's use of force, or at least seriously fragmenting hierarchy and control. Low salaries for policemen practically ensure that that they have to find additional strategies to supplement their income. It is common for policemen to have a *bico* (second job), many as private security. In these positions, the lines between official and private uses of force are often blurred. A survey by the Infoglobo institute, for instance, found that in 1996, 60 percent of the policemen who were interviewed said that they had a second job. Of these 54.6 percent worked as private security, where they often used their police badge and official weapon (Caldeira 1997, 146). At times, the Rio state government itself has essentially sought to sell its ability to use violence. Rio's governor Marcello Alencar, for instance, proposed charging businessmen a special tax, which came to be called the *imposto caça-bandido* (criminal-hunting tax), in order to reequip the police and increase police salaries (122)

It is common knowledge that Rio's police are often deeply involved in crime. In Caxambu and other favelas, for instance, it is so common for policemen to extort drug dealers that the practice has its own name, the *polícia mineira*. When policemen "do a mineira," they arrest a real or suspected drug dealer and demand a ransom in order to release him, sometimes keeping his weapons or drugs in order to resell them to other drug dealers.

The knowledge that sectors of the police are deeply involved in the very crimes that they are supposed to repress is not confined to favelas, but is widespread throughout the city. Sometimes police authorities themselves have publicly admitted this. César Caldeira notes a particularly notorious example that occurred in 1995. After a string of embarrassing revelations about police incompetence and complicity in kidnapping, Rio's governor reorganized the Divisão Anti-Sequestro (DAS), the specialized unit in charge of investigating kidnapping. When the newly appointed head of the DAS, detective Hélio Luz, assumed his office, he told the press: "Starting right now, the anti-kidnapping unit no longer kidnaps" (1997, 120). Luz also tried to prohibit the common practice of policemen associated with the DAS charging the families of kidnap victims for their services.

This pattern of impunity and corrupt policing means that many Brazilians—not just those who are poor or nonwhite—regard the police with suspicion and distrust. A victimization survey carried out by the Instituto de Segurança Pública, for instance, revealed that only 6.9 percent of those interviewed fully trusted the military police, while only 9.2 percent fully trusted the civil police (*O Globo*, August 19, 2008).[4] In such a context, it is clear that the police do not naturalize the power of the state, producing a docile population. Rather, they are widely seen as dangerous and unpredictable, to be avoided if possible.

The lethality of Rio's police and their pattern of policing—often modeled on counterinsurgency and not crime prevention—have in turn shaped how some analysts have understood the role of policing in deeply divided urban spaces such as Rio de Janeiro. One perspective has seen police violence as an indication of the Brazilian government's inability to control its own agents. Relying upon an underlying Weberian approach, some scholars have seen police violence, and the broader breakdown of Brazil's criminal justice system, as indicative of the state's failure to effectively monopolize its own use of force (Ahnen 2007; Brinks 2008; Hinton 2006; Macaulay 2007; Pereira 2008; Pinheiro 2000).

A second perspective has seen Brazil's pattern of abusive and often illegal policing of poor neighborhoods as a "solution" to the problem of a highly unequal society. This approach argues that the main purpose of the police is to patrol the divisions that separate the neighborhoods of the wealthy from those of the poor. According to Loïc Wacquant, neoliberal reforms and the shifting nature of the state have led to a "penal treatment" of the poor. Brazil, he argues, can be seen as a living laboratory for the use of "punitive containment as a political strategy for managing dispossessed and dishonored populations in the polarizing city" (2008, 57, 58).

If Rio's police produce such a high body count, and operate in such a militarized fashion, why focus on fleeting incidents such as Zeca and Nêgo's momentary face-off with the police? In this relatively innocuous and certainly mundane case, no one was arrested, no one was shot, and the police did not even directly interact with Zeca or Nêgo. They simply stared at each other across the street. But, as Winifred Tate points out, analysis of more extreme forms of violence—what she calls counting the dead—downplays less explicit, yet more pervasive, forms of violence, and risks separating violence from the larger social context (2007). As a result, as Luiz Eduardo Soares has argued, the full effect of the police upon everyday life is often not fully understood. As Soares puts it: "When life and death are in play, less serious forms of aggression do not seem as dramatic. However, it is dangerous to neglect the small 'violences' of everyday . . . because their effects, when they accumulate and are naturalized, end up being as devastating as the most barbarous crimes" (2000, 32).

The notorious lethality of Rio's police force has ensured that daily patrolling receives little analysis (an important exception is Ramos and Musumeci 2004). As a result, the full impact of the "small violences of everyday" is often left unexplored. It is equally problematic that assumptions about the relationship between the police and favela residents—such as the idea that the police are absent from favela communities—are left unchallenged. A more detailed examination of everyday police practices shows that policing is not always a failure of the state, nor does it necessarily succeed in imprisoning the poor. It also shows that although police interactions with favela residents are sporadic and irregular, the police exercise a pervasive impact upon the social identities and daily lives of favela residents; even if this impact is partial and contested, it lasts long after the police "invasion" has ended.

Incomplete Criminalization and the Disruption of Daily Life

An ethnographic understanding of the effects of policing in poor neighborhoods like Caxambu can benefit from Sally Engle Merry's analysis of criminalization. Merry points out that one of the things that the police and other agents of the state attempt to do in poor neighborhoods is to redefine common practices as crime, in effect criminalizing aspects of daily life. Criminalization is not simply a legal or institutional process, but is embedded in a larger socioeconomic and cultural context. As Merry states: "the criminalization of everyday life . . . takes shape on a rhetorical terrain" (1998, 15). Merry points out that this process is partial and contested, and does not always succeed. Yet even when criminalization is only partially successful it is often "powerful in reconstituting racial and gender ideologies" (36). Drawing upon Merry's approach, the questions to be examined are: What is the rhetorical terrain that policing operates upon? Are attempts to redefine social practices successful or not? If not, what other effects does criminalization have? Do the police reconstitute local racial and gender identities, and if so how?

Looking at everyday incidents of policing in Caxambu, it is clear that the police do not succeed in redefining social practices as crime, much less do they naturalize the power of the state. But they do have powerful effects, suddenly disrupting and abnormalizing daily life, reshaping how residents of Caxambu see themselves and their neighborhood.

For example, one afternoon I stopped by the morro's residents' association to talk to Clara, the association's secretary, and Seu Lázaro. As I was standing in the doorway, an unmarked black car sped up the hill, and I heard someone shout out: "Don't move, *fiquem aí* (stay where you are)." The car screeched to a halt, and two policemen, wearing black tee shirts with *força tarefa* (task force) written on them and carrying automatic rifles, jumped out. They searched Beto, Juninho, and Renato, who were standing around Juninho's car, which they had been spending most of the morning repairing.

The police made the three young men line up with their hands against the top of the car, and went through their pockets. After searching them, and finding nothing, a policeman thoroughly searched Juninho's car, looking under and between the seats. Two other policemen walked around looking menacing and searched the area where people often sit in the shade of a big mango tree and around the nearby public telephone, apparently looking for drugs. After the police left, Seu Lázaro told me that one of the policemen was Ralfe, who was well known in the area and used to be a regular uniformed military police before becoming part of the special *força tarefa* (task force) investigating drug-related crime. Clara later told me that he was notorious in the area for beating up boys in the neighborhood and trying to frame them for dealing drugs.

In this case, the police did not succeed in convincing Juninho and his friends that what they were doing was a crime. But they did suddenly transform the public space of the hillside from one of leisure and mudane tasks—such as attempting to fix a car—into a militarized zone of emergency. The police shifted the space of the morro from one of social intimacy—a sort of semidomestic space, almost an extension of the home—to one of anonymity and danger. Many residents of Caxambu see police actions as failing to respect local uses of space, automatically assuming that the street is a space of danger, rather than familiarity, and often disregarding distinctions between public and domestic spaces. For instance, one day I asked Seu Vander, a seventy-year-old retired man, what he thought about an infrastructure project carried out by the municipal government that was paving many of Caxambu's streets. He told me:

> If you go to the police station and ask them, they'll say that it improved a thousand percent. For them it improved a thousand percent. All the alleys are paved and everything. For them it's better. But for the rest? What's the improvement? The police show up, invade someone's house, do what they want. That's not improvement. I'm not seeing any improvement. We're the same favelados. They come in, but they don't beat anyone. I'm not going to say that. But *porra* (shit), just them entering your house, people who live near you are going to see and say, porra, they invaded Vander's house. They invaded José's house, Pedro's house. Porra, that's a humiliation.

Particularly significant in Seu Vander's comments are the connections that he drew between the police, domestic spaces, and male honor. Police invasions of local favela homes, he said, were not simply illegal, but were a humiliation. He complained that when the police invade someone's home—which he defined as male spaces, as "José's house, Pedro's house"—other people see this happening. Many observers have noted the strong connections between adult male status and the home. For instance, the verb *casar* (to marry) derives from the word *casa* (home) (Rebhun 1999, 114). The connection between a man's honor and his control over his home has at times even been enshrined in law: historian Peter Beattie notes that Brazilian law has limited the power of authorities to enter homes in the daytime (2003, 242). For Seu Vander, then, police actions did more than simply violate his right to privacy: they challenged his masculine identity and violated local status distinctions by confusing him, a respectable adult man, with a common criminal. Nêgo likewise complained that the police were "humiliating" people for no reason when they confused them with bandidos.

What people such as Seu Vander consistently point to is how the police treat people in the morro with no regard for the law or for local distinctions or markers of status. Rather, the fact of living in a favela exposes all residents to a blanket form of criminalization. Luiz Antonio Machado da Silva and Márcia Leite have also observed that when favela residents critique the police, they highlight a "variable" form of citizenship that allows the police to act violently toward favela residents without fear of punishment, while very different treatment is accorded to residents of other parts of the city (2007, 573). Criticism of police actions can be seen, then, as an implicit critique of forms of discrimination that divide the city into the *favela* and the *asfalto* (the "regular" city). "In other words, what residents of favelas criticize," Machado da Silva and Leite state, "is not police violence per se, but their lack of selectivity" (2007, 572).

The police's lack of selectivity does not simply mean that favela residents accept police violence that they feel accurately targets "real" criminals. In an experiential sense, the police are seen as respecting no rules, as operating with no clear logic. Favela residents feel that they cannot predict how or when the police might act or who they might target, and worry that they could be harmed by actions over which they have no control. Because of this unpredictability, a fear of police violence lingers over everyday life, even when the police are not present.

One morning, for instance, I went to talk with Zeca, who was standing in front of the residents' association chatting with Seu Ismael, who was sitting on a folding chair on the sidewalk. When I walked up, Zeca said, "Something smells terrible." I said that it smelled like something was burning, then realized that it was marijuana and caught Seu Ismael chuckling at my naivité. Zeca turned to Seu Ismael and said, "You know, the other day I came up the hill and there was this guy—this white guy who I'd never seen before in the morro—smoking a big joint right in front of my house. I walked over to him and said, 'Excuse me, but this is a *casa de família* (family home), could you please go somewhere else?' The guy got pissed off, and said: 'Shit, this is a favela.' I said 'Yes, and I'm a *cria do morro* (I'm from here), and you should respect me because of that.' The guy was really angry, and walked off cursing. It's a real problem, though," he said, turning to me. "If a guy like that is smoking in front of a house and the police drive up, the police are going to assume that the people in the house are also bandidos, and will invade the house and hassle them too. But what can you do," he said, turning to Seu Ismael, "the police don't respect anyone and no one can complain."

The Rhetorical Terrain of Policing and the "War Metaphor"

Though the residents of Caxambu perceive the police as acting without any predictability or selectivity, this does not mean that the police operate outside of any ideological or rhetorical framework. For the police, their interactions with favela residents are organized by a set of discourses and practices rooted in images of warfare. The war metaphor pictures favelas as occupied enemy territory ruled by organized crime syndicates and characterized by an alternative set of social codes. Police often compare their actions to those carried out in international war zones and emphasize, in particular, the heavy weaponry of the drug dealers. For instance, a newspaper article interviewed a sergeant who had been with the police for eighteen years. The sergeant said that he still feels *um aperto no coração* (an ache in his heart) every time he leaves his home. He compared patrolling favelas in Rio's northern zone to war, stating: "It's a hypocrisy to state that we're as well armed as the drug dealers. Walking around a favela in the northern zone is like walking in Kosovo. Confrontation is constant, but we have to deal with it" (*Jornal do Brasil*, October 8, 1999).

Another policeman, Captain Pimentel, who was part of the military police's elite Batalhão de Operações Especiais (BOPE, Special Operations Battalion), a group sent to carry out the most intense and confrontational operations, made several remarkably candid remarks in the documentary film *Notícias de uma Guerra Particular* (News from a Private War) (Salles and Lund 1999). Pimentel said that ever since he was a little boy he wanted to be a policeman, and then had the following exchange with his off-camera interviewer:

PIMENTEL: I wanted to be able to participate in armed actions (*numa ação armada*). I ended up participating not in one, but in hundreds. Even if I had been in the army I might not have had this opportunity.
INTERVIEWER: Would you like to have participated in a war?
PIMENTEL: Look I . . . I am participating in a war. I participate in a war. The only difference is that at the end of every day I go home.

The war metaphor that frames policing is also often visible in the Brazilian media. One of many countless examples was an article in the *Globo* newspaper that compared violence in Rio to the war in Iraq. The article stated: "In the past twenty-four hours, violence in Rio has caused more deaths than attacks on the coalition forces commanded by the United States in Iraq. In Iraq, nine people were killed between the day before yesterday and yesterday, including Iraqis who worked for the US forces. In Rio, fourteen were killed" (*Globo*, "Pior do que no Iraque," January 23, 2004).[5]

In addition to carving out Rio's favelas as spaces of warfare, the war metaphor depicts drug dealers as enemies and, in the typical tradition of war narratives, as almost different species of humans (or, indeed, as subhumans). For example, the commander of the military police of Rio stated: "You don't have to be a sociologist to realize that the criminals of today are willing to kill in order to steal R$20 [about US$10 at the time] on a bus, or even to set fire to a human in order to escape from the police. . . . Our feeling is that we are dealing with a new generation of murderers who have nothing to lose" (*O Globo*, June 16, 2000).

The way that the police speak about their actions in favelas also marks off these communities as distinct from the "regular" city: the police often describe their actions in favelas as *caçando bandidos* (hunting criminals), and the favela is often seen as a free-fire zone. The result is that policing of favelas has taken on a distinctly militaristic outlook and strategy. Captain Pimentel, for instance, wryly remarked that the BOPE's extensive experience in combat has made it "probably the most efficient urban combat force in the world."

The militaristic outlook of the police became visible in a scandal that erupted in 2003 when people living in Laranjeiras, a wealthy neighborhood in Rio, complained about the chants that the military police were using during their training. In a letter to the *Globo* newspaper, a resident of the neighborhood said that while they were running in the neighborhood, members of the military police's special BOPE unit chanted the following:

Bandido favelado
não se varre com vassoura
se varre com granada
com fuzil, metralhadora

[Favela bandit
Isn't swept up with a broom

He's swept up with a grenade
With a rifle or a machinegun]

The letter writer pointed out that this chant was a reworking of a famous song by Geraldo Vandré called "Cantiga Brava," which protested against the military dictatorship (*O Globo* 2003).

But if the police view patrolling favelas as combat, they are also sometimes unclear about what ultimate goal or underlying logic might be at work. Unlike most wars, in this one there is often no larger overarching strategy or clearly defined ideologies that are contending for superiority. The result, for at least some policemen, is a sense that the war has become an end in itself. As Captain Pimentel stated: "The police today are living a private war where you kill a trafficker and the trafficker ends up hating the police. The traffickers kill a policeman and you end up hating the traffickers. The thing continues at that level . . . it's almost a private war."

Favela Residents' Views of Police

While the police sometimes see favelas as distinct spaces cut off from the rest of the city, favela residents tend to speak of the police as radically other. Favela residents and the police employ a similar schemes of classification, which draw sharp boundaries between two groups of people. In the process, they both militarize the space of the favela, regarding each other as different and distinct sorts of people, two sides engaged in a conflict against each other. But this rhetoric, like the depiction of Caxambu as a big family where everyone gets along, is only partially true. Often, the lines that divide residents, drug traffickers, and the police are blurred.

The way that favela residents publicly describe the police can be seen as analogous to Nogueira's idea of the racial dynamics at work in the prejudice of origin. That is, rather than recognizing a spectrum of differences and similarities between favela residents and the police, people in Caxambu tended to place themselves and the police in radically separate groups having little in common. For instance, one day Clara, the secretary of the residents' association, told me that a group of people had formed a *chapa* (electoral slate) to run against the current leadership of the residents' association. The group was led by Walter, a man who often coached a soccer team for kids in the neighborhood. Clara told me that Walter had asked her to be part of the new group, but that she had turned him down. "After all," she said, "he's a *polícia* (policeman). Worse than that, an ex-polícia. They retired him because the police thought that he wasn't right in the head. But I know that he's only acting crazy when he wants to. *Você nunca pode confiar nessa raça* (you can never trust those people). They're worse than bandidos. Bandidos you see grow up, you go to school with them, you know who they are and what they're going to do. But you don't know the police. You never know what they're going to do."

Two elements of Clara's sharp categorical distinction between the regular people of the morro and the police deserve emphasis. First, Clara characterized the police by their unpredictability and their social foreignness: favela residents, she said "don't know" the police and can't predict their actions. Second, Clara views the police as a distinct and separate type of people. The police, she said were a *raça*, meaning a race or breed, that couldn't be trusted. The dynamic at work when favela residents talk about the police mirrors police depictions of favelas and favela residents: in both cases there is a pronounced hardening of status distinctions. Rather than recognizing police as sharing much in common with them—after all, many policemen are poor, dark-skinned, and live in neighborhoods like Caxambu—favela residents highlight stark differences, seeing policemen as strangers or even a different breed. This public presentation of attitudes toward the police, though, is the flip side of the unstated public secret that the lines between favela residents, drug traffickers, and the police are often blurred. Many policemen, especially lower-level members of the military police, are often poor and nonwhite. In fact, the military police have often been seen by black and mixed-race people as an institution that holds open the possibility of upward social mobility (Sansone 2002). The military police, the saying goes, recognize no color other than blue (the color of their uniform).

And while the police are feared, favela residents at the same time demand greater provision of public security from the state (Machado da Silva and Leite 2007). In addition, while the police as an institution are regarded as "other," individual policemen—such as Ralfe, the policeman that Seu Lázaro pointed out to me—are often well known. For Clara, the ironies and contradictions went even deeper: her father was a retired policeman who, Clara told me, boasted of his participation in a notorious pre-dictatorship police death squad.

Why, then, do favela residents draw such a sharp line between themselves and the police? Part of the answer is that favela residents are reacting to the hardening of social relations that the police impose upon the favela by deploying an equally hard logic that denies any commonality between themselves and the police. If the police are going to treat everyone in the neighborhood as a criminal, and are going to explicitly single out skin color as a marker of hierarchical status—indeed of differential citizenship—then favela residents respond in kind by removing policemen from their imagined social community. The police can then become the stigmatized outsiders, subjects of complaints that cannot otherwise be uttered, a contrast upon which senses of belonging can be built. Unlike the police, favela residents (or so this logic goes) treat everyone with respect.

Particularly sharp, here, is the contrast between the police and local drug traffickers. Bandidos, Clara said, "you see grow up." Drug dealers are social intimates, if dangerous ones, potentially violent but predictable. The police, however, "humiliate people for no reason," as Nêgo stated. Depicting the police as dangerous outsiders thus fits with the injunction against speaking negatively about drug traffickers. If it is not permissible to voice criticism of local drug dealers, the dangerous intimates, then it is allowable to criticize the outsider. Concerns about insecurity, and fear of being unfairly targeted for violence, can be displaced onto the police, disguising the knowledge that drug traffickers too often act unpredictably.

Perverse Symbiosis and the Coproduction of Insecurity

The perception that favela residents have of the police as an arbitrarily violent and corrupt force is often seen as one of the factors that enable drug traffickers and organized crime. Leeds, for instance, quotes the former head of the military police in Rio, Colonel Carlos Magno Nazareth Cerqueira, as stating that police corruption and arbitrary violence are the "greatest weapon that organized crime has at its disposal to allow it to operate freely" (1996, 64).[6] Soares puts the point eloquently: "It's possible to see why police terror is more feared than the barbarism of drug traffickers when it's understood that the police disdain rules and enjoy an ad hoc morbid creativity, while traffickers restrict themselves to codes and subordinate their practices to a public and intelligible order" (Soares 2000, 40).

Less commonly noticed, though, is how police disorder goes hand in hand with drug-trafficker order. That is, rather than seeing the police and drug traffickers as opposites, one group acting arbitrarily while the other functions according to clear rules, it is more accurate to see the two as symbiotically related, acting together to produce (in)security, which they can attempt to manipulate for their own interests.

Rampant corruption among some sectors of the police ensures that at times the lines between organized crime and some sectors of the police hardly exist at all. The drug trade and the accompanying sale of weapons in Brazil are big business. Given the low salaries of most policemen and a pervasive pattern of impunity for police who break the law, it is hardly surprising that some units of the police have been easily corrupted. In fact, local drug gangs and elements of the police sometimes act together against rival drug traffickers or against other police forces. In many cases, urban violence has become an end in itself, a "war machine" where predation and profit making take precedence over occupation of territory or control of populations (Mbembe 2003, 32).

Arrangements between the police and the drug dealers are often made between the drug gang and particular policemen. Different policemen, or members of different battalions, might have no arrangements at all or might attempt to negotiate separate deals. Indeed, I heard stories about competition and rivalry among policemen over who was getting the best deal. (Stories about violent conflicts between corrupt policemen and honest ones, or about corrupt policemen battling against each other in favelas, are not uncommon). When policemen are assigned to patrol new communities, the arrangements between the drug dealers and corrupt policemen need to be renegotiated. This often creates a new period of instability and violence as the police step up repression against the drug trade in order to encourage drug dealers to enter into relations of bribery, while the drug dealers hold out as long as they can.

At the beginning of my period of field research in Caxambu, the local drug dealers had an "arrangement" with some military policemen. The police would enter the morro to pick up their bribes and would rarely disturb the drug dealers or harass the neighborhood's residents. In May and June 1999, however, this changed. When the new governor, Anthony Garotinho, was elected, his new secretary for public security, Luiz Eduardo Soares, was committed to restructuring the police forces. Among his attempts at reform, Soares reassigned police commanders to different districts, seeking to make the police more accountable and efficient.

But because of the perverse symbiosis between drug dealers and corrupt policemen, the effect was exactly the opposite. In the neighborhood where Caxambu is located, a new commander was appointed to head the local battalion of the military police, and he reassigned policemen to patrol new areas. This meant that all of the prior arrangements between the police and the drug dealers were disrupted and had to be renegotiated. Along with this change, there was an attempt to create a new promotion system based on statistical analysis of arrest rates and crime statistics. This provoked extended period of tension and violence in Caxambu, as new policemen harassed drug dealers in order to convince them to pay bribes (and, according to some people, they were asking more money than the prior policemen), and the police arrested teenagers suspected of being drug dealers in order to boost their arrest statistics (often using this as a pretext to extort bribes).

Relations of corruption, though, were not the only ties between drug traffickers and elements of the police. Rather, police-induced chaos was the grounds for drug-trafficker authority, providing the insecurity upon which trafficker security could be built. As police actions targeted young men, harassing them and publicly displaying their vulnerability, they allowed the local drug traffickers to display their greater respect. As the police hardened local social relations, treating local spaces as militarized zones of criminality, they allowed drug traffickers to depict themselves as operating according to the soft logic of intimacy and common belonging. Indeed, it was hard not to feel as if the actions of police and drug traffickers were co-producing disorder, each creating subjects upon whom their power could be exercised.

One afternoon, for example, I was speaking with some residents of Caxambu while we were sitting on benches at the top of the hill that the neighborhood is built on. A police car suddenly drove up and two armed military policemen got out. After searching several people, the police-men walked down the street to a small plaza, where the other policeman was searching three young men, who were loudly complaining. After the police let them go, one of the men, Juninho, walked up the hill. The police-man yelled at him to go away and leave the street, and Juninho responded angrily, "Where do you want me to go? I live here, I don't live in Copaca-bana [a wealthy neighborhood]."

Juninho then quickly walked away from the policeman, who with one hand on his revolver began to run after him. The policeman grabbed Jun-inho from behind, knocked him on the ground and began kicking him. Two women from the neighborhood—one of them Juninho's aunt—tried to intervene and pleaded with the policeman to leave Juninho alone, saying that he was a *trabalhador* (worker) and not a *bandido* (criminal). From the desperation of their pleas it was clear that they feared that the policeman might shoot Juninho on the spot. The second policeman told the one threatening Juninho that they should leave. They got into their car and drove off, while Juninho picked himself up, dusted himself off, and walked to his house.

Juninho had in fact once been a drug dealer but had been trying to find a regular job and extricate himself from the drug trade. The local drug dealers knew that after being harassed by the police and being unable to retaliate, it was tempting for Juninho to return to the drug trade, where he would have the weapons and support to resist such humiliation. They did not hesitate to appear in the neighborhood after the police had left and complain loudly about how disrespectful the police were. The perceived vulnerability to police violence generates deep anxieties for favela residents such as Juninho and Nêgo, who feel disrespected and humiliated by the police, yet who have struggled to avoid joining the "other side."

Policing and the Prejudice of Criminalized Space

When favela residents such as Juninho, Nêgo, and Seu Vander talk about their interactions with the police, they consistently highlight how the police disrupt daily life and humiliate them, and consistently identify forms of misrecognition. Juninho sarcastically wondered if the police "misrecognized" him as a resident of Copacabana, a wealthier neighborhood. Nêgo complained that the police misrecognized him as a criminal, and Seu Vander complained that the police misrecognized his adult male authority over his home.

This perception of police misrecognition, in turn, is connected to a sense that the police also misrecognize how racial dynamics should function. Instead of seeing the public spaces of the morro as areas of social intimacy, where distinctions of color should matter little, the police saw public spaces as zones of criminality, disregarding differences between bandidos and workers and treating everyone as a criminal. Instead of seeing racial differences as relatively unimportant, the police imposed hierarchical binaries. Viewing policing in this way—as the active imposition of categories and attempts to resignify spaces—helps illuminate the relationship between the criminalization of the neighborhood and processes of racial formation.

Observers of race relations in Brazil have frequently pointed out that discourses based on crime and alleged criminality have long been a central aspect of how Brazilians think about race (Adorno 1999; Fry 2000). The sociologist Sérgio Adorno notes: "In common sense, black citizens are seen as potential disturbances to the social order, despite the existence of studies that have challenged the supposed greater contribution of blacks to crime" (1996, 283). This long tradition that associates blacks with crime can be traced back to the criminal anthropology of Cesare Lombroso, which found its Brazilian counterpart in the early twentieth-century scholarship of Raimundo Nina Rodrigues (Schwarcz 1993, 207–213; Skidmore 1993, 57–62).

Nancy Scheper-Hughes notes, for instance, that crimes committed by the poor are "are viewed as race crimes, as naturally produced." She states that poor black men are "are freely referred to as 'bandits' because crime is 'in their blood'" (2006, 153). But perhaps it would be more accurate—and more in keeping with local understandings of crime and race—to reverse the equation: rather than seeing blackness as making a person a criminal, criminalization "makes" a person black.

For example, in their analysis of the 1988 national census, Michael Mitchell and Charles Wood found a correlation between skin color and victimization by the police. Men who identified themselves as *pardo* (brown, or of partial African descent) were only slightly more likely to be assaulted by the police than white men. But men who identified themselves as *negro* (black), were 2.401 times more likely to be assaulted by the police than white men (1999). One is tempted to reverse the implicit causality and ask: does being black make a person more vulnerable to police violence, or is vulnerability to police violence at least partially constitutive of the subjectivity of *negros*? In other words, does police violence make a person black?

Favela residents seem to be pointing to this when they complain about how harassment by the police unfairly imposes the prejudice of crime on themselves and their neighborhood. The prejudice of crime interacts in complex ways with the prejudice of skin color. Sometimes blackness and criminalization overlap. In other cases, the prejudice of criminality operates autonomously, and criminal is seen as an almost racialized type. In yet other cases, the space of the favela is the key factor.

Cases where criminalization overlaps with racialization are fairly common. One afternoon, for example, as I walked out of my house I saw a police car parked at the bottom of the hill and a group of worried people standing near the public telephone discussing something in hushed, urgent whispers. After a short while Seu Mário, an older man, separated from the group and walked toward the police car. I walked over and asked what was going on. Seu Lázaro, who was standing in the group of people, told me that the police had arrested Tião, Seu Mário's son. "What happened?" I asked. Regina told me: "The police came up the *escadão* [a steep alleyway staircase] and saw Tião, and decided to arrest him." "What was he doing?" I asked. "He wasn't doing anything," Regina said, "he was a *negão* (big black guy) wearing a *cordão* (big gold chain), who was walking around in the middle of the day."

Although Regina used an explicitly racial term, and clearly identified race as a main reason why Tião was detained, the other factors she mentions should not be ignored. In addition to his skin color, Regina mentions Tião's gold chain and the fact that he was walking around the morro in the middle of the day. Both factors are potential indicators to the police that Tião might have been a drug dealer: he appeared to have greater access to income than most other favela residents, and appeared to have no regular daytime job. In Brazil's racial classification system, money supposedly "whitens" (Harris 1964, 59). In the criminalized space of the favela, though, greater wealth both criminalized and darkened Tião. Borrowing Nogueira's terms, the "prejudice of mark" was combined with, and perhaps heightened by, the "prejudice of crime."

In other cases, the prejudice of crime operates autonomously, and criminality is understood as powerfully determinative biological trait, one that leads to bandits often being perceived as distinct types of people. For example, as part of a project seeking to understand the racial component of crime, researcher (and police officer) Jorge da Silva asked middle-class residents of Rio if they thought there was discrimination in the criminal justice system. One respondent stated: "I don't think one thing has anything to do with the other. I'm also poor; my father was poor . . . and I didn't turn out a criminal (*não dei pra bandido*). . . . It's that those people appear to have that instinct (*essa gente parece que já tem o instinto*)" (Silva 1997, 103). Criminality, in this understanding, emerges as an essentialized and biologized trait, which can manifest itself independently of a person's social status or physical appearance. While these three traits—that is, phenotype, class status, and place of residence—are understood as often coinciding, they appear to be seen as independent variables.

Those who are the targets of criminalization draw upon—while critiquing—essentialized and biologized understandings of crime. Another one of Silva's respondents, a dark-skinned resident of a favela, complained about the police, stating: "I think it's wrong that the PM [the military police] can beat people up without asking for their documents. They show up already firing their guns. From them, the brother of a criminal (*bandido*) is a criminal, the mother of a criminal is a criminal" (Silva 1997, 103). Ironically, in a society that has never had a clear ideology of hypodescent, this person is identifying a one-drop rule of criminality.

For residents of Rio's favelas, though, the most powerful pattern occurs when the prejudice of mark overlaps with the stigma of criminalized space. This is how policing shapes the way that young men like Nêgo who live in poor neighborhoods understand structures of racialized difference. Social difference is seen as constructed not only on the basis of the prejudice of color (in Nêgo's terms, *por causa da cor*) but also on the basis of the prejudice of crime (in his terms, "not everyone who lives in the favela is a traficante"). Policing is the mechanism by which the prejudice of mark is connected to the prejudice of crime, and this experience is sharpest when the police treat the favela as criminalized space. For example, Alex, a dark-skinned nineteen-year-old who lived in a part of Caxambu known as the Wild West because of frequent shoot-outs between police and drug dealers, told me the following: "Sometimes the police beat up people who have nothing to do with it [who don't deal drugs]. Just because we live in the morro, where are we going to hang out? We're going to hang out in the morro. . . . sometimes they [the police] show up and they don't even want to know. They think that because you're in the morro, because you're wearing . . . I don't know, a nice pair of shorts or something, that you're a *traficante*."

Conclusion: Thanking the Guys Who Are in Charge

When police violence is seen ethnographically, in all its complexity, it is hard to depict as simply part of a "deep logic of punitive containment" (Wacquant 2008, 58). Instead, the police and the drug dealers jointly disorganize favela life. Rio's policy of "pacification" of favelas, begun in 2008, marks both significant shifts in police practices, yet also significant continuities. Although the police pacification policy has changed the nature of relations between the drug dealers and the police, it has, if anything, only deepened the impact that the police have had on daily life.

Although I cannot ethnographically evaluate the impact of the pacification policy in Caxambu, the changes that Unidades de Polícia Pacificadora (Units of Police Pacification), commonly known as UPPs, have made are striking. The police presence in pacified favelas is supposed to be permanent. The police are now supposed to carry out community policing, and not the militarized patrolling that was the case when I lived in Caxambu. Rio's authorities have also changed the jurisdictions of the military police and civil police, creating overlapping "integrated security areas" where the two forces can cooperate, and creating joint financial incentives to minimize rivalries between the two forces.

It is crucial to point out, however, that while the co-production of disorder has been transformed, favelas continue to be deeply militarized and criminalized. When they occupy favelas, the police, in a strange sort of mimesis, take over many of the roles exercised by local drug gangs and the residents' associations. Local drug traffickers, for instance, often organized baile funk parties. The police in many favelas have prohibited such parties or have prohibited the type of music that can be played at them (though the legal basis for this prohibition is unclear). Like the drug delears, the police are attempting to control local forms of sociability, although in this case they only allow practices that they see as civilized and respectable. The residents' associations were often the bridge between favela residents and city services. The UPPs now occupy that role. Drug-trafficking organizations were also often deeply involved in regulating the provision of "informal" services in favelas, such as internet connections, cable television, and alternative transportation. With the UPPs, these services are now regulated by the police until, presumably, they are no longer provided on an informal basis.

This sort of continuing symbiosis is perhaps best symbolized by an observation made by Monique Carvalho in the pacified favela of Borel. Walking through Borel, she saw that several walls in the morro that had been painted with the letters CV now bore the initials UPP. Carvalho notes the irony of the police mimicking the graffiti used by the traficantes, and states: "The interpretation that can be made, since it is a similar practice, is the following: the UPP is saying to residents that the police now dominate the area" (2013, 297).

As Luiz Antonio Machado da Silva has pointed out, such police practices might contribute to a deep "policification" of favelas, which only deepens the sense that they are distinctive and different urban spaces (2010). As they regulate local services, ban dance parties, and mediate between favela residents and the state, the police seek to impose order upon favelas. The precondition for all these services, though, is the logic of militarized occupation: social services and public order are seen as only possible after favelas have been pacified. Further, as Machado da Silva points out, the UPP policy does not fundamentally challenge notion that public order is best achieved through police coercion; it merely reduces the amount of truculence used by the police (2010, 6). Sonia Fleury likewise observes that in the pacified favela of Santa Marta, the rhetoric of an expansion of citizenship rights is contradicted by a daily reality of a deeply militarized neighborhood (2012).

What, then, has policing done? Sally Engle Merry has argued that the police are often only partially successful in recasting social practices as crimes (1998, 36). More important is how police practices reshape identities and daily practices as they impose social anxieties upon marginalized groups. As Alex, Nêgo, Clara and the other residents of Caxambu clearly stated, being associated with a criminalized neighborhood—with the space of the morro—has become a fundamental component of experiences of discrimination. Experiences of racial discrimination—and race itself—appear to be increasingly shaped by spatial and criminalized criteria. Although money might "whiten," living in a poor neighborhood produces a prejudice of crime, making one a potential criminal, and "blackening." Although the UPP policy of pacification alters the nature of police presences in favelas, it does little to change the notion that these are criminalized zones of difference, even deepening this sense of alterity by subjecting favelas to different forms of policing.

As policing ties the prejudice of color to the prejudice of criminalization, it makes broader patterns of marginalization clear, leading favela residents to critique the variable forms of citizenship that abnormalize their lives. This process does not go uncontested. In their daily life, though, favela residents are faced with the dilemma of how to live within a structure of marginalization that they clearly perceive, yet are often powerless to do much to alter. The recent pacification policy does little to alter this overall structure of relative powerlessness.

Sometimes the only response is to point to the absurdity of a life forcibly organized by those who deliberately disorganize daily routines. For example, one morning I saw Seu Zé, a retired man in his sixties, standing on the sidewalk across from the residents' association. I went over and chatted with him, and Seu Lázaro walked up. A car with three civil policemen drove past, and Seu Lázaro said: "Those are police, aren't they?" I said yes, because I could see that they were wearing black vests with "civil police" written on them. Seu Zé walked over to a house next to where we were talking and opened the gate, telling the people there, including two teenage drug dealers, that the police had come by. Seu Lázaro joked with Seu Zé about running from the police, saying that he was too old to get far.

Seu Zé laughed, and said that a few days ago he had been framed (*enquadrado*) by the police. He told a funny story that I can't retell in his clipped, wry manner. But it went something like this:

> The police drove by and pointed a gun at me, saying stop right there. I did what they said, because they're the guys in charge (*são eles que mandam*). Then I asked them whether they really wanted me to stay still, or turn to turn around, since I had my back to them. They said: "No, turn around." I turned around and said, "Here are my documents." They said: "We don't want to see your documents, we know who you are," and then asked, "Where do you live?" I said, "Right over there, do you want me to show you?" But they said no. After a couple of minutes I asked them if I could go. They said I could, and I said, "Thank you very much." I was happy that they'd helped me figure out who I am and where I live, and was thanking them for that. I asked them if they wanted to know why I was thanking them, but they ignored me and drove off.

Seu Lázaro said that Seu Zé was really being a *sacana* (wise-ass) with the police. Seu Zé, with his sarcastic smile, responded: "No, they're the bosses. I was just doing what they told me to do. After all, they had an automatic rifle pointed at me."

6

Conclusion

"It Was Here That Estela Was Shot"

> In conditions of modernity, place becomes increasingly *phantasmagoric*: that is to say, locales are thoroughly penetrated by and shaped in terms of social influences that are quite distant from them.
> —Anthony Giddens (1990, 19)

A Conversation with Zeca

One afternoon I was interviewing Zeca. We began talking while sitting on the sidewalk at the top of the hill, leaning against the rough concrete wall of the local Catholic church. Although everyone referred to the building as the *igrejinha* (the little church), the local Catholic parish had abandoned the building long ago. What remained was a large, two-story brick building with broken windows and a badly leaking roof, half of which was occupied by the residents' association. In front of the church was a large ten-foot-high concrete cross decorated with red light bulbs. The local drug dealers made sure that at night the light bulbs always shone brightly, as a sign that the Comando Vermelho (Red Command) controlled drug dealing in the morro. People would occasionally light candles at the foot of the cross, and at times the drug dealers would stash small plastic bags of marijuana or cocaine in the cracked bricks at its base.

As Zeca and I talked, a teenager on a motorcycle zoomed up and down the street that climbed the ridge of the hill up to where we sat at the top. The motorcycle driver stopped and talked with another teenager sitting across the street from us, who handed him bags of cocaine or marijuana. Swinging his motorcycle in a tight arc he then sped down the hill to make a sale. It was hard to talk with Zeca because of the noise from the motorcycle and the loud baile funk music playing on a nearby boombox. So Zeca suggested that we walk over to the landing of his house, built adjacent to the downhill side of the church.

We climbed up and over the low wall that separated his house from the church and talked while standing on the roof of Zeca's half-finished house, looking across at the Guanabara Bay and the Rio-Niterói bridge in the distance. Toward the end of our conversation I asked Zeca if he thought that in the future Caxambu would change. He told me:

ZECA: You know what's going to end? Something important that used to happen in the *morro*? There's no longer going to be that thing of the police showing up and shooting, grabbing, and killing innocent people. Understand? That's going to stop. . . . Now if they show up shooting we're going to be able to speak up. . . . We'll be able to speak up.

BEN: Yeah, that's important . . .

ZECA: Yeah, because in the past lots of people were killed here. You know why? The police would show up in the morro, *pá, pá, pá* [the sound of gunfire] shooting, beating people up, understand. Beating up people who had nothing do with *marginalidade* (crime), people who lived here in the morro because of difficulties, because they had to. . . . But the police, maybe because they didn't know this, thought that everyone in the morro was a criminal. Now that's going to change. . . .

BEN: But the police stopped and searched me the other day.

ZECA: You can be sure that this is going to change. Today they search you. But in the past they'd show up and beat people up. . . . Lots of people were killed.

BEN: Yeah, people talk about a girl who was killed here.

ZECA: Yeah, Estela. It was here that Estela was shot, right in front of that gate across the street. Right there. There was a kid who was in the middle of the street right there. . . . I was right here, I saw the whole thing. . . . The police came up the hill and the kid ran away and they opened fire. *Pá*, the police-man fired his gun and Estela was shot in the head and killed. Yeah, Estela, that was her name.

Shifts and Continuities in the Drug Trade and Phantasmagorical Spaces

The transnational drug trade is inherently dynamic and shifting, as are all transnational organized crime enterprises, perhaps best thought of as mutable networks responding to shifting patterns of demand and repression (Nordstrom 2007). Drug dealing in Rio's favela is no exception. As I was conducting my research, the local drug trade was undergoing major transformations, as the relatively hierarchical and coherent structures of the 1980s and 1990s were becoming far more decentralized and fragmentary. In the past few years, the Rio state authorities have also dramatically changed their approach to public safety.

The state of (in)security in Rio's favelas continues to change, creating new forms of unpredictability for Rio's favela residents. Indeed, perhaps the only constant is change and unpredictability. But as I have argued throughout this book, paying attention only to the larger-scale, more dramatic events often obscures the continuities in how violence and insecurity permeate daily life. Zeca's comments, remembering where Estela was shot by the police in 1987, show how large-scale shifts in transnational illegal economic structures or policing strategies can shape the meanings attached to local places. At the same time, though, when they talk about their neighborhood, the residents of Caxambu contribute to forms of public memory that persist in remembering durable patterns of exclusion, even while they hope for a better future.

Caxambu was one of the last holdouts of the "old school" Comando Vermelho favelas more common in the early 1990s. Dê, the "owner" or main drug dealer, exerted substantial control over the dealers under his command, most of whom were locals, imposing a fairly strict code of conduct. He cultivated cordial ties with more powerful drug dealers from a nearby favela, and there was relatively little internal rivalry. The drug trade, and hence the overall security situation, people often told me, was "stable." The only exception to this sense of relative stability, as Zeca loudly pointed out, was fear over police shootings.

This situation, though, was relatively short-lived, changing at the end of my major period of fieldwork and even more since then. Dê's arrest toward the end of my major period of fieldwork signaled the beginning of larger changes to come. As major owners like Dê were killed or imprisoned—a result of a hard-line approach to crime by Rio's authorities—the drug trade became increasingly fragmented. Younger leaders assumed control, and with the shift in leadership came increased internal rivalries. In Caxambu, a new, younger leadership took over while Dê was in prison, and several traffickers were expelled after a fairly short-lived struggle for leadership. This echoed larger fragmentation within the Comando Vermelho, and increased competition with its two major rivals, the Terceiro Comando and the Amigos dos Amigos.

At the same time, two other major changes were occurring. In the 2000s, *milícias* (militias) appeared on the scene. These organizations were composed of off-duty firemen, municipal guards, and policemen, and offered to "protect" poor neighborhoods from drug traffickers and other criminals (McLeod-Roberts 2007; Zaluar and Conceição 2007). Milícias represented the expansion of privatized security from Rio's wealthy neighborhoods to poorer parts of the city. These paramilitary organizations also had some roots in poor neighborhoods in the western part of Rio, where off-duty policemen and others associated with the state's public security apparatus had long violently imposed a certain type of tranquility (Mesquita 2008).

Unlike drug-trafficking organizations, the milícias counted upon close—though unofficial—ties with the state. Perhaps ironically, they also assumed a role similar to organized crime syndicates in the United States and Europe: while milícias did not openly tolerate drug trafficking in neighborhoods that they controlled, they did organize and tax many of the other semi-legal and informal economic activities in poor neighborhoods, such as local transportation. As the milícias came to power in some neighborhoods, driving out local drug dealers, they further disrupted the city-wide drug trade. Drug traffickers expelled from milícia-controlled areas moved into other favelas, where they did not have as many local connections, and favelas that had not previously been as important to the drug trade assumed a new strategic role.

The second major change was in patterns of policing. In 2008, the Rio state public security authorities inaugurated the Unidades de Polícia Pacificadora (UPP, Units of Police Pacification) (Carneiro 2012; Peres 2011). The UPP policy is a contradictory blend of a militaristic approach to policing—one closely modeled on classic counterinsurgency strategies—and community policing. UPP programs begin with a massive "invasion" of favelas by the police, sometimes with the assistance of the army. Following classic counterinsurgency strategy of "clear, hold, and build," security forces expel drug traffickers and establish a permanent presence in the newly "pacified" favelas.[1] These military operations draw upon both the "high impact" policing strategies popularized by William Bratton, former chief of police in New York and other American cities, and the experience that Brazil's military forces have gained while participating in the United Nation's Peace Force in Haiti (Carneiro 2012). Despite the massive military presence, there have been relatively few fatalities.

A militarized approach permeates this policy: favelas are seen as territory recovered from an enemy. Media reports on major UPP operations often show the police raising the Brazilian flag over neighborhoods depicted as newly "liberated." After the occupation of the Vila Cruzeiro favela, José Maria Beltrame, Rio's secretary of public security, told the press (*Globo On-Line*, November 26, 2010): "Our main objective is to retake territory. For years, the hills of Rio have been used as safe harbors by criminals, who committed barbarities and ran away, like cowards, to the favela. It's important to arrest them, confiscate drugs and weapons, but it's essential to take away their territory. Today we broke through a wall imposed by this war."

At the same time, the UPP program proposes extending government services to favelas, and having the police shift their roles from repressing crime to working with the community. In this instance, the Rio authorities are building not on counterinsurgency, but rather on several longstanding projects of favela-based community policing (Mesquita Neto and Loche 2003; Muniz et al. 1997). It remains to be seen if these two contradictory approaches can be melded and, indeed, if the Rio state government has the will and resources to invest in what favela residents truly want: real citizenship and full integration into the city's economic, political, and social structures.

The UPPs larger goal is to work in this direction by fully integrating Rio's favelas into the rest of the "regular" city. If the UPP policy continues after Rio hosts the 2016 Olympic Games and meets this larger goal, the effects could be profound. As I have argued, favelas are a product of marginalization, poverty, and racism, and yet as informal neighborhoods are the solution that Rio's poor have found to the obstacles that confront them. If favelas become "regular" neighborhoods, the effects could be profoundly contradictory. On the one hand, regularization might mean improved property values, land tenure security, better provision of basic urban amenities like garbage collection and sewage, and greater access to goods and services. At the same time, rising home prices and real estate values could displace favela residents, and the greater penetration of the formal economy and government regulations could lead to higher prices for goods and services and greater competition for favela-based entrepreneurs. Already, Rio's newspapers have noted that wealthier people are beginning to buy or rent properties in the city's southern zone favelas, many of which have stunningly beautiful ocean views. Most profoundly, "pacification" might integrate favelas into the rest of the city, but does little to alter larger structures of inequality. The contradiction, as Luiz Antonio Machado da Silva has pointed out, is clear: the pacification policy proposes "integrating" favela residents into a society that remains highly unequal (2010).

(In)security and the Semiotization of Place

Changes in drug trafficking, policing, and in state policies mean that the state of (in)security that I experienced in Caxambu has now assumed a new shape. While milícias never materialized in Caxambu, a UPP police unit was set up in the neighborhood in 2011. Zeca's comments to me about where Estela was shot, though, show that even as the security situation in Caxambu shifts, violence and insecurity have deeply marked the neighborhood, shaping public memories and imposing meanings on spaces—meanings and memories that are often phantasmagorical, visible only to those who have the eyes, and memories, to see them, yet perhaps even more powerful exactly because they are not tangible.

As Alan Feldman has argued, violence semiotizes spaces, bodies, and objects, imbuing them or perhaps forcing upon them new meanings (1991, 6–7). For Zeca and many other residents, violence has semiotized Seu Lázaro's front gate, the spot where in 1987 the police drove up the hill on a weekday afternoon and shot at a drug dealer, missing him but killing a girl who was playing on the street. Dona Elsa would also often point out to me the place just a few steps away where Ramão, a notorious *bandido* (drug dealer), was killed by the police after a prolonged shoot-out in her house in the early 1980s. The meanings attached to such spaces are, in fact, quite complex. They do not merely reproduce a sense of terror or fear. The spaces of Caxambu are shaped by intangible large-scale forces of exclusion, and sharper and more direct forms of violence perpetrated by the police and drug traffickers. Yet while these forces attempt to disembed local social relations, subjecting daily life in Caxambu to forces far beyond the neighborhood, this process is only partial. For example, a young graffiti artist from Caxambu chose to paint a large mural of the neighborhood, with its distinctive water tower, on the wall just to the right of Seu Lázaro's gate, where Zeca told me Estela had been shot. The unfinished mural was crowned by a simple slogan: *Paz* (peace).

I offer, then, two final examples of meanings that the residents of Caxambu attached to the public spaces at the top of the hillside. First is a statue of former president Getúlio Vargas, which was placed on a concrete column just uphill from the place where Estela was shot.[2] The second is a large cross, located across the street from the statue of President Vargas and in front of an abandoned church, visible from far down the hill. Looking at the phantasmagorical meanings assigned to these spaces of the *pracinha* (little square), as everyone called the public area at the top of the hill, serve as final examples of both how the sense of (in)security in Caxambu is experienced, and yet how knowing how to live in Caxambu meant deploying social tactics that insist on maximizing local social agency, pride, and autonomy.

Getúlio and the Cross

Many of the residents of this part of Caxambu saw the small bronze bust of President Getúlio Vargas, or simply Getúlio as everyone referred to it, as a special emblem of Caxambu's past. Dona Nilza and Dona Arlinda, sixty-year-old sisters, told me one version of this story. I interviewed them with Zeca, and as we talked Dona Arlinda's daughter-in-law, Clarice, aged thirty-seven, also joined in the conversation:

> DONA NILZA: Look, I remember when Getúlio Vargas came here to the *praça* [the square around the water tower]. I was a girl, a child . . .

CLARICE: Really, he came here?

DONA NILZA: . . . when he came I lived on the other side of the hill. Everyone came up to the top of the hill yelling: "Look, Getúlio is in the morro." All the homes here had pictures of Getúlio. My mother did, everyone liked Getúlio.

BEN: He came to inaugurate the water tower?

DONA NILZA: Yeah. . . . [Changes her mind]. No, his bust. He came to inaugurate it. And there was a big party here in the morro, everyone without shoes, running around.

CLARICE: So you mean that the bust is old?

DONA ARLINDA: Ah, very old.

DONA NILZA: Look, there it was just *barro* (clay or mud). Just with him in the middle. . . . That church wasn't there. It wasn't there. There weren't as many homes. It was a *praça* of mud, hard-packed mud.

Dona Nilza's story reveals the personal connections that some of Caxambu's residents feel with the statue of Getúlio: she did not speak of the statue as an inanimate object, but as a person, as Getúlio himself. Though other residents claimed that the statue was placed on the hill after President Vargas's death, in Dona Nilza's version she has perhaps found a way of reconciling the language that residents use when speaking of the statue with historical memories. Residents often referred to the statue as Getúlio, and insisted that "he" be treated with respect (for instance, Dona Elsa became upset when some neighborhood kids painted the bust different colors). By Dona Nilza's reasoning, this must be because Getúlio himself was responsible for placing the statue in the neighborhood. Dona Nilza also associated the statue with memories of the neighborhood's early days when the streets were all mud. In this way, the statue established a link between Caxambu's early history and the former president.

The memories attached to the statue of Getúlio can be seen as another social tactic: part of an implicit social critique that contrasts the current exclusion of Caxambu's residents from larger socioeconomic structures with a past where the state was seen, in however patronizing a form, as caring for the poor. Vargas, residents often told me, was a president who "really tried to do something for the suffering workers of Brazil." By emphasizing that such a powerful man had visited their neighborhood, residents were drawing a contrast with current politicians, who were seen as corrupt and dishonest and as having no interest in the neighborhood. Pedro, for instance, told me that Getúlio was "the greatest statesman in Brazil. He brought progress to Brazil. Not to enrich himself like other politicians but to try to stop the massacre of the poor." Because the statue evoked memories of Vargas's populist ideology—his strategy of building a political base through extending assistance to the working class—Getúlio also was a symbol of Caxambu's workers.

The stories and memories that Getúlio's statue evokes also emphasized the importance of jointly sharing in the experience of Caxambu's streets. When the statue was removed from the square below the water tower because a city-funded project was widening the road, Nete, a woman in her mid-thirties, came into the residents' association to joke about the missing statue, saying that she was worried that Getúlio had been kidnapped. Clara, the association's secretary, told her that Getúlio was being kept in the residents' association building and would be cleaned before being placed once again in the square. "Oh good," Nete replied, "Getúlio has been around here so long that he has been rained on, has sat in the sun and has even been shot (*já tomou chuva, sol, e até bala*). So you should make sure that he looks good."

Perhaps most important, though, the statue of Getúlio symbolized how residents of Caxambu struggled to attempt to resist the neighborhood's social invisibility and criminalization. President Getúlio Vargas was famous as a populist who built his support through appeals to Rio's working class. Linking Caxambu to Vargas's memory was a way to insist that the residents of Caxambu were not criminals, but hard-working *trabalhadores* (workers). Similarly, pointing out that a president had visited Caxambu—and in fact had visited the very top of the hill, deep inside the neighborhood and, by the 1980s, one of the most strategic spots for warehousing drugs and guns— was a way to insist that Caxambu had its own, distinctive, and valuable history, one not subsumed by media portrayals of "violent favelas."

If the statue of Getúlio was a symbol of Caxambu's workers, and of the neighborhoods resistance to criminalization, then the cross can be seen as a far more ambivalent object, one that reflects the complexities of Caxambu's state of (in)security. The meanings and memories attached to the cross were complex and contradictory: the same object was both a sign of Caxambu's religiosity and traditions, and yet also a symbol of the Comando Vermelho drug organization's control of the morro.

Older residents told me that a small wooden chapel had long stood at the top of the hillside and that a cross, initially a wooden one, was placed outside the chapel. Before Padre Giovanni and a group of local Catholics had transformed the wooden chapel into a brick church, community *reza-deiras* (prayer leaders) conducted services in the chapel and would watch over and protect the image of Saint Sebastião, the patron saint of Rio de Janeiro to whom the chapel was dedicated. The wooden church collapsed in the 1970s, but the cross remained on top of the hill, and local women kept the images of saints in their homes. As a result, the cross was not just a symbol of Catholicism but was also associated with memories of specific local religious practices and with the morro's past.

Yet the cross also symbolized the Comando Vermelho-Jovem (CV-J, Young Red Command). It is unclear when the cross became associated with the CV-J, or even whether it was appropriated as a deliberate part of the gang's takeover of the morro. But this practice of using hilltop crosses as a symbol of the Comando Vermelho is not unique to Caxambu. For example, when the Brazilian army occupied several of the city's favelas in 1994, paratroopers landed on the top of the hillside of the Morro do Borel and demolished the cross at the hill's peak (Resende 1995, 108–109).[3] This is deeply ironic, as the planting of crosses was originally a marker of the Portuguese colonization of Brazil, and one of Brazil's original names was "Terra de Vera Cruz," or "Land of the True Cross."

Although they are stigmatized for living in a favela, the residents of Caxambu also live in a neighborhood that is marked by dense kinship ties and a strong sense of belonging. This sense of identity is intimately tied to the space of the morro itself. As the neighborhood has grown over decades, it has been shaped by, and has also transformed, the neighborhood's networks of social relations. As a result, residents of Caxambu see their neighborhood as a place of social intimacy and pride. Yet Caxambu is the target of various forces that seek to shape, control, and alter the neighborhood. Residents also have to contend with the drug gang that seeks to control the neighborhood's space, and with the police who do not patrol the neighborhood but occupy it or carry out "invasions." But other forces intervene as well. For example, while I lived there, a city-sponsored urban redevelopment project dramatically changed parts of Caxambu, removing homes, widening streets, building new recreation areas, and improving basic infrastructure.

The everyday violence that marks daily life in Caxambu and in Rio's other favelas does not merely destroy or undermine systems of meaning but also creates particular types of subjectivities, affects how parts of the hill are used, and influences the shape of memories, ways of speaking, and the embodied experience of the neighborhood. Violence both disrupts some forms of order and also constitutes others: creating particular norms, infusing spaces with particular meanings, connecting residents of distant communities through the dynamic and transnational flows of illegal commodities, and structuring new types of subjectivity, social practice, and urban form. Yet none of these effects are completely stable or naturalized, and the ways of living that I have analyzed are all aimed at addressing the unpredictability and uncertainty that is generated by violence.

Conclusion: Phantoms and Experiences of (In)security

The violence and sociospatial exclusion that mark Caxambu generate meanings and create memories that are attached to particular places. Caxambu's streets are now paved, but they continue to hold memories of dirt and mud, and thus of struggle and discrimination. Getúlio Vargas's populist and protectionist policies have long since been overwhelmed by current neoliberalism. The Catholic Church's attempts to help organize poor communities in the 1970s have receded in the wake of conservative retrenchment in the Church and harsh attacks by drug dealers on independent favela social movements. But the memories and meanings that Caxambu's residents attach to their neighborhood resist social invisibility and blanket criminalization, though without directly challenging—without *batendo de frente* (hitting straight on)—the more powerful. By remembering and forgetting, by marking spaces with different emotions and social meanings, by refusing to allow the meanings of the hillside to be determined by more powerful forces, the residents of Caxambu insist that their neighborhood is their own: the product of their labor, a sign of their identity, and a source and repository for their memories.

Yet these memories and meanings overlap and abut, shaping and being shaped by, a space of both danger and fear, and of pride and social intimacy. Some ghosts have assumed a more permanent presence than others. The drug dealers, like the state, were sometimes phantasmagoric entities, evoked frequently by the residents of the morro but not always visibly present. The markers of the drug trade were permanent: the CV-J and PJL graffiti tags on the walls; the occasional bullet holes pock-marking walls; and the large cross on the top of the hill lit up with red light bulbs. But these markers often evoked the local drug traffickers more by their absence than their presence. It was always eerie, for example, to pass by a wall spray-painted Comando Vermelho—PJL, and see no drug dealers present, but only kids kicking a soccer ball or women on their way up the hill from work or grocery shopping.

The sense of (in)security that marked daily life in Caxambu was built out of these contradictory meanings and fleeting memories, more felt and experienced than discursively constructed. Knowing how to live in such a neighborhood meant attempting to sense when safety might tip over into danger, of learning how to cope with ambiguity and uncertainty. For instance, one evening my wife and I were walking back to Caxambu after having had a few beers with Clara and her boyfriend at a bar in the neighborhood below the hillside. The streets of the working-class neighborhood below Caxambu were often empty and somewhat spooky at night. Usually whenever I began walking up Caxambu's steep alleys I relaxed, knowing that we would not be robbed or harassed in the morro.

This particular night, though, when we got to the bottom of the *escadão*, the large stairway that led up the hill, I noticed that the small bar at the entrance to Caxambu was closed. Heading up the stairs, I began to notice that fewer people than usual were outside. About halfway up the stairway, we got to a small open space, and I noticed Careca, a teenage drug dealer, standing in the alley looking down the hill, with a revolver tucked into the waistband of his shorts. I said "hello," but he didn't respond, which was not unusual. As my wife and I walked further up the hillside, I noticed that Careca was following a few steps behind us. As we continued to climb further up the stairs, Careca continued to shadow us. We finally turned the corner into the main street, and finally got to the gate that led into the homes owned by Seu Nogueira, our landlord. I fumbled with my keys and unlocked the gate.

When we stepped inside our house, my wife told me: "What was going on? You practically ran up the stairway." I hadn't even noticed that I'd sped up. I only knew that I'd had a vague premonition that things weren't quite normal. Maybe it was too cold that night for people to hang out in the alley, socializing as usual. Maybe the police had come into the neighborhood earlier that evening, and people went inside as a precaution. Maybe there was an interesting movie or *telenovela* on television. Maybe it was all of these together. It was hard to tell what, if anything, was going on. When I asked about it the following morning, no one seemed to think that anything unusual had happened. It was the ordinary mix of comfort in familiar surroundings and apprehension about danger, daily routine, and lurking unpredictability.

Notes

Chapter 1   "To Live Here You Have to Know How to Live"

1. This name and the names of all the individuals in this book are pseudonyms. In Portuguese the letter x is pronounced like 'sh,' so Caxambu is pronounced ka-sham-boo'. I chose the name Caxambu because many of the early residents of the neighborhood came from the city of Caxambu and other parts of the southern part of the state of Minas Gerais. Caxambu is also a name given to the music and dance also known as *jongo.* Older residents recalled that jongo parties were often held in the neighborhood.
2. I lived in Caxambu for a year and a half in 1998 and 1999, and then returned to conduct more research in 2001.
3. In Portuguese, he said: "Pra morar aqui é preciso saber viver." This wasn't some piece of neighborhood lore. He was quoting a song by Brazilian singer Roberto Carlos featured in a popular nightly *telenovela* (soap opera).
4. Following the lead of Caxambu's residents, I will generally use *morro* to refer to Caxambu, and *favela* as the more generic term for squatter neighborhoods throughout Rio.
5. In analyzing the hyper-real favela, I am drawing upon Alcida Ramos's concept of the hyper-real Indian (Ramos 1994).
6. The head drug trafficker in Rocinha, known as Nem, was arrested three days before the occupation. Nem was a member of the Amigos de Amigos (ADA) criminal organization, which seized control of Rocinha in 2004 after a violent confrontation with the Comando Vermelho.
7. The actual process of implementing a UPP in Rocinha was, in fact, fraught and complicated. The police occupation lasted for almost a year before the UPP post was set up in September 2012. During that time, there were shootouts between the police and drug dealers, and between rival drug gangs, as a gang that had been expelled from Rocinha sought to reclaim territory from the weakened local gang. There were also allegations of police violence, including the arrest of three

policemen accused of having raped a local woman. After the UPP was set up, some residents protested after Amarildo Souza, a local man who worked as a bricklayer and had no known connections to drug dealing, was arrested by the police, taken to the UPP base, and then never reappeared.

8. Rio de Janeiro was Brazil's capital city for nearly two hundred years until 1960, when the capital was transferred to the newly built city of Brasília. This loss of political prestige—and federal government jobs—was compounded by economic shifts in the 1970s and 1980s, as the manufacturing sector declined.

9. Rio de Janeiro refers to both the city of Rio de Janeiro and the state of the same name. Unless otherwise specified, when I use "Rio," I refer to the city. In 2009, the state of Rio accounted for 83 percent of Brazil's petroleum production and 50 percent of its natural gas (Fernández and Renault 2011, 117).

10. According to a survey of residents of favelas where UPPs had been established, carried out by the Instituto Brasileiro de Pesquisa Social, 93 percent of favela residents said they felt their neighborhood was safe, while 68 percent said that they feared that drug-dealing gangs might return (*O Globo*, February 20, 2010).

11. Caxambu was occupied by the police in 2011, and a UPP police post was set up four months later. The main UPP base was set up in a neighboring favela, but a UPP "advanced police base" was set up on the street that I lived on when I did my fieldwork.

12. There have been claims that police have sometimes dumped the bodies of homicide victims across municipal lines, and homicides where the bodies are never found are not counted.

13. Homicide rates steadily increased during the 1980s, reaching a peak in the late 1990s and early 2000s. By 2004, homicide rates in Rio leveled off or even began to fall (Waiselfisz 2007).

14. The proportion of young victims of homicide is so large that according to Waiselfisz, if victims aged fifteen to twenty-four were not included in the calculation of homicide rates, Brazil's nationwide homicide rates would have actually fallen slightly between 1980 and 2004 (Waiselfisz 2007, 69).

15. For example, in 1998 the homicide rate for males in Rio between the ages of fifteen and twenty-nine was 280 per 100,000. Guatemala and El Salvador's murder rates during the late 1980s, when the countries were at war, were 150 per 100,000. In the 1990s, war-torn Colombia had a nationwide homicide of 89.5 per 100,000, higher than Rio's overall homicide rate, but lower than the homicide rate in some of Rio's neighborhoods, and lower than the homicide rate for young men in Rio (Huggins 2000, 114).

16. Statistics that break down homicide by race are rare, but in the wealthier neighborhoods of the Zona Sul, Barra, and Tijuca, blacks and *pardos* (or mixed-raced individuals) are 18 percent of the population, but 66.6 percent of the victims of homicide (*Jornal do Brasil*, April 21, 2001).

17. A disproportionate percentage of the victims of police shootings are black: although they are 8 percent of the population of the city of Rio according to official statistics, between January 1993 and July 1996, blacks were 30 percent of those killed by the police (Cano 2010, 37).

18. *Carioca* means someone or something from the city of Rio de Janeiro.

19. This perspective, and my own, owes a great debt to Pierre Bourdieu, who

emphasized how structures of exclusion are made to seem natural as they are embedded in daily habits and familiar spaces (Bourdieu 1977).

Chapter 2   "Now You Know What It's Like"

1. When I first visited Caxambu, people often thought I was there to buy drugs. Later on this became a running joke: one afternoon, Seu Lázaro pointed out three young white men in brand-new soccer shirts walking up the hill. He told me: "Look, your brothers are coming to do business with the *malandros* (the drug dealers)."
2. On the history of the Peace Corps in favelas in Rio, see Valladares 2005, 104–112.
3. For histories of Rio's favelas, see Abreu 1987; Burgos 1998; Leeds and Leeds 1977; Parisse 1969; Perlman 1976; Pino 1997; Valla 1986; Valladares and Ribeiro 1994; and Zylberberg 1992.
4. In 1897, this hillside was occupied by soldiers who had returned to Rio from a military campaign in Brazil's northeast. They built shacks on the hillside, near the army's parade grounds, while they demanded their back pay. Perhaps because the hill was similar to one named Favela Hill in Bahia, where the soldiers had fought, it came to be known as the Morro da Favela. The term *favela* then quickly became a generic term for other similar squatter neighborhoods.
5. He also discovered that shacks had been built by soldiers, who then sold or rented them, showing that even from this early period there was already a de facto real estate market in the city's favelas despite the lack of legal land ownership (Abreu 1994, 37).
6. This historical legacy echoed down to my research. At one point while I was carrying out fieldwork, I agreed to help Caxambu's Residents' Association register elderly residents for free flu shots. This project was an utter failure: many elderly residents refused to register for the flu shots, telling me how much they distrusted the public health system.
7. For interpretations of the history of samba, see Hertzman 2013; Moura 1983; and Vianna 1995.
8. The intersections of race, class gender, and sexuality are beyond my concerns here. For three insightful treatments, though, see Burdick 1998; Edmunds 2010; and Goldstein 2003.
9. Between 1947 and 1954, the Fundação Leão XIII carried out projects in thirty-four favelas (Leeds and Leeds 1977, 199). They were active near Caxambu, helping to set up a now defunct Residents' Association and running a health clinic just below the hill, also long since abandoned. Residents of Caxambu remembered the health clinic, but no one could tell me much about the Fundação's other activities.
10. This policy was not carried out without opposition. For example, one of Zé Kéti's most famous songs, "Opinião" (Opinion), composed in 1965, protested the removal of favelas. Part of the song goes: "Podem me bater / Podem me prender / Mas daqui do morro eu não saio não" (You can beat me / You can arrest me / But I won't leave the morro). For a biography of Zé Kéti, see Lopes 2000.
11. When I did my fieldwork in Caxambu, people still talked about Dênis da Rocinha, Isaías do Borel, and Beato Salu of Mangueira as "good" *traficantes* who "respected" favela residents.

12. They included: Rogério Lemgruber (Bagulhão), who became a leader of the CV, and Escadinha (José dos Reis Encina), who controlled the drug trade in the favela of the Morro do Juramento (Amorim 1993, 143). Other important drug dealers who joined the CV were Dênis da Rocinha, Cy de Acari, Isaías do Borel, and Beato Salu.

13. By the end of 1985, the CV controlled drug trafficking in 70 percent of the favelas of the city of Rio (Amorim 1993, 167). This dominance, though, was short lived: in the late 1990s, the CV fractured into several competing groups and also lost control over neighborhoods to rival organizations.

14. It also came to light that the daughter of Moreira Franco's vice governor was having a love affair with Meio-Quilo, a drug trafficker from the favela of Jacarezinho (Amorim 1993, 27).

15. Nilo Batista became the governor of the state of Rio in April 1994, when Brizola stepped down to run for president.

16. Surprisingly, one of the groups calling for a temporary state of emergency, which would allow the federal army to assume control over internal security, was the Rio de Janeiro chapter of the Ordem dos Advogados do Brasil (OAB), Brazil's equivalent of the bar association and a major critic of the military dictatorship (Caldeira 1996, 53).

17. In November 1994, two thousand soldiers participated in the first part of Operation Rio, during which the army occupied the favelas of Dona Marta, Mangueira, Dende, Andaraí, and Borel, and set up roadblocks around several other favelas. In January 1995, the army invaded the Complexo do Alemão, and military forces surrounded the Complexo da Maré (Resende 1995).

18. What was not reported was the army abuse of some favela residents. According to Human Rights Watch, in the favelas of Borel and Chácara do Céu troops tortured detainees with electrical current, near drowning, and severe beatings (Human Rights Watch 1995, 71).

19. General Cerqueira's appointment was highly controversial among human rights activists and the political left. During the military dictatorship, General Cerqueira was a regional commander of the army's notorious DOI-CODI intelligence unit and led the operations that resulted in the death of guerrilla leader Carlos Lamarca.

20. Police killings of civilians increased from sixteen per month before General Cerqueira took office to thirty-two per month after he assumed control of the police (Human Rights Watch 1997, 92–93). This period also saw an increase in the deaths of policemen, though the rate did not equal the increase in the number of civilians killed by the police.

Chapter 3   A Familiar Hillside and Dangerous Intimates

1. According to the *Oxford English Dictionary*, one definition of the English word "familiar" is "of or pertaining to one's household," reflecting the word's roots in the Latin "familiār-is," though this meaning is now rare.

2. Research on female participation in the drug trade is scarce. Robert Gay's book on a woman who was the girlfriend of several drug traffickers is one exception, as is Mariana Barcinski's analysis based on interviews with five women who were directly involved in drug dealing. Both Gay and Barcinski argue that although women suffer

greatly in this male-dominated world, women involved in drug trafficking are not passive victims but exert considerable agency and influence (see Barcinski 2009; Gay 2005).

3. Dona Joana is referring here to the global Spanish flu epidemic, which broke out in 1918 and killed over forty million people worldwide.

4. Dona Joana's father probably arrived before 1920, since she refers to the worldwide Spanish flu epidemic of 1918. Another longtime resident, Seu Amaro, told me that his father purchased his plot in 1914. Both stated that when their parents moved to Caxambu there were already other homes on the hillside.

5. In the late 1990s, the average per capita income in Caxambu, was R$127 (US$60), less than half that of the surrounding neighborhood and among the lowest in the city (Lima 1999). There was no reliable census information on racial identities.

6. Though he denied that racism existed in the morro, Zeca also told me that when he was a teenager he couldn't date a neighborhood girl because her mother refused to let her date "people of my color."

7. Dona Carmen, who was very dark-skinned, adopted a fair-skinned blond boy who was abandoned by his parents. She told me one afternoon: "*Coitadinho* (poor kid), he's going to be so sad when he realizes that he's white."

8. For a history of these churches, see Chestnut 1997.

9. The term *viciado* applies only to those who use cocaine, marijuana or other drugs. Alcoholics are not usually called viciados.

10. According to a study by the Observatório de Favelas research group, one-fifth of the young people working in drug gangs whom they followed were killed over the course of two years, most of them by the police (BBC News, November 25, 2006).

11. Research on women who participate in the drug trade indicates a similar mix of motives: women mention both external causes for their participation, such as a lack of other economic options, and also the status and respect they gain (Barcinski 2009).

12. Ellen Moodie notes a similar phenomenon in El Salvador, where one response to urban crime was an emphasis upon being *listo* (street-smart or cunning) (Moodie 2010, 104).

Chapter 4   Tubarão and Seu Lázaro's Dog

1. The transcription is from the Brazilian hip-hop webzine www.culturaderua.cjb .com. The translation is mine.

2. The term that MV Bill uses is *sangue bom*, literally "good blood," a slang expression similar to the American terms *home boy*, *brother*, or *good guy*. In this context, though, he refers to the head of the local drug gang.

3. This is a reference to a Brazilian adage: *em boca fechada não entra mosca*, or "flies can't get in a closed mouth," which warns against the consequences of a loose tongue.

4. The term X-9 comes from an American comic book, published in Brazil from the 1940s through the 1990s, which featured a character named Secret Agent X-9.

5. A funk song called "X-9 Torrado" (Toasted X-9) by Cidinho and Doca, which I often heard in Caxambu, described how traffickers kill informants by placing tires

over them and burning them alive. The chorus was: "smell of burning tires / busted carburetors / a wasted X-9."

Chapter 5   "The Men Are in the Area"

1. Nêgo's pseudonym is a racial term, meaning black person. It is also often used as a term of endearment. Nêgo's real nickname was a similar racially coded term.
2. In 1821, almost half of Rio's population (46 percent) was enslaved, and together with freed persons, people of color made up the bulk of Rio's population. In 1849, Rio had the largest slave population of any city in the Americas (Karasch 1987, 61–62, 65).
3. When the dictatorship ended, control over the military police reverted to the democratically elected state governors.
4. Distrust of the police has deep historical roots: Marcos Bretas, for instance, shows that at the beginning of the twentieth century both the elite and the urban poor had a negative vision of the police (1997, 46, 55–56).
5. Of course the comparison in the article is problematic since it compares overall deaths in Rio to deaths of US coalition forces, and not overall fatalities in Iraq.
6. Colonel Nazareth Cerqueira was tragic example of the violent divisions within Rio's police force: an active proponent of police reform and a critic of militarized policing, as well as one of the highest-ranking Afro-Brazilians, he was murdered in suspicious circumstances in 1999.

Conclusion

1. The phrase "clear, hold, and build" comes from US General David Petraeus's *Field Manual 3–24 on Counter-Insurgency*, published in 2006. While I do not know whether Brazilian public security officials read Petraeus's report, several of the Brazilian army officials who participated in the UPP program had extensive peacekeeping experience in Haiti, and were surely knowledgeable about international military strategy.
2. Getúlio Vargas assumed power in a military coup in 1930, and was deposed by the military in 1945. He was then elected president in 1951 and served until his suicide in 1954 (Levine 1998).
3. Residents of Borel and the local Catholic priest protested this action. Residents of Borel told me that the cross had been erected by the church and had nothing to do with the drug dealers. It is interesting, though, that the army was so sure of the association that it symbolically marked its takeover by demolishing the cross (see also Resende 1995).

References

Abreu, Maurício de A. 1987. *Evolução Urbana do Rio de Janeiro*. Rio de Janeiro: Jorge Zahar.
————. 1994. "Reconstruindo uma história esquecida." *Espaço e Debates* 14 (37): 34–46.
Adorno, Sérgio. 1996. "Racismo, criminalidade violenta, e justiça penal: Réus brancos e negros em perspectiva comparativa." *Estudos Históricos* 9 (18): 282–300.
————. 1999. "Racial Discrimination and Criminal Justice in São Paulo." In *Race in Contemporary Brazil*, edited by Rebecca Reichmann, 123–138. University Park: Pennsylvania State University Press.
Agamben, Giorgio. 1995. *Homo Sacre*. Stanford, CA: Stanford University Press.
————. 2005. *State of Exception*. Chicago: University of Chicago Press.
Ahnen, Ronald. 2007. "The Politics of Police Violence in Democratic Brazil." *Latin American Politics and Society* 49 (1): 141–164.
Alquéres, José Luiz. 2011. "A Evolução do Ambiente de Negócios no Rio de Janeiro." In *Rio: A Hora da Virada*, edited by André Urani and Fabio Giambiagi, 60–72. Rio de Janeiro: Elsevier.
Alvito, Marcos. 2001. *As Cores de Acari*. Rio de Janeiro: Editora FGV.
Amorim, Carlos. 1993. *Comando Vermelho*. Rio de Janeiro: Editora Record.
Andreas, Peter. 1999. "When Policies Collide." In *The Illicit Global Economy and State Power*, edited by H. Richard Friman and Peter Andreas, 125–141. New York: Rowan and Littlefield.
Andrews, George Reid. 1991. *Blacks and Whites in São Paulo, Brazil 1888–1988*. Madison: University of Wisconsin Press.
Arias, Enrique Desmond. 2006. *Drugs and Democracy in Rio de Janeiro*. Chapel Hill: University of North Carolina Press.
Arias, Enrique Desmond, and Daniel Goldstein, eds. 2010. *Violent Democracies in Latin America*. Durham, NC: Duke University Press.
Arias, Enrique Desmond, and Corinne Davis Rodrigues. 2006. "The Myth of Personal Security: Criminal Gangs, Dispute Resolution, and Identity in Rio de Janeiro's Favelas." *Latin American Politics and Society* 48 (4): 53–81.

Athayde, Celso, MV Bill, and Luiz Eduardo Soares. 2005. *Cabeça de Porco*. Rio de Janeiro: Objetiva.

Austin, J. L. 1975. *How to Do Things with Words*. 2nd ed. Cambridge, MA: Harvard University Press.

Auyero, Javier. 2000. "The Logic of Clientelism in Argentina: An Ethnographic Account." *Latin American Research Review* 35 (3): 55–81.

Ballibar, Etienne. 1991. "Is There a 'Neo-Racism'?" In *Race, Nation, Class*, edited by Etienne Balibar and Immanuel Wallerstein, 17–28. London: Verso.

Barcinski, Mariana. 2009. "Protagonismo e Vitimização na Trajetória de Mulheres Envolvidas na Rede do Tráfico de Drogas no Rio de Janeiro." *Ciência & Saúde Coletiva* 14 (2): 577–586.

Basso, Keith H. 1996. *Wisdom Sits in Places: Landscape and Language among the Western Apache*. Albuquerque: University of New Mexico Press.

Beattie, Peter. 2003. "Slavery and Soldiering in Brazil from 1850 to 1888." In *Changing Men and Masculinities in Latin America*, edited by Matthew Gutmann, 234–255. Durham, NC: Duke University Press.

Benchimol, Jaime. 1990. *Pereira Passos: Um Haussman Tropical*. Rio de Janeiro: Prefeitura da Cidade do Rio de Janeiro.

Benjamin, Walter. 1978. *Reflections: Essays, Aphorisms, Autobiographical Writings*. Translated by Edmund Jephcott. New York: Schocken Books.

Bourdieu, Pierre. 1977. *Outline of a Theory of Practice*. Cambridge: Cambridge University Press.

Bourgois, Philippe. 1996. *In Search of Respect: Selling Crack in El Barrio*. Cambridge: Cambridge University Press.

———. 2004. "The Continuum of Violence in War and Peace: Post–Cold War Lessons from El Salvador." In *Violence in War and Peace: An Anthology*, edited by Nancy Scheper-Hughes and Philippe Bourgois, 425–434. Oxford, UK: Blackwell.

Bretas, Marcos Luiz. 1997. *Ordem na Cidade: O Exercício Cotidiano da Autoridade Policial no Rio de Janeiro, 1907–1930*. Rio de Janeiro: Rocco.

Brinks, Daniel. 2008. *The Judicial Response to Police Killings in Latin America*. Cambridge: Cambridge University Press

Burdick, John. 1993. *Looking for God in Brazil: The Progressive Catholic Church in Brazil's Religious Arena*. Berkeley: University of California Press.

———. 1998. *Blessed Anastacia: Women, Race, and Popular Christianity in Brazil*. New York: Routledge.

Burgos, Marcello Baumann. 1998. "Dos Parques Proletários ao Favela-Bairro." In *Um Século de Favela*, edited by Alba Zaluar and Marcos Alvito, 25–60. Rio de Janeiro: Editora FGV.

Butler, Judith. 1993. *Bodies That Matter*. New York: Routledge

Cabral, Sérgio. 1996. *As Escolas de Samba do Rio de Janeiro*. Rio de Janeiro: Lumiar Editora.

Caldeira, César. 1996. "Operação Rio e Cidadania." In *Política e Cultura: Visões do Passado e Perspectivas Contemporâneas*, edited by Elisa Reis, Maria Tavares de Almeida, and Peter Fry, 50–74. São Paulo: Editora Hucitec.

———. 1997. "Segurança Pública e Sequestros no Rio de Janeiro, 1995–1996." *Tempo Social* 9 (1):115–153

Caldeira, Teresa. 2000. *City of Walls: Crime, Segregation, and Citizenship in São Paulo*. Berkeley: University of California Press.

Caldeira, Teresa, and James Holston. 1999. "Democracy and Violence in Brazil." *Comparative Studies in Society and History* 41 (4): 691–729.

Cano, Ignácio. 1997. *The Use of Lethal Force by Police in Rio de Janeiro*. Rio de Janeiro: ISER.

———. 2010. "Racial Bias in Police Use of Lethal Force in Brazil." *Police Practice and Research* 11 (1): 31–43.

Cardoso, Ruth C. L. 1984. "Creating Kinship." In *Kinship Ideology and Practice in Latin America*, edited by Raymond Smith, 196–203. Chapel Hill: University of North Carolina Press.

Carneiro, Leandro Piquet. 2012. *"The Politics of Pacification in Rio de Janeiro: A Study in Leadership and Innovation."* Working paper, Lemann Dialogue, Kennedy School of Government. Cambridge, MA: Harvard University.

Carvalho, José Murilo de. 1997. *Os Bestializados: O Rio de Janeiro e a República Que Não Foi.* Rio de Janeiro: Companhia das Letras.

Carvalho, Monique Batista. 2013. "A Política de Pacificação de Favelas e as Contradições Para a Produção de Uma Cidade Segura." *O Social Em Questão* 16 (29): 285–308.

Cerqueira, Carlos Magno Nazareth. 1996. "Remilitarização da Segurança Pública." *Discursos Sediciosos* 1 (1): 141–168.

Certeau, Michel de. 1984. *The Practice of Everyday Life.* Translated by Steven Rendall. Berkeley: University of California Press.

Chandler, Billy Jaynes. 1978. *The Bandit King: Lampião of Brazil.* College Station: Texas A&M University Press.

Chestnut, R. Andrew. 1997. *Born Again in Brazil.* New Brunswick, NJ: Rutgers University Press.

Civico, Aldo. 2008. "Portrait of a Paramilitary." In *Engaged Observer: Anthropology, Advocacy, and Activism*, edited by Victoria Sanford and Asale Angel-Ajani, 131–146. New Brunswick, NJ: Rutgers University Press.

Coelho, Eduardo Campos. 1988. "Da Falange Vermelha a Escadinha: O Poder Nas Prisões." *Presença: Revista de Política e Cultura* 11: 106–114.

Costallat, Benjamim. 1990 [1924]. *Mistérios do Rio.* Rio de Janeiro: Prefeitura da Cidade do Rio de Janeiro, Secretaria Municipal de Cultura.

Da Matta, Roberto. 1991 [1979]. *Carnivals, Rogues, and Heroes.* Notre Dame, IN: University of Notre Dame Press.

———. 1997. "Tem Pente Aí: Reflexões Sobre a Identidade Masculina." In *Homens*, edited by Dario Caldas, 31–50. São Paulo: SENAC.

Davis, Diane. 2006. "The Age of Insecurity: Violence and Social Disorder in the New Latin America." *Latin American Research Review* 41 (1): 178–197.

Davis, Mike. 2007. *Planet of Slums.* New York: Verso.

di Leonardo, Micaela and Roger Lancaster. 1997. "Introduction," in *The Gender and Sexuality Reader*, edited by Roger Lancaster and Micaela di Leonardo, 1–10. New York: Routledge.

Do Rio, João. 1997. *A Alma Encantada das Ruas.* Edited by Raúl Antelo. São Paulo: Companhia das Letras.

Dowdney, Luke. 2003. *Children of the Drug Trade.* Rio de Janeiro: 7 Letras.

Durham, Eunice. 1980. "A Família Operária." *Dados* 23 (2): 201–213.

Edmunds, Alexander. 2010. *Pretty Modern: Beauty, Sex, and Plastic Surgery in Brazil.* Durham, NC: Duke University Press.

Faoro, Raymundo. 1980. *Os Donos do Poder: Formação do Patronato Político no Brasil.* 10th ed. Rio de Janeiro: Editora Globo.

Feitlowitz, Marguerite. 1999. *A Lexicon of Terror: Argentina and the Legacies of Torture.* Oxford: Oxford University Press.

Feldman, Allen. 1991. *Formations of Violence: The Narrative of the Body and Political Terror in Northern Ireland*. Chicago: University of Chicago Press.

Fernández, Eloi, and Alfredo Renault. 2011. "Rio, Capital da Energia." In *Rio: A Hora da Virada*, edited by André Urani and Fabio Giambiagi, 111–122. Rio de Janeiro: Elsevier.

Ferreira, Sergio Guimarães. 2011. "Segurança Pública no Rio de Janeiro: O Caminho das Pedras e dos Espinhos." In *Rio: A Hora da Virada*, edited by André Urani and Fabio Giambiagi, 73–99. Rio de Janeiro: Elsevier.

Filho, Aziz, and Francisco Alves Filho. 2003. *Paraíso Armado: Interpretações da Violência no Rio de Janeiro*. São Paulo: Garçoni.

Fischer, Brodwyn. 2004. "Quase Pretos de Tão Pobres: Race and Social Discrimination in Rio de Janeiro's Twentieth-Century Criminal Courts." *Latin American Research Review* 39 (1): 31–59.

———. 2008. *A Poverty of Rights: Citizenship and Inequality in Twentieth-Century Rio de Janeiro*. Stanford, CA: Stanford University Press.

Fleury, Sonia. 2012. "Militarização Do Social Como Estratégia de Integração—O Caso da UPP do Santa Marta." *Sociologias* 14 (30): 194–222.

Fonseca, Claudia. 1986. "Orphanages, Foundlings, and Foster Mothers." *Anthropological Quarterly* 59 (1): 15–27.

———. 1991 "Spouses, Siblings and Sex-Linked Bonding." In *Family, Household and Gender Relations in Latin America*, edited by Elizabeth Jelin, 133–160. London: Kegan Paul.

———. 2002. "Philanderers, Cuckolds and Wily Women." In *Changing Men and Masculinities in Latin America*, edited by Matthew Gutmann, 61–83. Durham, NC: Duke University Press.

Fontaine, Pierre-Michel, ed. 1985. *Race, Class, and Power in Brazil*. Los Angeles: Center for Afro-American Studies, University of California.

Foucault, Michel. 1977. *Discipline and Punish: The Birth of the Prison*. Translated by Alan Sheridan. New York: Vintage Books.

———. 1991. "Governmentality." In *The Foucault Effect*, edited by Graham Burchell, Colin Gordon, and Peter Miller, 87–104. Chicago: University of Chicago Press.

Freyre, Gilberto. 1945. *The Masters and the Slaves*. Berkeley: University of California Press.

Fry, Peter. 2000. "Politics, Nationality, and the Meanings of 'Race' in Brazil." *Daedalus* 129 (2): 83–118.

Garriott, William, ed. 2013. *Policing and Contemporary Governance: The Anthropology of Police in Practice*. New York: Palgrave Macmillan.

Gay, Robert. 1994. *Popular Organization and Democracy in Rio de Janeiro: A Tale of Two Favelas*. Philadelphia: Temple University Press.

———. 1999. "The Broker and the Thief: A Parable (Reflections on Popular Politics in Brazil)." *Luso-Brazilian Review* 36 (1): 49–70

———. 2005. *Lucia: Testimonies of a Brazilian Drug Dealer's Woman*. Philadelphia: Temple University Press.

Geertz, Clifford. 1973. *The Interpretation of Cultures*. New York: Basic Books.

———. 1995. *After the Fact*. Cambridge, MA: Harvard University Press.

Giddens, Anthony. 1990. *The Consequences of Modernity*. Stanford, CA: Stanford University Press.

Gilbert, Alan. 1998. *The Latin American City*. London: Latin America Bureau.

Gilroy, Paul. 1987. *"There Ain't No Black in the Union Jack": The Cultural Politics of Race and Nation*. Chicago: University of Chicago Press.

Goldstein, Daniel. 2003. "'In Our Own Hands': Lynching, Justice, and the Law in Bolivia." *American Ethnologist* 30 (1): 22–43.

———. 2004. *The Spectacular City: Violence and Performance in Urban Bolivia.* Durham, NC: Duke University Press.

———. 2010. "Toward a Critical Anthropology of Security." *Current Anthropology* 51 (4): 487–499.

———. 2012. *Outlawed: Between Security and Rights in a Bolivian City.* Durham, NC: Duke University Press.

Goldstein, Donna. 2003. *Laughter Out of Place: Race, Class, Violence, and Sexuality in a Brazilian Favela.* Berkeley: University of California Press.

Graham, Richard. 1990. *Patronage and Politics in Nineteenth-Century Brazil.* Stanford, CA: Stanford University Press.

Green, Linda. 1998. *Fear as a Way of Life.* New York: Columbia University Press.

Gutmann, Matthew. 2003. "Introduction." In *Changing Men and Masculinities in Latin America*, edited by Matthew Gutmann, 12–16. Durham, NC: Duke University Press.

Hanchard, Michael. 1994. *Orpheus and Power: The Movimento Negro of Rio de Janeiro and São Paulo, 1945–1988.* Princeton, NJ: Princeton University Press.

Harazim, Dorrit. 1994. "A Centrífuga do Medo na Cidade." *Veja*, November 23.

Harris, Marvin. 1964. *Patterns of Race in the Americas.* New York: Walker.

Hasenbalg, Carlos, and Nelson do Valle Silva. 1999. "Notes on Racial and Political Inequality in Brazil." In *Racial Politics in Contemporary Brazil*, edited by Michael Hanchard, 154–178. Durham, NC: Duke University Press.

Hautzinger, Sarah. 2007. *Violence in the City of Women.* Berkeley: University of California Press.

Hinton, Mercedes. 2006. *The State in the Streets: Police and Politics in Argentina and Brazil.* Boulder, CO: Lynne Rienner,

Herzfeld, Michael. 1996. *Cultural Intimacy.* London: Routledge.

Hertzman, Marc. 2013. *Making Samba: A New History of Race and Music in Brazil.* Durham, NC: Duke University Press.

Holloway, Thomas H. 1993. *Policing Rio de Janeiro.* Stanford, CA: Stanford University Press.

Holston, James. 1991. "Autoconstruction in Working-Class Brazil." *Cultural Anthropology* 6 (4): 447–65.

Holston, James, and Arjun Appadurai. 1999. "Introduction: Cities and Citizenship." In *Cities and Citizenship*, edited by James Holston, 1–20. Durham, NC: Duke University Press.

Huggins, Martha. 1985. *From Slavery to Vagrancy in Brazil.* New Brunswick, NJ: Rutgers University Press.

———. 2000. "Urban Violence and Police Privatization in Brazil: Blended Invisibility." *Social Justice* (Summer): 113–134.

Human Rights Watch. 1995. *Human Rights Watch World Report.* New York: Human Rights Watch.

———. 1997. *Police Brutality in Urban Brazil.* New York: Human Rights Watch.

ISER. 1997. *Mapa de Risco da Violência no Rio de Janeiro.* Rio de Janeiro: Instituto de Estudos da Religião.

Jackson, Michael. 1989. *Paths toward a Clearing: Radical Empiricism and Ethnographic Inquiry.* Bloomington: Indiana University Press.

Karasch, Mary. 1987. *Slave Life in Rio de Janeiro, 1808–1850.* Princeton, NJ: Princeton University Press.

Kleinman, Arthur. 1997. "The Violences of Everyday Life: The Multiple Forms and Social Dynamics of Violence." In *Violence and Subjectivity*, edited by Veena Das, Arthur

Kleinman, Mamphela Remphele, and Pamela Reynolds, 226–241. Berkeley: University of California Press.

Koonings, Kees, and Dirk Kruijt, eds. 1999. *Societies of Fear: The Legacy of Civil War, Violence, and Terror in Latin America.* London: Zed Books.

Kottak, Conrad. 1967. "Kinship and Class in Brazil." *Ethnology* 6 (4): 427–443.

Leeds, Anthony, and Elizabeth Leeds. 1977. *Sociologia do Brasil Urbano.* Rio de Janeiro: Zahar.

Leeds, Elizabeth. 1996. "Cocaine and Parallel Polities." *Latin American Research Review* 31 (3): 47–83.

Lefebvre, Henri. 1991. *The Production of Space.* Translated by Donald Nicholson-Smith. Oxford, UK: Blackwell.

Leite, Márcia Pereira. 1998. "O Rio de Janeiro em Pauta." *Cadernos de Antropologia e Imagem* 6 (1): 103–121.

———. 2008. "Violência, Risco e Sociabilidade nas Margens da Cidade." In *Vida Sob Cerco,* edited by Luiz Antonio Machado da Silva, 115–142. Rio de Janeiro: Editora Nova Frontera.

Levine, Robert. 1998. *Father of the Poor? Vargas and His Era.* Cambridge: Cambridge University Press.

Lima, José Matias de, ed. 1999. *Pesquisa Sócio-Económica das Comunidade de Baixa Renda: Resultados da Pesquisa de Domicílios; Rio de Janeiro*: Prefeitura da Cidade do Rio de Janeiro/Secretaria Municipal do Trabalho.

Lopes, Nei. 2000. *Zé Kéti: O Samba sem Senhor.* Rio de Janeiro: Relume Dumará.

Lovell, Peggy. 1994. "Race, Gender, and Development in Brazil." *Latin American Research Review* 29 (3): 7–35.

Lutz, Catherine, and Donald Nonini. 1999. "The Economies of Violence and the Violence of Economies." In *Anthropological Theory Today,* edited by Henrietta Moore, 72–113. Cambridge, UK: Polity Press.

Macaulay, Fiona. 2007. "Justice Sector and Human Rights Reform under the Cardoso Government." *Latin American Perspectives* 34 (5): 26–42.

Machado da Silva, Luiz Antonio. 2004. "Sociabilidade Violenta: Por uma Interpretação da Criminalidade Contemporânea no Brasil Urbano." *Sociedade e Estado* 19 (1): 53–84.

———. 2010. "Afinal, Qual é a das UPPs?" *Observatório das Metrópoles,* March 2010, 1–7, accessed June 12, 2013. http://www.observatoriodasmetropoles.ufrg.br.

Machado da Silva, Luiz Antonio, and Márcia Pereira Leite. 2007. "Violência, Crime e Polícia: O que os Favelados Dizem Quando Falam Desses Temas?" *Sociedade e Estado* 22 (3): 545–591.

Magnani, José. 1998. *Festa no Pedaço.* São Paulo: Hucitec.

Massey, Doreen. 1994. *Space, Place, and Gender.* Minneapolis: University of Minnesota Press.

Mbembe, Achille. 2001. *On the Postcolony.* Berkeley: University of California Press.

———. 2003. "Necropolitics." *Public Culture* 15 (1): 11–40.

McLeod-Roberts, Luke. 2007. "Paramilitary Games." *NACLA Report on the Americas* 40 (4): 20–25.

Meade, Teresa. 1997. *"Civilizing" Rio: Reform and Resistance in a Brazilian City, 1889–1930.* University Park: Pennsylvania State University Press

Merry, Sally Engle. 1998. "The Criminalization of Everyday Life." In *Everyday Practices and Trouble Cases,* edited by Austin Sarat, Marianne Constable, David Engel, Valerie Hans, and Susan Lawrence, 14–39. Evanston, IL: Northwestern University Press.

Mesquita, Wania Amélia. 2008. "'Tranquilidade' sob Uma Ordem Violenta." In *Vida Sob Cerco,* edited by Luiz Antonio Machado da Silva, 227–248. Rio de Janeiro: Editora Nova Frontera.

Mesquita Neto, Paulo, and Adriana Loche. 2003. "Police-Community Partnerships in Brazil." In *Crime and Violence in Latin America*, edited by Hugo Fruhling, Joseph Tuchman, and Heather Golding, 179–204. Washington, DC: Woodrow Wilson Center Press.

Misse, Michel. 1997. "As Ligações Perigosas." *Contemporaneidade e Educação* 2 (1): 93–116.

———. 2006. *Crime e Violência no Brazil Contemporâneo*. Rio de Janeiro: Lumen Juris.

Mitchell, Michael, and Charles H. Wood. 1999. "Ironies of Citizenship in Brazil: Skin Color, Police Brutality, and the Challenge to Democracy in Brazil." *Social Forces* 77 (3): 1001–1020.

Moodie, Ellen. 2010. *El Salvador in the Aftermath of Peace*. Philadelphia: University of Pennsylvania Press.

Moore, Sally Falk. 1987. "Explaining the Present: Theoretical Dilemmas in Processual Anthropology." *American Ethnologist* 14 (4): 727–736.

Moura, Roberto. 1983. *Tia Ciata e a Pequena África no Rio de Janeiro*. Rio de Janeiro: FUNARTE.

Moore, Robin Dale. 1997. *Nationalizing Blackness: Afrocubanismo and Artistic Revolution in Havana, 1920–1940*. Pittsburgh, PA: University of Pittsburgh Press.

Muniz, Jacqueline, Sean Larvie, Leonarda Musumeci, and Bianca Freire. 1997. "Resistências e Dificuldades de Um Programa de Policiamento Comunitário." *Tempo Social* 9 (1): 197–213.

Nagengast, Carole. 1994. "Violence, Terror, and the Crisis of the State." *Annual Review of Anthropology* 23: 109–136.

Neate, Patrick, and Damian Platt. 2006. *Culture Is Our Weapon: Making Music and Changing Lives in Rio de Janeiro*. New York: Penguin.

Neuwirth, Robert. 2004. *Shadow Cities*. London: Routledge.

Nogueira, Oracy. 2006 [1954]. "Preconceito Racial de Marca e Preconceito Racial de Origem." *Tempo Social* 19 (1): 287–308.

Nordstrom, Carolyn. 1992. "The Backyard Front." In *The Paths to Domination, Resistance, and Terror*, edited by Carolyn Nordstrom and JoAnn Martin, 260–274. Berkeley: University of California Press.

———. 2004. *Shadows of War*. Berkeley: University of California Press.

———. 2007. *Global Outlaws: Crime, Money, and Power in the Contemporary World*. Berkeley: University of California Press.

O'Donnell, Guillermo. 1993. "On the State, Democratization, and Some Conceptual Problems." *World Development* 21 (8): 1355–1369.

O'Neill, Kevin, and Kendron Thomas, eds. 2011. *Securing the City: Neoliberalism, Space, and Insecurity in Postwar Guatemala*. Durham, NC: Duke University Press.

Parisse, Luciano. 1969. *Favelas do Rio de Janeiro: Evolução, Sentido*. Rio de Janeiro: Pontifícia Universidade Católica do Rio de Janeiro.

Parker, Richard G. 1991. *Bodies, Pleasures, and Passions: Sexual Culture in Contemporary Brazil*. Boston: Beacon.

Parnell, Philip, and Stephanie Kane. 2003. *Crime's Power: Anthropologists and the Ethnography of Crime*. New York: Palgrave Macmillan.

Penglase, Ben. 1994. *Final Justice: Police and Death Squad Homicides of Adolescents in Brazil*. New York: Human Rights Watch.

———. 2005. "The Shutdown of Rio de Janeiro." *Anthropology Today* 21 (5): 3–6.

———. 2007. "Barbarians on the Beach: Media Narratives of Violence in Rio de Janeiro, Brazil." *Crime Media Culture* 3 (3): 305–325.

———. 2008. "The Bastard Child of the Dictatorship: The Comando Vermelho and the Birth of Narco-culture in Rio de Janeiro." *Luso-Brazilian Review* 45 (1): 118–145.

———. 2009. "States of Insecurity: Everyday Emergencies, Public Secrets, and Drug Trafficker Power in a Brazilian Favela." *PoLAR: Political and Legal Anthropology Review* 32
(1): 407–423.

———. 2011. "Lost Bullets: Fetishes of Urban Violence in Rio de Janeiro, Brazil." *Anthropological Quarterly* 84 (20): 411–438.

Penglase, Ben, and Stephen L. Kass. 1993. "The Killings at Candelária and Vigário Geral."
News from Human Rights Watch/Americas, November. New York: Human Rights Watch.

Pereira, Anthony. 2008. "Public Security, Private Interests, and Police Reform in Brazil." In
Democratic Brazil Revisited, edited by Peter Kingstone and Timothy Power, 185–208.
Pittsburgh, PA: University of Pittsburgh Press.

Peres, Leandra. 2011. "A New Approach to Citizen Security in Brazil: Rio's Pacifying Police
Units." Woodrow Wilson Center, March 16, accessed April 18, 2001. http://www
.wilsoncenter.org

Peres, Maria Fernanda Tourinho. 2004. *Violência por Armas de Fogo no Brasil*. São Paulo:
Núcleo de Estudos da Violência, Universidade de São Paulo.

Perlman, Janice. 1976. *The Myth of Marginality: Urban Poverty and Politics in Rio de Janeiro*.
Berkeley: University of California Press.

Pinheiro, Paulo Sérgio. 2000. "Democratic Governance, Violence, and the (Un)rule of Law."
Daedalus 129 (2): 119–143

Pino, Julio César. 1997. *Family and Favela: The Reproduction of Poverty in Rio de Janeiro*.
Westport, CT: Greenwood.

Rafael, Antônio. 1998. *Um Abraço Para Todos os Amigos*. Niterói: EDUFF.

Ramos, Alcida. 1994. "The Hyperreal Indian." *Critique of Anthropology* 14 (2): 153–171.

Ramos, Silvia, and Leonarda Musumeci. 2004. "Elemento Suspeito." *Boletim Segurança e
Cidadania* 3 (8): 1–16.

Rebhun, Linda. 1999. *The Heart Is Unknown Country*. Stanford, CA: Stanford University
Press.

Reichmann, Rebecca, ed. 1999. *Race in Contemporary Brazil: From Indifference to Inequality*.
University Park: Pennsylvania State University Press.

Resende, Juliana. 1995. *Operação Rio*. Rio de Janeiro: Scritta.

Ribeiro, Luiz César de Queiroz. 1996. "Rio de Janeiro: Exemplo de Metrópole Partida e Sem
Rumo?" *Novos Estudos CEBRAP* 45: 167–182.

Rodgers, Dennis. 2006. "Living in the Shadow of Death: Gangs, Violence, and the Social
Order in Urban Nicaragua, 1996–2002." *Journal of Latin American Studies* 38 (2):
267–293.

Rosaldo, Renato. 1989. *Culture and Truth: The Remaking of Social Analysis*. Boston: Beacon.

Salles, João Moreira. 2001. "Sarajevo e Rio: Duas Guerras Distintas," *Jornal do Brasil*, September 24.

Salles, João Moreira, and Kátia Lund. 1999. *Notícias de uma Guerra Particular*. Documentary
film. Rio de Janeiro.

Sansone, Livio. 2002. "Fugindo Para a Força: Cultura Corporativista e 'Cor' na Polícia Mili-
tar do Estado do Rio de Janeiro." *Estudos Afro-Asiáticos* 24 (3): 513–532.

———. 2003. *Blackness without Ethnicity*. New York: Palgrave Macmillan.

Santos, Boaventura de Sousa. 1977. "The Law of the Oppressed: The Construction and
Reproduction of Legality in Pasargada." *Law & Society* 12: 5–126.

Sarti, Cynthia. 1992. "Família Patriarcal Entre os Pobres Urbanos?" *Cadernos de Pesquisa* 83:
37–41.

Scarry, Ellen. 1985. *The Body in Pain: The Making and Unmaking of the World*. Oxford: Oxford University Press.

Scheper-Hughes, Nancy. 1992. *Death without Weeping: The Violence of Everyday Life in Brazil*. Berkeley: University of California Press.

———. 2006. "Death Squads and Democracy in Northeast Brazil." In *Law and Disorder in the Postcolony*, edited by Jean Comaroff and John Comaroff, 150–187. Chicago: University of Chicago Press.

Scheper-Hughes, Nancy, and Philippe Bourgois, eds. 2004. *Violence in War and Peace*. Oxford, UK: Blackwell.

Schwarcz, Lilia Moritz. 1993. *O Espetáculo das Raças*. São Paulo: Companhia das Letras.

Sento-Sé, João Trajano. 1998. "Imagens da Ordem, Vertigens do Caos—O Debate Sobre as Políticas de Segurança Pública no Rio de Janeiro nos Anos 80 e 90." *Arché* 7 (19): 41–73.

Sheriff, Robin. 2001. *Dreaming Equality*. New Brunswick, NJ: Rutgers University Press.

Silva, Jorge da. 1997. "Representação e Ação dos Operadores do Sistema Penal no Rio de Janeiro." *Tempo Social* 9 (1): 95–114.

Silva, Nelson do Valle. 1985. "Updating the Cost of Not Being White in Brazil." In *Race, Class, and Power in Brazil*, edited by Pierre-Michel Fontaine, 42–55. Los Angeles: Center for Afro-American Studies, University of California.

———. 1999. "Racial Differences in Income: Brazil, 1988." In *Race in Contemporary Brazil*, edited by Rebecca Reichmann, 67–82. University Park: Pennsylvania State University Press.

Silva, William da. 1991. *Quatrocentos Contra Um*. Rio de Janeiro: Vozes.

Skidmore, Thomas. 1993. *Black into White: Race and Nationality in Brazilian Thought*. Durham, NC: Duke University Press.

Slater, Candace. 1982. *Stories on a String: The Brazilian Literatura de Cordel*. Berkeley: University of California Press.

Soares, Luiz Eduardo. 2000. *Meu Casaco de General: Quinhentos Dias no Front da Segurança Pública do Rio de Janeiro*. Rio de Janeiro: Companhia das Letras.

Soares, Luiz Eduardo, and Leandro Piquet Carneiro. 1996. "Os Quatro Nomes da Violência." In *Violência e Política no Rio de Janeiro*, edited by Luiz Eduardo Soares, 13–58. Rio de Janeiro: ISER / Relume Dumará.

Stahlberg, Stephanie. 2011. "*The Pacification of Favelas in Rio de Janeiro*." Working paper, Center on Democracy, Development, and the Rule of Law. Palo Alto, CA: Stanford University.

Stoll, David. 2008. "Human Rights, Land Conflicts, and Memory of the Violence in the Ixil Country of Northern Quiché." In *Human Rights in the Maya Region*, edited by Pedro Pitarch, Shannon Speed, and Xóchitl Leyva Solano, 187–206. Durham, NC: Duke University Press.

Surin, Kenneth. 2001. "The Sovereign Individual and Michael Taussig's Politics of Defacement." *Nepantla* 2 (1): 205–219.

Tate, Winifred. 2007. *Counting the Dead: The Culture and Politics of Human Rights Activism in Colombia*. Berkeley: University of California Press.

Taussig, Michael. 1986. *Shamanism, Colonialism, and the Wild Man*. Chicago: University of Chicago Press.

———. 1992. *The Nervous System*. New York: Routledge.

———. 1999. *Defacement: Public Secrecy and the Labor of the Negative*. Stanford, CA: Stanford University Press.

Thoumi, Francisco. 2005. "The Colombian Competitive Advantage in Illegal Drugs." *Journal of Drug Issues* 35 (1): 7–26.

Turner, Victor. 1957. *Schism and Continuity in an African Society.* Manchester, UK: Manchester University Press.

———. 1967. *Forest of Symbols: Aspects of Ndembu Ritual.* Ithaca, NY: Cornell University Press.

Twine, Frances Winddance. 1998. *Racism in a Racial Democracy.* New Brunswick, NJ: Rutgers University Press

Valla, Victor Vincent, ed. 1986. *Educação e Favela: Políticas Para as Favelas do Rio de Janeiro, 1940–1985.* Petropolis: Vozes.

———. 1994. "Reconstruindo Uma História Esquecida: Origem e Expansão Inicial das Favelas do Rio de Janeiro." *Espaço e Debates* 14 (37): 34–46.

Valladares, Lícia do Prado. 1978. "Working the System: Squatter Response to Resettlement in Rio de Janeiro." *International Journal of Urban and Regional Research* 2 (1): 12–25.

———. 2005. *A Invenção da Favela.* Rio de Janeiro: Editora FGV.

Valladares, Lícia do Prado, and Rosa Ribeiro. 1994. "The Return of the Favela: Recent Changes in Intrametropolitan Rio." *Urbana* 14–15: 59–73.

Vianna, Hermano, 1995. *O Mistério do Samba.* Rio de Janeiro: Editora UFRJ.

Wacquant, Loïc. 1993. "Urban Outcasts: Stigma and Division in the Black American Ghetto and the French Urban Periphery." *International Journal of Urban and Regional Research* 17 (3): 366–382.

———. 2008. "The Militarization of Urban Marginality: Lessons from the Brazilian Metropolis." *International Political Sociology* 2: 56–74.

Wafer, James. 1991. *The Taste of Blood: Spirit Possession in Brazilian Candomblé.* Philadelphia: University of Pennsylvania Press.

Wagley, Charles. 1964. "Luso-Brazilian Kinship Patterns." In *Politics of Change in Latin America,* edited by Joseph Maier and Richard Weatherhead, 174–189. New York: Praeger.

Waiselfisz, Julio. 2007. *Mapa da Violência dos Municípios Brasileiros.* Brasília: Organização dos Estados Ibero-Americanos para a Educação e Ciência e a Cultura.

Warren, Kay. 2002. "Toward an Anthropology of Fragments." In *Ethnography in Unstable Places,* edited by Carol Greenhouse, Elizabeth Mertz, and Kay Warren. Durham, NC: Duke University Press.

Wilson, William Julius. 1987. *The Truly Disadvantaged.* Chicago: University of Chicago Press.

Winant, Howard. 1992. "Rethinking Race in Brazil." *Journal of Latin American Studies* 24 (1): 173–192.

Wolf, Eric. 1956. "Aspects of Group Relations in a Complex Society: Mexico." *American Anthropologist* 58: 1065–1078.

Wood, Charles, and José Alberto Magno de Carvalho. 1988. *The Demography of Inequality in Brazil.* Cambridge: Cambridge University Press.

Woortman, Klaas. 1982. "Casa e Família Operária." *Anuário Antropológico* 80: 119–150.

Yúdice, George. 1994. "The Funkification of Rio." In *Microphone Fiends: Youth Music and Youth Culture,* edited by Andrew Ross and Tricia Rose, 193–217. New York: Routledge.

Zaluar, Alba. 1985. *A Máquina e a Revolta.* São Paulo: Brasiliense.

———. 1994. *Condomínio do Diabo.* Rio de Janeiro: Editora UFRJ.

———. 2000. "Perverse Integration: Drug Trafficking and Youth in the Favelas of Rio de Janeiro." *Journal of International Affairs* 53 (2): 653–671.

———. 2004. *Integração Perversa.* Rio de Janeiro: Editora FGV.

Zaluar, Alba, and Isabel Siqueira Conceição. 2007. "Favelas Sob o Controle das Milícias no Rio de Janeiro." *São Paulo em Perspectiva* 21 (2): 89–101.

Zaluar, Alba, and Alexandre Ribeiro. 1995. "Drug Trade, Crime, and Policies of Repression in Brazil." *Dialectical Anthropology* 20: 95–108.

Zilberg, Elana. 2011. *Space of Detention: The Making of a Transnational Gang Crisis between Los Angeles and San Salvador.* Durham, NC: Duke University Press.

Zylberberg, Sonia. 1992. *Morro da Providência: Memórias da "Favela."* Rio de Janeiro: Prefeitura da Cidade do Rio de Janeiro.

Index

abnormalization: concept, 29; drug traffickers' use of, 125–126; local ideologies reshaped in, 135–136; police use of, 137–139; strategies of, 107–108. *See also* drug traffickers–Caxambu residents relationships; order/disorder continuum; police–Caxambu residents relationships

Abreu, Maurício de A., 45, 77–78

Acari, Cy de, 182n12

"Acender as Velas" (Light the Candles, samba song), 48

Adorno, Sérgio, 139, 159

Afro-Brazilians: favelas as symbol of traditions, 8; homicide rate for, 14–15, 180n16; police killings of, 15–16, 180n17; religions of, 85, 89–90, 122

Agamben, Giorgio, 115

Alencar, Marcello, 57, 58, 144, 145

Alquéres, José Luiz, 11

ambivalences: lived experience of, 21–22; in terms for drug trafficking, 31–33; toward local drug dealers, 93–99. *See also* (in)security; uncertainties

Amigos de Amigos (ADA), 31, 168, 179n6

Andaraí favela, 182n17

Argentina: language impacted by dictatorship, 31

asfalto (asphalt, "official" city): Caxambu contrasted to, 37, 82–84. *See also* Rio de Janeiro (city)

Assembleia de Deus (Assembly of God), 85

asymmetrical exchange model of authority, 106–107, 111–112, 114

Austin, J. L., 71

authority: asymmetrical exchange model of, 106–107, 111–112, 114; *domínio do tráfico* (domination of the drug trade) model, 106, 114. *See also* Brazilian state; drug traffickers; security forces

bandidos (criminals): alterity of, 91; familial rhetoric of, 72, 92; police hunting of (*caçando bandidos*), 152; use of term, 31–32, 95; workers distinguished from, 88–93, 158. *See also* drug traffickers

Bangú neighborhood: homicide rate in, 15

Barcinski, Mariana, 182–183n2

barro (clay or mud), 80–81. *See also* streets

Basso, Keith H., 74–75

Batalhão de Operações Especiais (BOPE, Special Operations Battalion), 10–11, 13, 151, 152–153

batendo de frente (hitting head on): keeping head up while avoiding, 101–103, 175; in police–drug dealers relationships, 104

Batista, Nilo, 55, 182n15

Beattie, Peter, 149

Beira Mar, Fernandinho, 9

Beltrame, José Maria, 10, 169. *See also* Unidades de Polícia Pacificadora

About the Author

R. BEN PENGLASE is an associate professor of anthropology and Latin American studies at Loyola University Chicago. He earned his PhD in anthropology from Harvard University. Before becoming an anthropologist, he was a researcher for Human Rights Watch. He has published numerous articles on urban violence and insecurity in Brazil.

CPSIA information can be obtained
at www.ICGtesting.com
Printed in the USA
BVHW072155300820
587624BV00001B/76